MW00681386

THE ETHICAL CONTRIBUTION OF ORGANIZATIONS TO SOCIETY

RESEARCH IN ETHICAL ISSUES IN ORGANIZATIONS

Series Editors: Michael Schwartz and Howard Harris

Recent Volumes:

RESEARCH IN ETHICAL ISSUES IN ORGANIZATIONS
VOLUME 14

THE ETHICAL CONTRIBUTION OF ORGANIZATIONS TO SOCIETY

EDITED BY

MICHAEL SCHWARTZ

*Royal Melbourne Institute of Technology,
Melbourne, Australia*

HOWARD HARRIS

University of South Australia, Adelaide, Australia

DEBRA COMER

Hofstra University, Hempstead, NY, USA

United Kingdom – North America – Japan
India – Malaysia – China

Emerald Group Publishing Limited
Howard House, Wagon Lane, Bingley BD16 1WA, UK

First edition 2015

Reprints and permissions service
Contact: permissions@emeraldinsight.com

British Library Cataloguing in Publication Data
A catalogue record for this book is available from the British Library

ISBN: 978-1-78560-447-8
ISSN: 1529-2096 (Series)

Printed and bound by CPI Group (UK) Ltd, Croydon, CR0 4YY

ISOQAR certified
Management System,
awarded to Emerald
for adherence to
Environmental
standard
ISO 14001:2004.

Certificate Number 1985
ISO 14001

INVESTOR IN PEOPLE

CONTENTS

LIST OF CONTRIBUTORS

Peter Bowden	Department of Philosophy, University of Sydney, Sydney, Australia
Hugh Breakey	Institute for Ethics, Governance and Law, Griffith University, Brisbane, Australia
Tim Cadman	Institute for Ethics, Governance and Law, Griffith University, Brisbane, Australia
Paul A. Cimbala	Department of History, Fordham University, Bronx, NY, USA
Charles J. Coate	Department of Accounting, St Bonaventure University, St Bonaventure, NY, USA
Rebecca J. Glover	Department of Educational Psychology, University of North Texas, Denton, TX, USA
Howard Harris	School of Management, University of South Australia, Adelaide, Australia
Mark C. Mitschow	School of Business, SUNY College at Geneseo, Geneseo, NY, USA
Timothy O'Shannassy	Graduate School of Business and Law, RMIT University, Melbourne, Australia
Karen Palmunen	University of Saint Joseph, West Hartford, CT, USA
Charles Sampford	Institute for Ethics, Governance and Law, Griffith University, Brisbane, Australia.
Michael Schwartz	School of Economics, Finance & Marketing, Royal Melbourne Institute of Technology, Melbourne, Australia

Elizabeth C. Vozzola   Department of Psychology, University of
                             Saint Joseph, West Hartford, CT, USA

Manuel Wörsdörfer   Cluster of Excellence 'The Formation of
                             Normative Orders', Goethe University,
                             Frankfurt, Germany

INTRODUCTION

Organizations promote all sorts of activities. Almost every activity undertaken in the world today is reliant in some way or another on an organization. The majority of papers in this volume consider the ethical aspects of the activities undertaken by organizations and their impact on society. The last two papers in the collection are concerned with the impact of individuals, and recall an earlier volume (2013) in which moral saints and moral exemplars was the theme.

Organizations make contributions to society through the provision of goods and services. They are necessary to bring about tasks which could never be achieved by an individual acting alone. While that may be sufficient to justify the existence of organizations, it is not enough to ensure that organizations make an ethical contribution, or contribute to the ethical development of society. Organizations can make an ethical contribution and can be a positive force for good in the world, or they can contribute to less fortunate outcomes such as environmental pollution and the Global Financial Crisis. In this collection, the contributors explore two features of that contribution: integrity (or the lack of it) and the role of professions, and provide examples from finance, the military, social enterprise, and a range of professions.

An organization making a positive ethical contribution to society will be found to be acting with integrity – integrity that makes it a non-disruptive part of society and integrity that pervades its own inner institutional workings. Integrity is a difficult, disputed topic. Hugh Breakey, Tim Cadman, and Charles Sampford provide a comprehensive integrity framework of three elements with which the integrity of organizations can be assessed. As a framework it has been adopted by Transparency International, and in their paper Breakey, Cadman, and Sampford explore the links between individual and organizational integrity, seeking to draw insights about institutional integrity from the extensive literature on personal integrity. They conclude that the elements of consistency-integrity, coherence-integrity, and context-integrity – the three elements of the comprehensive framework – can be used to examine the extent of both personal and organizational integrity. This framework, they argue, can provide a unified, cross-disciplinary basis to guide not only current practice but also future research.

One aspect of integrity is morality. As Breakey, Cadman, and Sampford argue, one can have integrity in the sense of consistency and coherence (and even context) and yet that integrity may be aligned with evil. That a set of values is clearly stated and strongly held does not make them ethical. This is a topic taken up by Timothy O'Shannassy. Applying exemplary rules of governance does not of itself guarantee good governance. The practice of corporate governance, he argues, has to be looked at in the light of the organization's own ethics. How the organization views its mission and processes will affect the way in which it applies corporate governance standards. A better understanding of governance practices will make for better governance within the organization; it may also spread beyond that one organization through its impact on the practices of governance in the community and the understanding fostered there, perhaps even leading to changed rules and laws. O'Shannassy considers the impact that the widely employed theories of agency, stewardship, and resource dependence have on the process and form of corporate governance. If the corporation is ethical, has integrity, and takes governance seriously, then it will have an impact in society and governance will not be something that directors can turn on and off like a tap.

Time can change the contribution that an organization makes to society. As Breakey, Cadman, and Sampford say, integrity is context dependent. Most countries have an armed military force of one sort or another and they often have a significant impact on the economy, politics, and ethics of the nation. Michael Schwartz explores two different military organizations to examine their ethical contribution to society. The first is the Prussian Army and the second the compulsory military service scheme in Israel. The military has a role, he argues, to inculcate virtue. He draws attention to management guru Peter Drucker's discussion of the Prussian Army, which from its founding in 1640 had had a strong political and social role with a capacity to influence society, a role it had lost by the early twentieth century according to Drucker. The social role of compulsory military service has been much more resilient according to Schwartz.

Resilience and personal development are topics which form a bridge between the consideration of integrity and the discussion of the role of professions. Schwartz discusses the potential for ethical development and social cohesion that can come from military service as individuals learn how to establish trust and shared values. It is also a source of potential ethical conflict when individuals, soldiers one day and civilians the next, struggle to reconcile their differing roles. Reflection, making the values one's own, was an element of the comprehensive integrity framework discussed in the first paper in this collection, by Breakey, Cadwell, and Sampford, and it is an activity available to citizen soldiers as they seek to better understand themselves. The other papers which consider the development of self in individuals take as their examples the US president Abraham Lincoln and the Dutch woman Miep Gies, friend to the Frank family during the Nazi occupation.

What of organizations in the emerging gray sector, neither government, nor for-profit private sector businesses, nor non-profits or NGOs? Charles J. Coate and Mark C. Mitschow consider the place of benefit corporations which combine profit-making ventures with specific social objectives. These social enterprises can make an ethical contribution to society, Coate and Mitschow argue, and could replace some of the roles presently undertaken (ineffectively) by government. They particularly consider underserved aspects of US society and apply Catholic Social Teaching as a way to assess the contribution of benefit corporations. Recourse to key texts, including the 1891 encyclical *Rerum Novarum*, shows how the capacity for organizations to influence society and its ethical stance has been acknowledged for some time and that the opportunity for people to enter the "circle of exchange" considered an important responsibility of society in *Rerum Novarum* might be further expanded though benefit corporations.

The impact on society of the ethical dilemmas within 11 professions and disciplines is explored by Peter Bowden in his contribution. Many of these, he suggests, are unresolved questions which should be taken up by the relevant professional association as they cannot be answered by a generalist. It is once again for an organization to make an important ethical contribution to society, for, as Bowden concludes, the most commonly invoked ethical theories of utilitarianism, duty and virtue are often unable to provide clear direction, and discipline-specific codes might do a better job. The development of a code is described by Manuel Wörsdörfer. The Equator Principles are a voluntary finance industry benchmark which commit participating institutions to social and environmental standards in lending for major projects and their execution. Wörsdörfer describes not only the conception and formulation of the Equator Principles but also their impact on the ethical behavior of organizations and society. He shows how institutional and industry codes of conduct can help in the development of trust in important institutions and in the resolution of some of the dilemmas posed by Bowden. Interaction between organizations – the lending banks and the borrowing enterprises – are linked with society through the Principles which require engagement with stakeholder groups as part of the assessment and reporting provisions. This fosters a dynamic interaction between banks, NGOs, and civil society organizations through which the actions and values of the organizations contribute to society, and vice versa. In place for over 10 years, Wörsdörfer concludes that the Equator Principles have experienced rapid and widespread adoption, extending the practice of social and environmental assessment and protection in society. Membership, although not uniform, now includes some 80 lending institutions from the major economies of the developed and developing world.

Bowden, in his contribution to this volume which has already been mentioned above, also describes the development of an international network with ethical impact on society. Over 30 countries now have whistleblower protection systems, another form of institutional arrangement deliberately designed to impact ethical behavior.

A different story of institutional development is found in the establishment of the veterinary profession in France in the middle of the eighteenth century and its expansion throughout the world. Although it could have been an equestrian academy or a school to train workers to respond to a contemporary outbreak of a virulent animal disease, what was founded was a professional school with a commitment to contribute to society at the widest level and to develop within its students the capacity to observe and reflect. This recalls the link between reflection and integrity mentioned by Breakey, Cadman, and Sampford in connection with the comprehensive integrity framework. Howard Harris discusses the profession as an organizational form and how the profession has influenced not only veterinary practitioners but also the society in which they serve.

These papers have shown how many different forms of organizations have made an ethical contribution to society. That there would be a contribution from benefit corporations, well-governed stock exchange listed companies, and even the professions might have been expected, but the contributors to this issue have shown that military forces and an association of international financiers can also make a contribution to ethics. Integrity in many forms pervades the discussion. Society will benefit from consistency in application of values, individuals from the integrity that comes from coherence in their own lives and thence in their contribution to society and all will gain from a reflection on the morality of their values.

The opportunity to examine the lives of two individuals whose stories are associated with ethics and integrity is taken up in the final two papers in this issue. Blasi's (2004) theory of the construction of a moral self is used by Elizabeth C. Vozzola, Paul A. Cimbala, and Karen Palmunen in an analysis of the turning point in Abraham Lincoln's career, the 1854 Peoria speech against slavery. It was an organizational act that roused Lincoln, the repeal by Congress of the Missouri Compromise, but the paper is principally concerned with Lincoln's moral development and with the impact that an individual, especially one who is seen as a moral exemplar, can have. The paper examines the speech itself and surrounding narrative to establish relevant themes, textual elements, and character traits. Lincoln, the contributors argue, was an exemplar who was engaged deliberately in collective undertakings in the wider world of politics and government. They found abundant evidence of the emergence of a central moral self, and its crafting into a politically compelling personal myth with the strength to support his subsequent challenges and achievements. It was to become, they argue, "a morally compelling national story."

The second exemplar is also an historical figure but not one engaged in public political debate. The Dutch citizen Miep Gies was a friend of the Frank family and the custodian of Anne Frank's diary after Frank had been captured by the Germans. The focus in this paper by Rebecca J. Glover is on moral motivation. The paper applies Frimer and Walker's (2009) reconciliation model and methodology in examining themes of agency and communion in the motivation of Miep Gies. Although Gies was not involved in public life in the same way as Lincoln she did provide an extensive narrative which could be examined. When examined, this showed the depth of motivation and integrity in Gies' life, such that she felt she had no choice other than to act as she did to help Otto Frank, his family and colleagues. That strength included a humility and benevolence, important Glover argues, in the development of Miep Gies' moral self.

These two papers show the value of the use of investigative techniques, developed for use with live respondents, when used in the "interrogation" of historical documents. It is another example of the research in ethical issues in organizations to which this journal is committed. The earlier papers show how organizations, too, can make ethical contributions to society and reminds readers that organizations can be a force for good in the world.

Michael Schwartz
Howard Harris
Debra Comer
Editors

REFERENCES

Blasi, A. (2004). Moral functioning: Moral understanding and personality. In D. K. Lapsley & D. Narvaez (Eds.), *Moral development, self and identity* (pp. 335–348). Mahwah, NJ: Erlbaum.
Frimer, J. A., & Walker, L. J. (2009). Reconciling the self and morality: An empirical model of moral centrality development. *Developmental Psychology, 45*(6), 1669–1681.
Schwartz, M., & Harris, H. (Eds.). (2013). *Moral saints and moral exemplars* (Vol. 10). Research in Ethical Issues in Organizations. Bingley, UK: Emerald Group Publishing Limited.

CONCEPTUALIZING PERSONAL AND INSTITUTIONAL INTEGRITY: THE COMPREHENSIVE INTEGRITY FRAMEWORK

Hugh Breakey, Tim Cadman and
Charles Sampford

ABSTRACT

In this paper, we present a conceptual and terminological system — what we term the 'Comprehensive Integrity Framework' — capable of applying to both personal and institutional integrity, and to different levels of institutions (including sub-institutions and institutional complexes). We distinguish between three sorts of integrity: consistency-integrity *(whether the agent's acts accord with her claimed values);* coherence-integrity *(whether the agent's character and internal constitution accord with her claimed values); and* context-integrity *(whether the agent's environment facilitates her living up to her claimed values). We then employ this conceptual system to explore similarities, differences and overlaps between personal and institutional integrity, drawing in*

The Ethical Contribution of Organizations to Society
Research in Ethical Issues in Organizations, Volume 14, 1–40
ISSN: 1529-2096/doi:10.1108/S1529-209620150000014001

*particular on moral philosophic work on personal integrity (on the one
hand) and on 'integrity systems' and public administration approaches to
institutional integrity (on the other).*

Keywords: Integrity; personal integrity; institutional integrity;
comprehensive integrity framework; integrity systems;
compartmentalization

INTRODUCTION

What is the relationship between personal integrity — the idea of integrity
applied to individual people — and institutional integrity — the notion of
integrity applied to organizations and regimes? Are the two types of integrity exactly the same, or quite dissimilar? Do they follow similar or different logics? Can reflecting on each type furnish us with insights about the
other? This paper aims to help answer these questions.

Specifically, we have two major purposes. The first is to provide a conceptual and terminological system — the 'Comprehensive Integrity Framework'.
The Framework is intended to help us think and speak about different
aspects of integrity, as that term applies to both individual persons and larger institutions. As with most such efforts of conceptual 'under-labouring',
the immediate goal is to illustrate the alternative ways of conceiving the core
concept, and to help theorists and practitioners avoid talking past one
another. In turn, the Framework can help people think systematically about
their own integrity, or that of the institutions to which they belong. As well,
the Framework can be used as a tool to assist in externally appraising the
integrity of a person, institution or institutional complex. It helps remind us
that integrity is a complex notion, implicating actions, words, reflection,
internal constitution, external pressures and more.

Our second purpose is to tease out some preliminary answers to several
of the key questions thrown open by the Framework. With the conceptual
Framework in tow, we broach such questions as: What insights about institutional integrity can we draw from the considerable philosophical work on
personal integrity? Why do institutions have a more formal, public process
for declaring the values and goals they endorse — and why does the law
take such a close interest in institutions' failures to comply with these
values? And — does an institution's pursuit of its own integrity encourage
(or thwart) its members' personal integrity?

The paper proceeds as follows: the first section, 'Basic Terms and
Concepts', advances the core of the Comprehensive Integrity Framework,

providing basic terminology and concepts applicable to both personal integrity and institutional integrity.[1] Building on this Framework, the second section, 'Personal Integrity', explores personal integrity in greater detail, surveying the considerable work done over the last few decades on the philosophy of personal integrity. The third section, 'Institutional Integrity', then applies this Comprehensive Integrity Framework to institutional integrity, drawing in particular on the 'integrity systems' approach developed by Jeremy Pope and Charles Sampford and widely utilized by Transparency International. In the last section, 'Differences and Reflections', we turn to some of the differences between personal and institutional integrity our analysis has unearthed, and offer some reflections on the reasons underlying these differences.

Throughout we use the term 'agent' as the subject of integrity, applying it to both individuals and institutions (though we recognize a lurking danger of anthropomorphizing institutions through employing this term). Institutions can be formal or informal, including government branches, companies and corporations, community groups, charities, intergovernmental organizations and so on. Large institutions (or 'complexes' of institutions) can contain many smaller institutions nested inside the larger entity. In all cases, however, there must be sufficient cohesion across the institution in question to make sense of speaking of it as an 'agent'.

BASIC TERMS AND CONCEPTS

Sampford was one of the first theorists to both distinguish and link individual and institutional integrity. While several different formulations were used (Preston & Sampford, 2002b), a recent summary highlights that ethics:

> ... involves asking yourself hard questions about your values, giving honest and public answers, and trying to live by those answers. If you do, you have integrity in the sense that you are true to your values and true to yourself ... *Institutional* ethics applies the same approach to institutions. It involves an institution asking hard questions about its value and values, giving honest and public answers, and living by them. Doing so for an institution is more complex than for an individual but it is both possible and necessary. The first vital questions that must be asked of any institution or organisation are: what is it for? Why should it exist? What justifies the organization to the community in which it operates, given that the community generally provides privileges? ... Asking those questions involves an institutional and collective effort under an organisation's own formal and informal constitutional processes (including getting acceptance from relevant outsiders − including shareholders and/or relevant regulators). An organisation has integrity if it lives by its answers. However, it does so in a different way to an individual. It cannot merely be a personal commitment but must be an institutional

commitment that involves creating mechanisms which make it more likely that the organisation keeps to the values it has publicly declared and to which it is publicly committed. These mechanisms are collectively called an 'integrity system'.[2]

This paper seeks to build on these ideas and to tease out various elements of integrity. Applied to either individuals or institutions, integrity can alert us to aspects of an agent's internal qualities (virtues and values), its external environment or its actual observable behaviour. This section will introduce the array of terms the Comprehensive Integrity Framework employs to capture the different notions of integrity focusing on each of these objects. Our approach in this section will be to largely stipulate terms — later sections will help illuminate the reasons behind these definitional decisions.

'Claimed Values'

The fundamental organizing concept for studying integrity is the agent's *claimed values* (the answers given to those 'hard questions'). As we will see in later sections, the nature, content, provenance and modes of realization of these claimed values differ for individuals versus institutions. Compared to individuals, institutions profess their values in more formal and public ways, and these values play a role in socially justifying the institution's existence and activities. But in both the individual and institutional cases, the basic concept and logic remain the same: the individual or institutional agent endorses certain virtues, norms, pursuits or goals as central to their identity, and displays these values through their public interactions — in what they proclaim, advertise, argue for and so on. The claimed values are what the agent professes to *stand for* (Calhoun, 1995). Integrity then hinges on the extent to which the individual holds true to those values.

Of course, claiming values does not itself entail integrity. If the agent does not claim to stand for any particular values or goals, or the values the agent claims to stand for are inconsistent, incoherent or evanescent, then that agent cannot possess integrity.[3] Equally though, possessing claimed values does not demonstrate integrity. The values are only *claimed*, and may not be truly endorsed by the agent. Even if they are endorsed, they may not be reflected in the way an individual agent acts or an institutional agent operates.

Comprehensive Integrity

As we define it, an agent enjoys *comprehensive integrity* if its activities, its deeply-held ethos and internal constitution, and its external relations all accord with its claimed values. This definition draws on the inter-related ideas that integrity involves acting in accord with one's publicly asserted values ('consistency') as well as being integrated ('coherent'). It also includes attention to the way the agent fits with its external environment ('context'). Comprehensive integrity requires coherence-integrity, context-integrity and consistency-integrity on an ongoing basis.

The remainder of this section explains these three key terms of consistency-integrity, coherence-integrity and context-integrity.

Consistency-Integrity

If an agent's activities[4] are consistent with its claimed values, then it displays what we term *consistency-integrity*. In this reckoning, the agent's activities are not considered piecemeal. For an agent to display consistency-integrity none of its activities, assessed over a considerable period of time, can clash with its claimed values. (For example, an agent cannot claim consistency-integrity if she avoids corruption or conflicts of interests 'most of the time'.)

Consistency-integrity focuses purely on the agent's activities, and compares these activities to the agent's claimed values. So understood, consistency-integrity does not demand that the activities are in fact motivated by the agent's claimed values. The activities must accord with the claimed values, but need not be performed on the *basis* of those values. For this reason we could say that an agent with consistency-integrity *acts with* or *displays* integrity, but we could not (on the basis of consistency-integrity alone) assert that the agent *possesses* integrity. For possessing integrity requires more than mere compliance, it requires having certain sorts of internal features such as intentions, dispositions and character. These make up the domain 'coherence-integrity'.

Coherence-Integrity

While consistency-integrity appraises the agent's *acts*, coherence-integrity refers to the agent's enduring *qualities*. For an individual, coherence-integrity applies to her character: does she have the type of stable values, virtues, emotional dispositions, willpower, reflective practices, decision-making processes and public persona that integrate ('cohere') together in order to promote her living up to the values she claims?

Similarly, for an institution coherence-integrity applies to the institution's internal qualities – in particular, its members' deeply-held values (insofar as those values impact upon the members' behaviour within the institution), and the nature of the institution's internal organizational arrangements. These 'internal organizational arrangements' answer such questions as: How does the institution make its decisions? How does it seek to ensure that the actions of its members further the values it claims? To what extent does it recognize the temptations and dilemmas faced by its members in performing their duties? What structures does it have for explaining its mission and what it means for its members and their actions? How does it police and encourage compliance with institutional decisions? Do the institution's policies for transparency, accountability and critical feedback promote its ability to live up to its claimed values? If the institution's internal organizational arrangements on decision-making, accountability, compliance and suchlike drive its successful implementation of its claimed values, then the institution will possess a high coherence-integrity.

We saw above that consistency-integrity compares an agent's actions with its claimed values. Over a period of time, what does the agent *do*? In contradistinction, coherence-integrity compares an agent's internal constitution with its claimed values. Rather than looking at activities, it looks at internal qualities and processes. It asks: What *is* the agent?

An agent might display consistency-integrity without possessing coherence-integrity. This could occur if the agent just-so-happens, as a result of external constraints or good fortune, to consistently comply with its claimed values, with little input from its own internal qualities. Less commonly, an agent could have reasonable coherence-integrity but still fail consistency-integrity, if in an extraordinary situation, perhaps under great pressure or with an unfortunate concatenation of unlucky events, an otherwise reliable agent fails to live up to its claimed values.

If the agent is internally constituted so as to consistently live up to its claimed values (i.e. constituted so as to display consistency-integrity), then it has coherence-integrity and we can say that the agent *possesses* integrity.

Context-Integrity

Context-integrity refers to the agent's surrounding environment and all the elements in the environment that impact upon the agent living up to its claimed values. These elements include other organizations, cultural norms, (economic, social and security) pressures, opportunities and temptations and so on. Two contextual factors prove especially relevant. The agent's *legal context* is made up by the overarching (domestic and perhaps international) laws and regulations governing the agent. And what we will call the agent's *organizational-context* is constituted by the institutions or institutional-complexes of which the agent makes up one part. When one agent (as an individual or 'sub-institution') forms part of a larger institution, we will say it is 'nested' in that larger entity.

We have just said context-integrity refers to environmental elements impacting on whether the agent lives up to their claimed values. But as the foregoing discussion of consistency-integrity and coherence-integrity implies, this phrase 'lives up to' is ambiguous. Do we mean that the agent's actions conform to what is *required by* their claimed values (with consistency-integrity), or that the agent's actions are performed *on the basis of* their claimed values (with coherence-integrity)?

Context-integrity can refer to the external environment's impacts on both types of integrity. Some elements in an agent's environment will cultivate changes to the agent itself, by encouraging certain virtues and decision-making methods, requiring agents to constitute themselves in various ways, or challenging them to rethink their values and how they achieve them. Other external elements can constrain an agent's behaviour irrespective of its internal qualities, through incentives to good behaviour (including reputational benefits and promotion), through coercive punishment triggered by non-compliance with specific rules, through channelling behaviour (making it easy to the right thing, hard to do the wrong thing), or limiting the agent's capacity to engage in certain acts. As a loose rule of thumb, and as we will see in more detail below, studies of context-integrity in the *personal* realm tend to target the former (coherence-integrity) question of promoting internal changes to the person's *character*. Context-integrity in the *institutional* realm, in contradistinction, hones in on the latter (consistency-integrity) issue of policing external compliance over the institution's *actions*.

The distinction between these two ways context can influence character versus behaviour can be seen through considering what would happen if overnight the context changed, and the external mechanism was no longer producing its previous effect. If the mechanism only produced compliance through coercive deterrence, then the agent will be left with no reason to comply when the coercion disappears. But if the mechanism produced genuine internal change to the agent, then the agent will still comply with the relevant values even if the mechanism disappears. Of course, this difference is not a bright-line distinction; an agent in an environment where its corrupt actions are immediately sanctioned may well come to invest its thoughts and energies in non-corrupt directions, and these inclinations may ultimately transform the agent's values and decision-making processes (an insight historically driving the development of the separation of powers (Breakey, 2014a, p. 38)).

Simplifying, there are three different ways a contextual factor, or the overall context, might relate to the agent's integrity (either coherence- or consistency-integrity). The context might, (a) facilitate and empower the agent's integrity; (b) thwart and retard the agent's integrity; or (c) align with the agent's integrity. In this last case, the surrounding environment does not directly promote the agent's integrity, but at least accords with it. Since the values of different peoples and diverse organizations can easily clash in at least some circumstances, aligning the external context with the integrity of a given agent can be an important task. For example, efforts to align the profession of medicine (as an external context) to the integrity of devoutly religious doctors opposed to abortion, constitute a difficult and controversial endeavour (Magelssen, 2012). The challenge here is to develop rules that allow the professional duties to align with personal integrity.

PERSONAL INTEGRITY

Over recent decades philosophical literature on integrity has developed rich resources for understanding the nature of personal integrity (especially, as we will see, its coherence-integrity). The Comprehensive Integrity Framework aims to incorporate many of the key insights uncovered by this literature. Recall that the Framework takes its fundamental formulation of integrity as an agent asking itself hard questions about its values, giving honest and public answers, and trying to live by those answers (Sampford, 2010). Other influential accounts of personal integrity argue for similar formulations. Dare (2010, p. 123), for example, holds that, '… what matters for integrity is that the agent has engaged in appropriate critical reflection upon the projects upon which they purport to ground their identity and that they are prepared to act upon that reflection'.

On this footing, integrity combines a number of distinct elements. It fundamentally involves *reflection* about how to develop and cohere one's *values* (asking 'hard questions about values'), the *sincerity* to publicly profess what one stands for ('giving honest and public answers'), and the *willpower* to ensure the results of one's reflections are realized in one's character and actions ('living by those answers'). By incorporating these four key elements of personal integrity – reflection, values-coherence, willpower and sincerity – the Comprehensive Integrity Framework can in an eclectic spirit incorporate many of the insights of prior theorists. As we will see below, the Framework also makes indirect room for a fifth element: *morality*.

Why is such eclecticism attractive? Why should we opt for a version of integrity incorporating these many disparate elements, rather than one reducing personal integrity to a single elemental core? First, each distinct theory furnishes evidence for the existence of its particular element. If integrity had *nothing* to do with reflectiveness, for example, then it would have been almost impossible for any theorists to craft a theory that defined integrity's essence in its reflectiveness. Second, as Benjamin (1990, p. 47) observes, we can get an idea of what integrity positively requires by considering what it negatively rules out – that is, by considering the types of behaviours and characters that paradigmatically fail to possess integrity. As we will see, each element explains different failures of integrity. As none of the elements can be straightforwardly collapsed into the others, this favours an inclusive approach.

Consistency-Integrity for Individuals

The distinction noted above between 'acting with' integrity (consistency-integrity) and 'possessing the virtue of integrity' (coherence-integrity) applies to both individuals and institutions (Dudzinski, 2004). That said, the philosophical literature on personal integrity focuses on the person's internal qualities of mind and character, and so on coherence-integrity. The mere fact of compliance, unless it is driven by the person's actual values and internal dispositions, can seem almost irrelevant to appraising personal integrity. This judgment drives W. H. Hindman's oft-quoted quip that, 'Integrity is doing the right thing when no one is looking'.

Coherence-Integrity for Individuals

As noted above, the rich literature on personal integrity focuses on internal character traits – the subject matter of coherence-integrity. In this subsection we detail the five core aspects of a person's coherence-integrity found in this literature: values-coherence, willpower, reflection, sincerity and morality. For expository ease, we will use as an example the character of 'Ingrid', who possesses integrity.

Values-Coherence

Perhaps the most obvious element of coherence-integrity involves holding 'integrated' values. Almost all accounts of integrity involve at least some measure of values-coherence, sometimes combined with one of the remaining four elements. This idea of 'values-coherence' can be cashed out in several ways. Values-coherence can be conceived as Ingrid integrating all of her preferences together so they press in a unified direction, or (in a more sophisticated variant) possessing integrated first- and second-order preferences, meaning that Ingrid's ordinary preferences accord with her preferences about what preferences she would like to have (Frankfurt, 1971). This idea reflects integrity as 'integration'. Alternatively, values-coherence can refer to Ingrid's most important commitments and 'ground projects', conceived as commitments she endorses or identifies with (Williams, 1973). This idea captures integrity as the pursuit of what is 'integral' to Ingrid.

Plausibly, both the integration and integral pictures alert us to key parts of what Ingrid reflects upon and epitomizes as she coheres her values (Cox, La Caze, & Levine, 2009; Dare, 2010). This values-coherence element follows pleasingly from the etymological root of integrity as 'unity' or 'completeness'. Ingrid has brought into harmony her key values; she has a clear, reliable identity and character. Complete consistency is not required, nor inflexibility, but Ingrid's values possess sufficient coherence to give direction to her life, and to allow her to take her values seriously, being committed to them wholeheartedly. Because Ingrid has values-coherence, she is not inconsistent, torn, self-loathing, self-alienated or capricious.

Willpower

By 'willpower' we refer to all of the emotional dispositions, habits of thought and qualities of character that together serve to ensure that Ingrid puts her values into action. These qualities ensure that Ingrid's values determine the decisions she makes, and that she follows through on those decisions by implementing them in her actions. Ingrid is not swayed from pursuing her values on the basis of temptations, distractions or fears. Through Ingrid's strong willpower, she thus displays the virtues (the emotional dispositions) of patience, decisiveness, assertiveness, diligence, courage, grit, dedication and conscientiousness.

Though theorists often subsume willpower into values-coherence, this capacity remains distinct (Benjamin, 1990, p. 48; Reginster, 1997, p. 294).[5]

'Willpower' does not refer to the content or coherence of Ingrid's prefer-ences, but instead to her psychological character – specifically her disposi-tion to feel certain emotions in certain situations, and how she responds when in the grip of those emotions. On this footing, integrity incorporates qualities of character and psychology, and essentially opposes the failures of diffidence and akrasia.

Reflection
As a person of integrity, Ingrid's values must be her own, actively and deliberately claimed by her. This requires that Ingrid has reflected on her commitments. She knows her values and that those values fit with her beliefs – and she takes some care that those beliefs are accurate. The values Ingrid endorses are not arbitrary but chosen on the basis of reasons; her values cohere at least partly because Ingrid has used her reflection to bring them into accord.

Ingrid's reflectiveness does not demand searching philosophical interroga-tion, nor rigorous logical coherence. But it does require that Ingrid's reflective attention to her values includes at least some basic epistemic virtues that serve to ensure that no one could say that she was in the grip of self-deception, or that she was shallow, wanton, manipulated, brainwashed or simply confor-mist. Equally, she is not merely addicted, irrationally fixated or obsessed, or monomaniacal. Ingrid beats her own path, and not that of others, and one of the things that makes it *her* path is that she has reflected on and endorsed her commitments. On this basis many commentators place reflectiveness at the core of personal integrity (Calhoun, 1995; Cox et al., 2009; Edgar & Pattison, 2011; Reginster, 1997; Scherkoske, 2010).

Sincerity
Ingrid stands for her values. Those who meet her know what she stands for. Her public persona reflects her actually-held values. Ingrid is honest and faithful, not just reliable but *trustworthy* (Graham, 2001, p. 246). People may disagree with aspects of Ingrid's values, but they know they can trust her implicitly and rely upon her to predictably behave on the basis of her known commitments. If Ingrid decides she must break a law, she will openly take responsibility for what she has done. Indeed, in a paradigm of integrity, she may announce her attentions to 'conscientiously object' to the law ahead of time.

Theorists locating integrity's essence in sincerity locate the paradigm integrity failures in being hypocritical and two-faced (Calhoun, 1995; Luban, 2003). Because roles and positions allow for abuse if the role-holder is not sincere, corruptness and abuses of power present as symptoms of hypocrisy, and so as signature failures of integrity (Huberts, 2014). The integrity here lies in the accord between word and deed, between the public persona and the internal commitment. This element explains why honesty remains at the centre of what is 'measured' in integrity tests (Audi & Murphy, 2006, p. 7).

Morality

Setting aside the specific virtue of sincerity, controversy surrounds the relationship between integrity and morality.

Importantly, nothing in the notion of integrity defined here demands specific moral content for Ingrid's values. So conceived, integrity is thus a process value rather than a substantive value.[6] In this way integrity resembles the traditional or 'thin' concept of the rule of law, which does not directly impact upon the content of the law, but oversees the processes by which it is applied and implemented (and thus constitutes an indirect restraint on the types of laws likely to be promulgated). Similarly, the process that integrity demands can carry significant consequences for the resulting values, even if it does not determine them. As Dare (2010, pp. 117–118) argues, when an ordinary person works to cohere their values, their common-sense moral sensitivities will be one part of the overall web of values that the person aims to cohere together, meaning that the process of attaining integrity will encourage the holding of (and having the courage to act upon) decent moral values. As well, the reflectiveness noted above, requiring consideration of the reasons for holding one's convictions, makes thoughtless embrace of evils less likely (Kerwin, 2012). To these points about values-coherence and reflectiveness we can add that the element of sincerity further restrains the types of values that the person of integrity will develop and cherish. Only in rare cases is a person with violently anti-social convictions in a position to sincerely stand for them in word and deed. These three constraints (values-coherence, reflection and sincerity) may not categorically rule out Ingrid holding evil values,[7] but it limits the likelihood of such a result. This allows our definition's eclecticism to capture many of the points raised in connection to the element of morality. In particular, several general intuitions about the relationship between integrity and morality bear mention, even if for our conceptual purposes we resist taking them as constitutive elements.

First, Ingrid has a personal moral stance; she possesses moral commitments, reasoning and sensibility and she takes all of these seriously. This does not tell us anything about the *content* of Ingrid's moral life: only that she *has* a moral life.

Second, as just observed, the constraints of values-coherence and sincerity strongly influence the type of moral convictions a person of integrity is likely to hold. This helps explain why, while people routinely apply the term to those they disagree with on moral or political issues (Cox, La Caze, & Levine, 1999, p. 520), it is almost never spontaneously applied to truly evil characters like Hitler.

Third, some commentators note the perplexing fact that, despite its seeming ethical desirability, a host of 'moral dangers' seem to follow from the values-coherence implied by integrity. These potential dangers include egoism, extremism, intolerance, fanaticism, moral blindness and more (Benjamin, 1990; Edgar & Pattison, 2011; Luban, 2003; Scherkoske, 2010). A hint of these worries lurks in Nietzsche's extolling of the integrity of his 'noble man':

> The noble type of man experiences *itself* as determining values; it does not need approval; it judges, 'what is harmful to me is harmful in itself'; it knows itself to be that which first accords honor to things; it is *value-creating*. (Nietzsche, 1989, p. 260)

While Nietzsche exalts in the glory integrity can infuse, he equally expresses the hubris that seems to lie within it. Despite these dangers, we do not usually apply the term to ideologues and extremists. One way or another (the precise mechanism is disputed (Calhoun, 1995; Cox et al., 2009; Scherkoske, 2010)), the intuitive application of integrity manages to skirt the serious moral dangers of taking one's own commitments to extreme levels – what Scherkoske (2012, p. 185) terms 'vicious steadfastness'. Again, our stance here, of taking personal integrity to involve the four elements of values-coherence, reflectiveness, sincerity and willpower, provides the beginnings of an answer. The requirement of integrating one's values (values-coherence), of subjecting them to a level of open and critical review (reflectiveness) and of being completely public about those values and their implications to one's community (sincerity), serves to make it extremely unlikely – though perhaps not impossible – that Ingrid exhibits brutal extremism.

Theorists locating integrity's essence in morality see integrity essentially opposed to being unprincipled, amoral, evil or tyrannical (Dudzinski, 2004; Graham, 2001).

Summation

As this overview illustrates, the most common understanding of integrity applied to individuals refers, as coherence-integrity, to the agent's persisting internal qualities. This coherence-integrity in turn is made up of four key elements (values-coherence, willpower, reflectiveness and sincerity) and carries consequences for the subject's substantive ethical position (a fifth element of morality). As we stressed, all these key elements are captured by the core idea that personal integrity involves Ingrid asking hard questions about her values, giving honest and public answers, and living by those answers.

Context-Integrity for Individuals

As well as exploring the substance of personal integrity (as coherence-integrity), theorists from a wide array of disciplinary perspectives have wrestled with the ways in which an individual's environment might erode her integrity (the question of context-integrity). Ingrid's social, political, organizational and economic milieu carries strong consequences for her internalization and harmonization of her claimed values, and on the internal qualities that contribute to her acting on those values.

Unlike the situation with institutional integrity (as we will later explore), studies of the impact of context on personal integrity do not tend to focus on compliance mechanisms like coercive external oversight (e.g. police enforcement of legal duties). That is, theorists are not interested in how external context works to enforce compliance – in our terms, how context-integrity helps drive a person's *consistency*-integrity. Rather, philosophers studying personal integrity focus on how the external environment, including the general culture but especially the organizational context, can help or hinder a member's capacity to develop and hold her own integrity – in our terms, how context-integrity impacts upon a person's *coherence*-integrity. (We will later (in the section 'Why isn't Coherence-Integrity a Focus for Institutions?') reflect on possible explanations for why institutional integrity focuses on consistency-integrity and compliance, while personal integrity hones in on coherence-question and character.)

This section develops the existing insights on how context-integrity, especially that provided by Ingrid's organizational context, can threaten Ingrid's coherence-integrity. That is, we outline the ways that institutions can encourage integrity failures such as personal distress, fragmentation, compartmentalization and rationalization. Our discussion here sets the groundwork for our later consideration (in the section 'Tensions between Institutional and Personal Integrity') of a key question that arises from reflection on the Comprehensive Integrity Framework's application to both individuals and institutions, namely, does *institutional integrity undermine or promote personal integrity*?

At the outset, note that the context-integrity of a member of a particular institution differs conceptually from that institution's coherence-integrity.

In other words, the way that Ingrid's institutional environment promotes *her* integrity conceptually differs from the way that the institution internally promotes *its own* integrity. By way of example, suppose Ingrid is a practicing doctor, and belongs to the relevant Medical Association. Ingrid's context-integrity describes how well her entire environment – including the professional association – contributes to her upholding and acting upon *her* claimed values. The coherence-integrity of Ingrid's professional association refers to how well its internal arrangements and member's values (including Ingrid's values) support the association living up to *its* claimed values.

With that distinction in mind, let us examine the ways that Ingrid's organizational context can impact upon her integrity. The literature provides us with a wealth of perspectives on the ways that institutions can work to undercut personal integrity, including from psychological and philosophical analysis of concrete case studies (Gioia, 1992), professional histories (Luban, 2003), major legal cases (Kerwin, 2012), fictional explorations (Breakey, 2014b), qualitative social science (Kelly, 1998) and more (MacIntyre, 1999; Rozuel, 2011). These studies alert us to different institutional pressures and the different types of personal fragmentation that can result from these.

Unfortunately for the integrity prospects for organization-members, it turns out that institutions can drive several distinct types of fragmentations. We distinguish four major categories, with several important sub-categories.

Compartmentalization
In the case of compartmentalization, the organization-member unthinkingly adopts the prevailing standards of his institutional role. (We will use the pronoun 'his' in this section to distinguish the fragmented person from Ingrid, who we will return to when we discuss 'Reflective Role-Endorsement' below.) The compartmentalizer does not ever step back from the institutional standards to evaluate them from a different point of view, either from his own life-perspective, or from the value-systems inherent in the other roles that he plays.

Compartmentalization rears its head in two ways, leading to two sub-categories.

Mild compartmentalization occurs when the organization-member has (for various reasons) failed to fully apprehend that his own values, especially his moral values, need to interrupt or otherwise impact on the institutional role he is following. Gioia (1992) describes a very personal example of mild compartmentalization in exploring his own role in Pinto Fires scandal. In charge of product recalls at Ford, Gioia explains how his job was made manageable by following 'scripts': cognitive processes that mapped existing knowledge onto a template for understanding and response. Unfortunately, his company's prevailing scripts failed to recognize ethically salient features of the Ford Pinto case — namely the small car's capacity to erupt into an all-consuming fire when impacted from behind. Gioia's personal values should have alerted him to this concern, but the significance of the scripts in making his job manageable proved a powerful impediment to him doing so.[8]

Total compartmentalization occurs when the organization-member is so engrained in following role-based scripts that they can scarcely fathom how their values in one role could impact upon their values in another. This extreme case emerges in Hannah Arendt's reflections on the Nazi 'desk-murderer' Adolph Eichmann (Kerwin, 2012), and in MacIntyre's (1999) exploration of his imagined character 'J' (who resembles Eichmann). In the case of mild compartmentalization, an agent like Gioia is able (when confronted with the reality of his actions) to 'snap out of it', and recognize that his values should have interrupted his script-following. But a character like Eichmann is incapable of such a realization. Compartmentalization so pervades his character that he can scarcely apprehend how he could criticize his role from an outside standpoint. There is no (mental or social) space available to him whereby such a critique could be made (MacIntyre, 1999). He is 'unthinking', as Arendt said of Eichmann (Kerwin, 2012).

Rationalization
Rationalization differs from compartmentalization inasmuch as the person adopting specific roles, and adhering to prevailing scripts, has not done so in an unthinking manner. To the contrary, the rationalizer has put at least some thought — and perhaps quite a lot of thought — into explaining why they adopt the particular role they do. While the mild compartmentalizer might be mortified at realizing what he has been a part of, the rationalizer is fully aware that his actions can be evaluated from a standpoint outside his specific role, and he has a story to tell about how that evaluation justifies his role. The rationalizer cares about his integrity — he actively perceives and publicly acknowledges the importance of some level of overall coherence across his values and actions.

The problem is that the rationalizer does not care *enough* about his integrity. The rationalizer's justifications for his role-based actions do not withstand any genuine rational scrutiny. The values he holds outside the institutional role *really should* impact upon his institutional behaviour; they should overthrow the feeble rationalization he offers. Explorations of professional ethics show how such rationalization can occur. In the context of the legal profession, Luban (2003) describes how social psychological processes (such as cognitive dissonance) can gull the lawyer into too-easily rationalizing away their immoral practices and eroding their initial idealism. In the context of nursing, Kelly (1998) recounts how noble client-focused ethics can be usurped by an insular in-group loyalty, rationalized by its adherents through a perceived need to survive and prosper as part of the team. ('Us-against-them' narratives often pervade stories of integrity failures (Gioia, 1992), promoting loyalty to the organization or group above other personally held values.)

Single-Minded Workaholic
The single-minded workaholic has placed his work-role as the centrepiece of his life, and made everything else subservient to it. The values used in his work-role are the values that he takes as definitive of his very person. For the workaholic, there is no perceived gap between his professional ethos and his everyday values — and to the extent gaps do arise, it is the everyday ethos that must give way.

What prevents the single-minded workaholic from having integrity? Cécile Rozuel draws on the work of Jung, and also of Goffman, in showing the inherent fragility and imbalance of a person who has taken his role's values to be his true core (in Jung's terms, who has taken his 'persona' to be his 'ego'). More broadly, as we define him here, the single-minded workaholic fails to have integrity because the way he goes about the ruthless purging of his 'life' values is unsustainable. Life, and events outside his work, must still go on. He must eventually deal with life-issues such as partners, family, children, bereavement, loneliness, friends, religion, health and the wider society, and the institutional values purpose-built for his role may prove hopeless for navigating such realms. The workaholic ostensibly denies the significance of these wider concerns. But unless he is truly a monomaniac,[9] life will inevitably intrude on his working existence. When it does, his deeply-held but unrecognized values rear their heads and level their demands at him, unearthing inconsistencies that were always present. In Breakey's (2014b, pp. 72–73) exploration of role ethics in the television series *The Wire*, the character of Jimmy McNulty exemplifies such a workaholic: McNulty is totally dedicated to his police-work and its values and goods, to the point where his life falls apart. Eventually McNulty realizes his wrenching position. 'The things that make me good at this job', he laments, 'make me wrong for everything else'. In the series' final seasons

McNulty retreats from being a detective to the lower pressures, and happier existence, of a uniformed cop walking his beat.

The Morally Torn
Perhaps the saddest ramification of institutional processes on personal integrity comes in the form of the morally torn. Such a person, like the rationalizer, is aware of a significant gap between their ordinary values and their institutional role. Unlike the rationalizer however, the morally torn has too much integrity to sweep the issue under the carpet. But he is unwilling to leave the institution itself — perhaps because of the personal costs of doing so, or perhaps because he knows that things will be worse in the institution if he does not remain within it. Yet he does not have the power to change the institution's practices, and his personal involvement in activities he disagrees with. This chasm between his actions and values leads him to 'moral distress', as Kelly describes in the context of the nursing profession (Kelly, 1998). The morally torn person does not have integrity, and awareness of this very fact emotionally torments him. (Such a person is, however, a candidate for having integrity in the future. Perhaps he will need to change his occupation or at least his institution, or perhaps with time and experience he will acquire the power and support necessary to reform it. But his felt anguish at failing to have integrity — a failure that currently leaves him morally torn — may ultimately lead him to achieve true integrity.)

The distinctions between these four groups are important. The mild compartmentalizer does not *notice* the clash with his other values. The total compartmentalizer cannot *even conceive* of a clash with his other values. The rationalizer *fails to treat seriously* the acknowledged clash with his other values, while the single-minded workaholic has *distorted* all his other values in a forlorn attempt to align them with his role. The morally torn worker keenly *apprehends* the clash between his role and his values, but cannot or will not change either.

While these types of fragmentation differ conceptually, a single person can shift between them. For example, upon realizing he has been guilty of mild compartmentalization, a role-holder might for a time attempt rationalization. But his own reflections, or public challenges, might force him to give up the rationalization, collapsing into being morally torn. Over time, he may assuage his moral distress by becoming a single-minded workaholic.

What drives these different types of fragmentation? All institutions can potentially pose a threat to a person's integrity, treating them as mere cogs in a larger machine. But the literature unearths several signature pressures that drive the above fragmentations. These 'usual suspects' include:

- Institutional roles that suppress autonomous decision-making (Dolovich, 2010) or emotional responses (Gioia, 1992);
- Institutional roles heavily reliant on scripts to process and respond to information (Gioia, 1992);
- Institutional roles where the neophyte is thrown 'out of his depth', removing the capacity for self-confidence in his own values and evaluations (Kelly, 1998);
- Institutional roles and perceptions encouraging an us-and-them mentality (Gioia, 1992; Kelly, 1998);
- Institutional roles that involve lying, exaggerating, dissembling or advocating for positions one does not believe (Cox et al., 2009; Luban, 2003);
- The prevalence of clumsy metrics of quantified performance evaluation (Breakey, 2014b; Kelly, 1998);
- Resource and time constraints, including being continually forced in new directions for reasons of expedience (Breakey, 2014b; Gioia, 1992; Kelly, 1998);
- Institutional roles where small breaches are unpoliced, and can grow surreptitiously into larger violations (Luban, 2003);
- Institutional roles that don't allow space for raising concerns about practices, or that don't possess institutional space for integrity-preserving mechanisms such as (where appropriate) internal whistleblowing or conscientious objection mechanisms (MacIntyre, 1999; Magelssen, 2012);
- Societies with little space for reflection and activity in one realm to be linked to the values of another institution (and perhaps little overlap in the personnel of each realm) (MacIntyre, 1999);
- Modern societies of pluralism and dynamism, or where tensions exist between an institution and its wider community, making a consistent narrative difficult to hold (Benjamin, 1990, pp. 68–71; Breakey, 2014b).

Reflective Role-Endorsement
Of course, it is not all bad news. Simply because the values and practices a person employs in their organizational-role differ from the ones they use in other parts of their life does not necessarily mean the person fails to possess integrity. To the contrary, role-holders often perform vital tasks that cannot be done well without adopting distinct ways of behaving, valuing, feeling and thinking. Because these tasks can be important, either to an individual or to her society, Ingrid can have very good reason to take up the role necessary to fulfil her institutional task. In this case she resembles the 'rationalizer', who puts forward reasons explaining and justifying the clear gap between his ordinary values and his role-identity. The single but

profound difference, of course, is that in Ingrid's case the defence is a genuine, reasonable one, capable of being reflectively endorsed by Ingrid — and usually upheld and acknowledged by the wider society. Her defence is also bound to be a nuanced one, allowing Ingrid to take recourse to her own values where necessary, and to mitigate the role-identity in various principled ways.[10]

Contingency

What activities Ingrid performs, and what effects they have, emerge from both her coherence-integrity (who she is) and her context-integrity (what her environment is). But as well as these stable, ongoing factors, other events can occur that create new and unforeseen dynamics or pressures. In a given case, whether or not these events impact upon Ingrid's pursuit of her claimed values is a matter of 'contingency'. Contingency constitutes 'sudden shocks', unprepared-for exceptions and surprise events.

As we noted above, contingency (in the form of an unfortunate concatenation of unlucky events or extraordinary pressures) may create a situation where, despite an agent having solid coherence-integrity, she ultimately fails to perform with consistency-integrity.[11]

Together, the three causal elements of coherence-integrity, context-integrity and contingency determine Ingrid's activities and the extent to which they accord with her claimed values. As a result, in any given case, coherence-integrity, context-integrity and contingency together determine consistency-integrity (Fig. 1).

We do not include contingency only for the sake of completeness in the causal factors determining Ingrid's actions. Contingency matters to discussions of integrity. The greater Ingrid's coherence-integrity, and the healthier her context-integrity, the greater the *resilience* she will display to contingency's slings and arrows, and their capacity to impact upon Ingrid living up to her claimed values.

INSTITUTIONAL INTEGRITY

While much philosophical attention has surrounded personal integrity over the last few decades, institutional integrity remains comparatively less studied. Despite this, ordinary speakers routinely apply the term 'integrity' to

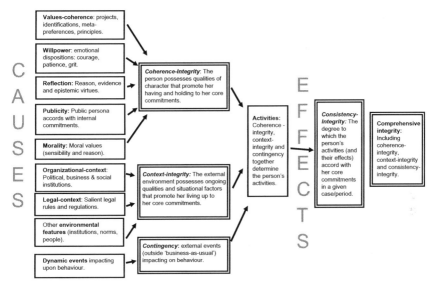

Fig. 1. Personal Integrity Conceptual Map.

institutions, companies and organizations. 'In fact', as Audi and Murphy (2006, p. 5) describe, 'integrity has appeared in 20 percent of company mission statements and is the most frequently mentioned value in corporate values statements'.

The application of the term 'integrity' to institutions seems appropriate to the extent we can view institutions as agents; collectively, institutions issue statements, make decisions, comply with norms and undertake actions. But the term 'integrity' can also apply in a descriptive sense to inanimate objects, and its employment in this respect also reflects some of what we might expect from the idea of institutional integrity. Dudzinski (2004, p. 300) explains: 'In the descriptive sense, the bridge has integrity because its purpose, design, and function are in harmony. ... A bridge would lack integrity if it was not reliable as a bridge and did not meet our expectations of bridges'. Wueste (2005) draws a similar link with health. Just as the idea of institutional integrity parallels in many respects to the normative concept of personal integrity, so too it captures many of the features of these descriptive meanings of the term.

In what follows we apply the Comprehensive Integrity Framework's terminology and conceptual analysis to institutional integrity, aiming to capture the thrust of both ordinary invocations of institutional integrity and recent theorising upon it.

'Claimed Values' for Institutions: The 'Public Institutional Justification' (PIJ)

What in the context of personal integrity are the relatively informal 'claimed values' becomes in the context of institutional integrity the more explicit and formal notion of the 'Public Institutional Justification' (PIJ). Usually including an account of the *raison d'être* of the institution (what it is 'for'), the PIJ is what the institution's members and representatives use to justify the institution and to show the public it deserves their support or at least tolerance (Preston & Sampford, 2002a, pp. 47–48). The PIJ justifies the risk the community takes in the creation of another institution whose powers could be abused and used against the community (Sampford, 2010). When the institution's actions, powers or existence are called into question, institutional members and representatives aim to re-establish its credentials by asserting its PIJ. While the PIJ is wholly chosen by the institution-members/representatives, it nevertheless reflects wider community values, as these are the audience for the justification. Like an individual's claimed values, the PIJ can be a mere fiction, little more than a slick public relations document. If so, it fails to genuinely justify the institution, and to contain 'honest and public answers'. To attain institutional integrity, an organization must not merely present a PIJ, but must live by it.

Many accounts of institutional integrity draw on this key organizing idea of the publicly asserted or acknowledged purpose of the institution (Preston & Sampford, 2002a, pp. 37–38; Wueste, 2005, pp. 15–22). As Buchanan and Keohane (2006, p. 428) observe, offering public justifications is itself a core part of an institution's achievement of integrity and transparency. Equally, the 'front page' test (Huberts, 2014, p. 46) is a well-known device that encourages both reflection on, and compliance with, the institution's PIJ.

Consistency-Integrity for Institutions

Paralleling consistency-integrity for individuals, if an institution's activities are consistent with its PIJ, then it has consistency-integrity and 'acts with' integrity. For institutions, consistency-integrity is arguably the key organizing concept: it is natural to ask whether the institution's acts accord with its words – and often much of social import hangs on the answer to this question. We can see this in talk of integrity *systems* (including external features like a free and vigorous press that act as a watchdog), integrity *violations*, and integrity *measures* (such as Crime and Misconduct Commissions). None of these notions focuses its attention on coherence-integrity and a concern for internal qualities like values and virtues. Instead, the focus lies with consistency-integrity – on whether or not the institution's actions accord with its PIJ. For example, an integrity breach or integrity violation does not occur when an institution possesses a vulnerable internal organizational arrangement. Rather, it occurs when the vulnerability manifests in an actual breach of a rule, or in a poor outcome. This is why, coming from a public administration background, Huberts (2014, p. 7) can assert (against the philosophers' focus on the internal intentions, character and values central to personal integrity) that, 'chiefly, however, the integrity concept concerns behaviour ...'.

Coherence-Integrity for Institutions

For institutions, coherence-integrity comprises two factors: (a) coherence on members' values (including moral values): the institution's members hold personal values that contribute to the institution pursuing its PIJ (this does not envisage full consensus but merely that individual members conceive of their role morality as being congruent with the institutional values[12]); and (b) coherence of internal organizational arrangements. 'Internal organizational arrangements' consist of the processes governing how the institution makes its decisions; the structures it uses for policing and encouraging compliance with those decisions; its policies on transparency, accountability and critical feedback; and any other arrangements that impact upon it living up to its PIJ. When working well, these internal organizational arrangements help create the PIJ and ensure that the institution pursues its PIJ.

In the ideal institution, these two factors of members' values and internal organizational arrangements ensure that the PIJ remains workable and acceptable to all those institution-members bound by the PIJ. An institution whose values and internal organizational arrangements cohere with its PIJ possesses high coherence-integrity, as all its pieces fit together and push in the same broad direction. Wueste (2005, p. 27) knits together values, purpose (PIJ) and coherence-integrity thus: 'in order to achieve the purpose, one has to comply with the normative constraints intrinsic to the enterprise, which is essentially the task of maintaining its integrity'. Ideally, the internal organizational arrangements of the institution reliably produce compliance with the PIJ even if the agents are not themselves saints. Alternatively, the internal arrangements may encourage the institution-members' formation of appropriate values and integrity. In the less ideal circumstance, an institution loses coherence-integrity if, 'its practices or procedures predictably undermine the pursuit of the very goals in terms of which it justifies its existence' (Buchanan & Keohane, 2006, p. 423).

In the last section's discussion of personal integrity, we noted five elements constituting coherence-integrity. We can draw on this philosophical work to illuminate aspects of institutional integrity, as each of these elements have analogues in the institutional context.

- *Values-coherence*: In assessing an institution's value-coherence, we ask: does the institution's stated PIJ reflect, or at least prove congruent with, the actual values held by its members, authorities and representatives? Does the institution actually possess a PIJ, or does its public relations department merely 'talk the talk' without the institution possessing a genuinely shared self-understanding of its values? Does its members' professional integrity promote the larger institutional integrity? We saw earlier that for personal integrity the idea of values-coherence refers to the existence and coherence of key values within an individual person. For institutions, values-coherence becomes the existence and coherence of 'member's values' across the institution.

- *Willpower*: Speaking of institutional 'willpower' is overly anthropomorphic, but nevertheless alerts us to a key issue. Merely possessing integrated values, without mechanisms to translate them into action, was insufficient to ensure personal integrity. For persons, this required willpower and virtuous emotions and dispositions. For institutions, this requires the 'internal organizational arrangements' mentioned above that ensure the institution makes its decisions based on its PIJ, and for the resulting decisions to be duly enacted.

- *Reflection*: Reflection plays a role both in the development of the PIJ and institution's values, and in the extent to which the institution's decisions and action correspond with its PIJ. Institutions possess reflection when they have decision-making and feedback processes that allow institution-members to inject values-based reasons into discussion and policy-making, and when the institution ensures that members understand the reasons for its decisions, rather than merely acquiescing in them.

- *Sincerity*: Sincerity requires the institution's actual behaviour tracks its public persona (its PIJ). Transparency and accountability (both internal and external) are key parts of the relevant internal organizational arrangements here (Buchanan & Keohane, 2006, p. 431). But the processes for decision-making are at least as important; for example, does the institution routinely apply a 'front page' test to its internal decision-making?
- *Morality*: The three moral facets of personal coherence-integrity implied: (i) possessing moral commitments; (ii) ensuring those commitments are not morally beyond the pale; and (iii) avoiding the moral dangers of egoism and extremism. Refracted onto institutions, the first facet is included in the idea of the PIJ: as a *justification* for the institution, the PIJ necessarily requires that moral concerns shape the institution's claimed values. Similarly, the PIJ's public nature usually ensures it will capture the second element of moral decency, because public scrutiny will not tolerate morally repugnant institutional behaviour. The third concern looms large for institutions too: moral danger threatens when the institutional interest becomes so strong that it swamps all other social and moral factors. This might occur when the institution, or its mission, is seen as sacred and demanding of unquestioned loyalty (such as a church, a charity or a state during war), when the institution's members believe that their well-being inextricably depends on the institution's flourishing and survival, and when members perceive the institution to be under attack. In all these cases, the interests of various individuals may attach so strongly to the institution as to overwhelm its pursuit of its PIJ – loyalty to the institution's survival and strength trump loyalty to the purposes the institution claims to pursue (in our terms, the risk is that members-values distort and swamp the larger coherence-integrity).

Context-Integrity for Institutions

Perhaps even more than the case with individual people, whether an institution will in fact behave in accord with its PIJ (i.e. whether it will have consistency-integrity) does not hinge primarily on its coherence-integrity. The behaviour of the institution will be substantially influenced by its external environment, including the institution's relationships to other organizations. The institution possesses 'context-integrity' if its external environment tends to facilitate the institution acting in accordance with its PIJ.

The importance of surrounding institutions for promoting consistency-integrity is a feature of many studies of institutional integrity (Buchanan & Keohane, 2006, p. 432). Indeed, in recent literature on integrity systems and accountability, focus has shifted from the existence of discrete anticorruption institutions to the overall network of interrelations between institutions. The network's primary goal is the promotion of integrity; combating its opposite (corruption) remains a secondary and derivative, though necessary, element (Sampford, Smith, & Brown, 2005). This attention to structuring external relations to achieve institutional integrity resurrects insights dating all the way back to ideas on the separation of powers, balance of powers, and checks and balances, arising in the work of Machiavelli, Locke, Montesquieu and other early modern political theorists (Breakey, 2014a; Rahe, 2011; Sullivan, 2006; Vile, 1998; Zuckert, 2012).

Nested Institutions
Context-integrity includes 'nested' relationships with larger institutions (or networks of institutions like the 'justice system'). An institution can be one part of a larger institutional complex that has its own PIJ and undertakes its own activities and tasks on a larger scale. In this case we will call the institution one 'sub-institution' nested within a larger 'regime'. An essential – even legally determined – part of the sub-institution's PIJ may be that the sub-institution plays an official part in the regime's pursuit of the regime's PIJ. In this case the sub-institution is a 'formal' part of the regime. When the sub-institution's PIJ accords closely with the regime's PIJ, the sub-institution's consistency-integrity will contribute to the regime's coherence- and consistency-integrity. Equally, a regime's coherence-integrity will facilitate the institution's context-integrity.

Alternatively, the sub-institution may link less officially with the larger regime; its PIJ may only accord indirectly with the regime's PIJ. In such cases it is only an 'informal' part of the regime. This may mean that while an informal sub-institution's activities tend to accord with the regime's PIJ, at some times its priorities will diverge, and its consistency-integrity (its actions in accord with its own PIJ) will run counter to the regime's consistency-integrity.

In either case the sub-institution may enjoy different sorts of relations with its larger regime and the other parts of that regime. As part of institutional design, the institution might relate antagonistically to other elements of the same regime, as occurs for example in some incarnations of the separation of powers (Rahe, 2011). Alternatively, the institution may have a supportive or 'associational' relation to other institutions surrounding it in the regime, with each acknowledging the others' role in securing the larger objective (Little, 2000, pp. 11–12).

Other Relations
An institution's context-integrity also includes reference to all the other bodies, individuals, norms, social factors, economic situations, standards, laws and institutional complexes, that impact upon the institution's pursuit of its PIJ. Some of these other bodies may promote, and others undermine, and others go to lengths to accord with, the institution's activities in compliance with its PIJ.

Integrity System

Together the internal qualities of the institution, and the qualities of its external environment, make up the institution's 'integrity system' (Preston & Sampford, 2002a). The integrity system thus combines the institution's coherence-integrity and context-integrity. It encompasses all the 'business-as-usual' operations and factors in the agent's world that impact on its performance.

Contingency

Contingency works in the same way as it does for individuals – namely, as including those unprepared for, sudden events that impact upon the agent's actions. Because it lies outside business-as-usual, such events are not part of the institution's 'integrity system' – but the more robust the integrity system, the more resilient the institution's integrity will be to these external shocks.

Scope and the Comprehensive Integrity Framework

The 'institution' chosen as the object of study can be larger or smaller. The conceptual system remains the same when scaled up or down. At the smaller scale (e.g. shifting from a specific organization to one of its subcommittees), relations or arrangements that previously featured under the organization's 'coherence-integrity' would then be considered as part of the subcommittee's external relations (and so a part of the 'organizational context' of its context-integrity). Likewise, when scaled up (e.g. from the organization to the larger regime complex of which it forms one part) relations

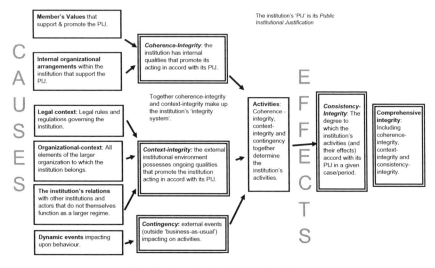

Fig. 2. Institutional Integrity Map.

and arrangements that were external context would now be captured within the internal organizational arrangements of coherence-integrity. In the proposed conceptual and terminological system, each different grouping can be focused upon as the institution under analysis (with the proviso that each institution must possess a PIJ) (Fig. 2).

DIFFERENCES AND REFLECTIONS

We have seen that the Comprehensive Integrity Framework maps personal and institutional integrity using the same terms and concepts. In so doing, the Framework has unearthed several revealing differences between, and interrelations amongst, the two applications of integrity.

Five of the following issues warrant reflection.

Individuals have 'Claimed Values', but Institutions Need a 'PIJ'

An institution's PIJ differs from an individual person's claimed values in several ways. Compared to claimed values, the PIJ has to be more formal, and often appears in a concrete form – a charter or creed or mission statement, or at least a slick public relations manifesto. As well, the PIJ is usually more publicly accessible than an individual's claimed values. Despite her personal integrity, Ingrid can be quite a private person, and it may only be when she is asked or expected to engage in some particular practice, or when someone voices an opinion on a particular topic central to her values, where her committed stance becomes clear. An institution's PIJ, contrariwise, is usually available for all to see. As one last point of distinction, the PIJ serves a particular purpose that personal claimed values need not — the PIJ aims to justify the institution's existence and activities. It is not just an uncompromising statement of the institution's purposes, but an apologia — a defence of its operations.

Why do these differences exist between an individual's 'claimed values' and the institution's PIJ? We offer three reasons. First, because institutions bring together several people, the process whereby shared values are debated, created, settled, changed, communicated and encouraged in new members needs to be a matter of public record. For organizations, the processes of reflection, decision and memorizing cannot happen in the same internal way possible in the case of personal integrity.

Second, institution's purposes must be far more interwoven with the law. To be properly registered and functional, certain associations require charters, churches perform specific sorts of tasks, and companies take on certain (e.g. fiduciary) responsibilities. These mean that various parts of an institution's PIJ may be reflected in, or required to be made explicit through, laws and regulations. Indeed, in many cases the PIJ and the codes and constitutions that apply and contextualize it need to be signed off by a minister, formally resolved at an AGM and so on.

Finally, PIJs need to give prominence to the issue of justification because institutions, far more than individual people, require legitimacy to exist and function — not least to justify the risk that the community takes that the institution's concentration of power, people and resources might be used against that community rather than for the values that constitute its PIJ. Institutions benefit greatly by being seen as legitimate and purposeful by their members — a voluntary organization that cannot justify itself to its own members is clearly under threat. But many organizations also require various types of legal and social privileges, or the support and patronage of parts of the local population, to survive and prosper. Individual persons do not require this level of justification; they have human rights preventing their liquidation — and rightly so. As well as not having any intrinsic moral worth, institutions possess more raw strength than a given individual acting alone. By 'raw strength' we refer to the sheer power and resources possessed by an institution that empower it to survive, expand, resist, compel, resource, reward, disrupt, threaten and influence (Breakey, 2014a, p. 32). Institutions draw together substantial economic, material and other resources, and if this power is employed for antisocial purposes it can constitute a far greater danger than that posed by an individual person. For this reason, policing institution's activities constitutes a particularly urgent social need.

For all these reasons, then, it should not surprise us that institutions come to possess a slightly different notion of claimed values – one more public and concrete, and more attuned to the specific business of validation: the Public Institutional Justification.

Why isn't Coherence-Integrity a Focus for Institutions?

The previous sections showed that studies of personal integrity honed in on the agent's internal qualities (coherence-integrity), while research into institutional integrity took the agent's actual behaviour (consistency-integrity) as the key concern. What is the reason for this difference of priority between the two applications of the same idea? Specifically, why do we hold institutions to account – even legally to account – for their actions in pursuit of their publicly stated purposes, but do not similarly hold persons responsible to the same degree? Why does personal integrity reside in the realm of supererogatory aspiration, while institutional integrity is a matter of law, regulation, constitutionalism and professionalism?

A large part of the answer, we submit, is that the institution's purpose structures its very existence. Legal entitlements, regulations and social expectations take their shape from the institution's purpose. Society and law respond differently to community organizations, churches, multinational corporations, small businesses and public services. Each of these institutions requires certain sorts of legal privileges and entitlements to function. So too, depending upon the type of resources the institution commands, each poses specific sorts of threats to individuals and communities. Social and legal practices thus need to respond to institutions very much based upon the institution's professed purpose.

For individual people, it is quite otherwise. The same law and the same rights, more or less, cover people with very different values and aspirations; Ingrid might totally revise her values without the law needing to accommodate such a shift in any way. The devout spiritualist, the enterprising entrepreneur, the dedicated artist, the social reformer – all of these can possess largely the same legal entitlements and obligations. This means that society does not require legal machinery or strong social sanctions to ensure that Ingrid acts in accord with her claimed values. Whether she does so or not is a matter for her own conscience, and for our social appraisal of her character.

Additionally, institutions almost by definition act on behalf of collectives. Corporations act on behalf of their shareholders; public administrators on behalf of taxpayers and citizens; and so on. The collective hands over its powers and resources to the institution on the condition that these invest-ments are to be used in a particular way, or for a particular purpose. Any action that breaches that purpose thereby wrongs the collective's members. For individual people, again, the situation differs. In the usual case, if Ingrid betrays her own values, the primary person who loses is Ingrid, and all her prior investments in those values. Others will not have the same cause for complaint; Ingrid is not abusing their investments. The powers and resources she is redirecting are her own. True, there are situations where Ingrid's self-betrayal will also harm others, perhaps her nearest and dearest, or those that have trusted her to live up to her values and supported her in doing so. But the general point remains that when an institution egregiously fails to live up to its PIJ, individual people's material investments are almost always mis-used. If Ingrid fails to live up to her specific claimed values, we can make no automatic presumption of an abuse of power.

For these two reasons, then, it makes sense for our concern with institu-tional integrity to focus on what the institution *does*. For an individual per-son outside of an institutional setting, on the other hand, our concern need not be legalistic or regulative, but a more social judgement about who that person *is*.

Claimed Values and the PIJ Differ from 'Members Values' for Institutions

The values and principles a person upholds and internalizes *just are* their claimed values. For individuals who possess integrity, we can read off the person's claimed values directly from their held values. The 'values-coherence' at the top-left-hand corner of Fig. 1 thus constitutes the 'claimed values' that form Ingrid's personal standard of integrity.

For institutions the relationship between the members' values and the PIJ proves less straightforward. 'Members' values' can relate to any norm, ideal or principle, held by any member of the institution, that ultimately helps the institution live up to its PIJ. This need not mean the norm itself forms part of the PIJ. Institution members can have values that promote the PIJ by comporting the member appropriately to various parts of the institution or environment around them. A member may have values that guide her engagement with any of the parts of her governing integrity system: with her colleagues, with the internal organizational arrangements, with the laws that regulate her, with the larger organizations to which she belongs, and with the community at large. In short, members' values may facilitate their interaction with every part of the integrity system described in Fig. 2.

By way of example, consider the public service as a profession. Drawing together prior research, Huberts (2014, pp. 84–85) lists an array of diverse values found in the public administration literature, categorized in terms of public servants' relationships with different agents and organizations. Translated into the language of the Comprehensive Integrity Framework, these public sector values can ensure proper action with respect to *internal organizational arrangements* within the public service itself (e.g. the virtues of innovation, timeliness and productivity); with respect to the *organizational context* provided by the elected politicians (e.g. the virtues of loyalty and responsiveness) and oversight regimes (e.g. openness and accountability); with respect to their *legal environment* (e.g. respect for rule of law, legality and equal treatment); and finally with respect to the *external context* of the stakeholder communities (e.g. citizen involvement, user orientation and professionalism). None of these values, important as they are, would actually feature as part of the profession's PIJ – but all of these values in various ways support the public sector in meeting its PIJ. Needless to say, the public sector *also* possesses values that relate directly to its PIJ, in the form of the sector's commitments to contribute to society (e.g. virtues such as promoting the common good, social cohesion, regime dignity and so on.). In this case we can see that the members' values of the public sector include values that directly parallel the sector's overall PIJ, as well as a multitude of operative norms that instrumentally aid the institution in securing the realization of that PIJ.

In sum, all the members' values (on the top left hand corner of Fig. 2), if they are to aid coherence-integrity, must support the pursuit of the PIJ. Sometimes, this will mean the member's values simply are part of the PIJ (as we saw with the public sector's values of the common good). Other times the member's values differ from the PIJ, but nevertheless work in support of it (such as with openness and respect for the rule of law). Again, this contrasts with the personal case, where Ingrid's claimed values will always form part of her values-coherence. Because Ingrid genuinely holds those values, they count as part of her claimed values.

Corruption and Abuse of Power Strikes at the Heart of Both Personal and Institutional Integrity

When we think of integrity failures, or the need for integrity measures, or when the term 'integrity' shouts from the news headlines, the subject of discussion almost always surrounds corruption or the abuse of power (Huberts, 2014, p. 8). The conceptual system provided above explains why this is so: namely, these types of behaviour represent striking violations of *both* personal and institutional integrity. They constitute a perform storm of integrity failure.

We have seen that personal integrity involves sincerity. When our person with integrity (Ingrid) deliberately and voluntarily joins an institution with clear and well-known practices, norms and values (and thus with a definite PIJ), Ingrid inculcates a social expectation that she will conform to those norms. Issuing from this social expectation, Ingrid's sincerity demands that she upholds those qualities – or publicly and explicitly refuses to do so, such as through conscientious objection. Ingrid's embrace of the institutional norms then becomes part of her own claimed values, and her professional integrity incorporates into her own integrity. Needless to say, rules against corruption and abuse of power will inevitably feature in the institution's norms – if an institution's PIJ explicitly endorsed and publicized its policies of abusing power, then they would no longer *be* abuses of power in the ordinary sense. As such, if Ingrid were to violate those norms, she would be not only betraying her own integrity and the professional integrity that forms part of it, but also undermining her institution's integrity. Little wonder, then, that abuse of one's institutional role constitutes the canonical example of a failure of integrity.

Tensions between Institutional and Personal Integrity

We noted earlier that an institution's coherence-integrity was not conceptually the same as the context-integrity of an institution-member (*qua* individual person, like Ingrid). We also surveyed ways that an institution might erode a member's integrity, resulting in their becoming a victim of compartmentalization or rationalization, or a single-minded workaholic, or morally torn.

Having provided an account of the nature of institutional integrity, our final question arises: What is the relationship between institutional and personal integrity? The values and practices of each individual member impact upon the institution's coherence-integrity, and the values and practices of the institution impact upon each individual member's context-integrity. This opens an intriguing question: do institutions with high (coherence) integrity inevitably promote their members' integrity? Or — to the contrary — does a high institutional integrity actually threaten the personal integrity of its members?

Three possible outcomes spring to mind. First, it may be that institutional integrity intrinsically clashes with personal integrity. After all, we might suppose that a fragmented institution, with little integrity, might be more beneficial to its members' integrity, precisely because its fragmentation and lack of control allowed more space for member's personal autonomy. More specifically, the institution might threaten its members' integrity if it can only achieve integrity by treating its members as little more than cogs in a larger mechanism, or if the institution's task required its members to suddenly shift in their convictions (undermining their values-coherence) or to systematically lie to others (undermining their sincerity).

A second possibility is that there is no tension whatsoever, and that an institution with integrity necessarily promotes and accords with the integrity of each of its members.

In fact, it is unlikely that either of these two absolute answers will prove correct. Because institutions possess very different PIJs, they can pursue very different instantiations of institutional integrity, and persons pursuing very different instantiations of personal integrity can wind up working for these institutions. Whether the two pursuits fit together will be a contingent, contextual question. Thus, a more likely (third) possibility emerges that certain specific types of institutions will (as they pursue their own institutional integrity) pose special challenges to certain specific individuals (as they pursue their own personal integrity).

While there are thus no hard and fast answers to the relationship between institutional and personal integrity, we can still make some general claims about the likely effects of institutional integrity on personal integrity. Recall that an institution with integrity has asked hard questions of its values, given honest and public answers, and does its best to live by those answers. Recall too that asking those hard questions will (ideally) mean involving the institutional members in the discussion and development of its PIJ.

The institution's development and commitment to the PIJ can facilitate the personal integrity of its members in several ways. First, the public nature of the PIJ means that institution-members, performing their required activities, can do so in a sincere fashion. Clients, stake-holders and the community are not being misled by the institution or its members.

Second, the public nature of the PIJ helps prospective members make an informed decision about whether they want to join the institution. Prospective members will be less likely to harbour an idealized or unrealistic notion of what the institution stands for. This does not mean that only prospective members whose values 'fit' the institution's PIJ will join. An entryist might join an organization precisely because they want to radically reform it. Others may want to take it in new directions. Still others may interpret the PIJ differently (indeed the PIJ may be subject to varied formulation at any one time and certainly over the longer term). These different interpretations of the PIJ and those who want to take it in new directions may prove vital for institutional dynamism and long-term institutional development.[13] While the publicity and honesty of the PIJ will thus not prevent divisions between members (and prospective members) about the PIJ's substance, such sincerity will diminish the shocks that a neophyte encounters on being exposed to the reality of practice at the coal-face (Kelly, 1998), which should in turn lessen the likelihood of 'morally torn' members.

Third, the institution's commitment to its PIJ in word and deed makes it likely that the PIJ actually does serve, to some extent at least, as a genuine justification of the institution to its community. This does not mean the PIJ, *qua* justification, is fully accepted by every stakeholder, but it does mean that the PIJ is more than a facile rationalization. As a result, an institution with integrity does not need to force its members into rationalizations. Why rationalize what you are doing when you have a sensible, public justification (the PIJ) on offer?

Equally, the fact that the PIJ is publically well known makes compartmentalization less likely. Recall that compartmentalization occurs when the institution-member does not (or cannot) reflect upon the values internal to their work from a perspective outside that work. But the PIJ, and its process of development, amounts to exactly such a perspective. An institution that sincerely holds its PIJ fully acknowledges that its internal workings and norms should be subject to critical inquiry from other perspectives, and it develops its PIJ precisely to mediate between the institution's goals and the community's priorities. In involving its members in the development and awareness of the institutional PIJ, an institution with integrity thus greatly reduces the prospects of compartmentalization.

As a general rule, then, we can conclude that institutions with integrity remove many of the pressures towards institution-members' compartmentalization and rationalization — two of the signature threats to members' personal integrity. Turing to the 'morally torn' integrity failure, the public nature of the PIJ removes some of the threats to personal integrity here, but it is doubtful that institutional integrity can entirely ameliorate this possible outcome. Real-world institutions must manage under resource- and time-constraints, and respond to specific events and sudden priorities, and these factors may ignite tensions between individual members wanting to do their own specific jobs 'the way they should be done', and the institution's pursuit of its goals within the existing constraints (Breakey, 2014b). As well, the solution an institution develops to a particular task, as found within its PIJ and its resulting practices, may not accord with the considered ethics of every institutional member. Examples of this clash would include medical practitioners who believe abortion falls outside proper patient care (Magelssen, 2012), or lawyers (especially criminal defence lawyers) who find that the 'zealous advocate' model of professional lawyer's ethics clashes with their ordinary moral commitments (Dolovich, 2010). Institutions that provide mechanisms for conscientious objection, internal whistle-blowing and the raising of formal objections, may help strike a balance between the needs of the institution and the individual in these matters.

But perhaps the largest threat to a member's personal integrity from the institution's integrity comes in the form of the 'single-minded workaholic'. To be sure, an institution with a reasonable PIJ will try to avoid setting up the type of 'us-against-them' mentality that so often serves to encourage single-mindedness. But other problems arise. Merely because an institution has reasonable, legitimate internal norms and values (justified through its PIJ) does not mean that those norms and values should permeate a member's life outside the organization. The norms might function well in allowing the institution to flourish without being good ways of managing one's personal life more generally. As well, the important and laudable work that the institution performs (in its successful pursuit of its PIJ) may encourage a member to prioritize her institutional role when she reflects on her own life and what she stands for. Sensitive to the importance of her institutional role, Ingrid conceives of herself foremost as a 'doctor', 'scientist' or 'humanitarian', for example. These factors can combine in tempting the institution-member to allow her institutional role-identity to swamp her other values and commitments – to allow the persona to masquerade as the person, to the detriment of her personal integrity (Rozuel, 2011).

While these thoughts are general and preliminary in nature, they suggest that institutions possessing great integrity manage to remove some of the key threats to their member's personal integrity (compartmentalization, rationalization and some forms of moral distress), but may pose special dangers in other ways (namely, the worthwhile goals they pursue may come to be so highly valued by the members that some members begin to devalue their lives outside the institution).

CONCLUSION

In this paper we have developed the Comprehensive Integrity Framework – a conceptual and terminological system for thinking about integrity in its both personal and institutional forms. Wielding this system facilitated us in considering the ways that insights into personal integrity can impact on institutional integrity, and vice versa. Equally, we uncovered intriguing differences in the way integrity functions in application to persons versus institutions.

Of course, these reflections may need to be revised in the light of further argument and research. Integrity as an unified, cross-disciplinary research subject is only beginning to come of age (Huberts, 2014). But we hope that the terminology and concepts we have introduced, and their ability to clearly map across the individual-institution-regime field, provide the language in which such explorations can occur, and so will help us improve our understanding of integrity as an integrated topic of research.

NOTES

1. Some distinguish between 'integrity', 'personal integrity' and 'moral integrity', but for our purposes here we consider these terms as synonymous. That is, we use the qualifier *personal* to contrast with *institutional*. For discussion, see: Graham (2001, pp. 240–241).

2. Sampford (2010, pp. 33–34). On 'integrity systems', see Preston & Sampford (2002b, pp. 41, 164, 171). Sampford initially described such sets of institutions as 'ethics regimes', observing the Queensland governance reforms of the early 1990s. The idea was picked up by the OECD and renamed 'ethics infrastructures' (OECD, 1996). Jeremy Pope, the founding CEO of Transparency International coined the term 'national integrity system' (Pope, 2000).

3. We set aside repugnant regimes, where public professions of what an agent stands for make it impossible to further the values articulated. Arguably, Oskar Schindler exhibited great integrity, but he could not be public about his driving values. This complication might require a new category of 'clandestine ("private"/ "silent") integrity'.

4. We use this term to cover individuals and institutions. We could use 'actions' to cover the former. The institutional equivalent of personal actions involves the way that the institution's power and resources are used by its leaders and members.

5. Of course, achieving values-coherence will limit the amount of genuine temptations on offer. However, aligning values does not remove the need for emotional fortitude. A person frightened of public speaking still needs courage (however much the speech aligns with her values).

6. Provided we understand sincerity as a process value, rather than a substantive value. The point is that (on the idea of integrity employed here) there is no *in principle* constraint on the content of the values the agent of integrity endorses.

7. Further restraints, inherent within the concept of integrity, capable of categorically ruling out such evils are possible, but they would extend beyond the core system we advocate here. This conceptual possibility is explored in: Hugh Breakey, 'Compromise despite conviction: Curbing integrity's moral dangers' (unpublished manuscript).

8. A similar case of script-following emerged during the famous Stanford Prison Experiment, where ethical values failed to intrude on the scientists' roles and scripts – requiring an external observer to call attention to the ethical violations involved. See also Rozuel's example of 'Amy' who 'does not really perceive that she compartmentalizes' (Rozuel, 2011, p. 694).

9. Of course, if such a person *really was totally* monomaniacal in his focus on the role, to the point where such life-issues are unlikely to ever intrude on his ambitions (he spurns family and any other social ties), then he would not be a 'single-minded workaholic' as we have defined him. His life may be narrow and pinched – but he is not fragmented, and may even have integrity (if he has reflectively endorsed and publicly professed his values).

10. Rozuel's case example of 'Vincent' is an exemplar of a reflective role-endorsement. (Rozuel, 2011, pp. 694–696). Dolovich's argument for revision of the lawyer's role of 'zealous advocate' aims to fashion a similar space for reflection: Dolovich (2010).

11. Thomas Nagel distinguishes several cases of 'moral luck'. One case involves external factors that shape one's own moral character (our category of context-integrity). Another type of moral luck (perhaps the paradigm case) concerns chance factors contributing to the success, failure and other consequences of one's attempted actions: 'Contingency' captures this source of moral luck (Nagel, 1979).

12. The greater the accord on such values, the more the members' values will promote the PIJ. Even so, it is hardly necessary to have complete harmony even on core principles; diversity, dynamism, dispute and dialogue can be healthy and helpful qualities. Good institutional practice will lead to a dialogue about values that in turn leads to convergence of values or an awareness of difference. The most dynamic institutions are constantly reinventing themselves as members propose new values to pursue. That said, the PIJ must have enough substance and widespread endorsement at any given moment to provide an appropriate standard for appraisal.

13. Consider western universities, the first of which predated the sovereign state by some 600 years and the limited liability joint stock company by 800 years and will probably outlive both. Such longevity was not attained by remaining gathering places for masters and their students. The same kind of points could be made for the Guild of Barber Surgeons, the Inns of Court and, of course, the Catholic Church which is nearly twice as old as universities.

REFERENCES

Audi, R., & Murphy, P. E. (2006). The many faces of integrity. *Business Ethics Quarterly*, *16*(1), 3–21.
Benjamin, M. (1990). *Splitting the difference: Compromise and integrity in ethics and politics*. Kansas: University of Kansas.

Breakey, H. (2014a). Dividing to conquer: Employing the separation of powers to structure institutional inter-relations. *Research in Ethical Issues in Organizations, 12*, 29–58.

Breakey, H. (2014b). Wired to fail: Virtue and dysfunction in Baltimore's narrative. *Research in Ethical Issues in Organizations, 11*, 51–80.

Buchanan, A., & Keohane, R. O. (2006). The legitimacy of global governance institutions. *Ethics and International Affairs, 20*(4), 405–437.

Calhoun, C. (1995). Standing for something. *Philosophy, 92*(5), 235–260.

Cox, D., La Caze, M., & Levine, M. (1999). Should we strive for integrity? *The Journal of Value Inquiry, 33*, 519–530.

Cox, D., La Caze, M., & Levine, M. (2009). *Integrity and the fragile self*. Aldershot: Ashgate.

Dare, T. (2010). Distance, detachment, and integrity. In T. Dare & W. B. Wendel (Eds.), *Professional ethics and personal integrity* (pp. 100–124). Newcastle upon Tyne: Cambridge Scholars Publishing.

Dolovich, S. (2010). Ethical lawyering and the possibility of integrity. In T. Dare & W. B. Wendel (Eds.), *Professional ethics and personal integrity* (pp. 125–185). Newcastle upon Tyne: Cambridge Scholars Publishing.

Dudzinski, D. M. (2004). Integrity: Principled coherence, virtue, or both? *The Journal of Value Inquiry, 38*, 299–313.

Edgar, A., & Pattison, S. (2011). Integrity and the moral complexity of professional practice. *Nursing Philosophy, 12*, 94–106.

Frankfurt, H. (1971). Freedom of the will and the concept of a person. *Journal of Philosophy, 68*, 5–20.

Gioia, D. A. (1992). Pinto fires and personal ethics: A script analysis of missed opportunities. *Journal of Business Ethics, 11*(5/6), 379–389.

Graham, J. L. (2001). Does integrity require moral goodness? *Ratio, 14*, 234–251.

Huberts, L. (2014). *The integrity of governance: What it is, what we know, what is done, and where to go*. Hampshire: Palgrave Macmillan.

Kelly, B. (1998). Preserving moral integrity: A follow-up study with new graduate nurses. *Journal of Advanced Nursing, 28*(5), 1134–1145.

Kerwin, A. (2012). Beyond the banality of evil: Conscience, imagination and responsibility. *Journal of Management Development, 31*(5), 502–514.

Little, L. (2000). Envy and jealousy: A study of separation of powers and judicial review. *Hastings Law Journal, 47*, 47–121.

Luban, D. (2003). Integrity: Its causes and cures. *Fordham Law Review, 72*(2), 279–310.

MacIntyre, A. (1999). Social structures and their threats to moral agency. *Philosophy, 74*, 311–329.

Magelssen, M. (2012). When should conscientious objection be accepted? *Journal of Medical Ethics, 38*, 18–21.

Nagel, T. (1979). Moral luck. In *Mortal questions* (pp. 24–38). Cambridge: Cambridge University Press.

Nietzsche, F. (1989). In W. Kaufmann (Ed. & Trans.), *Beyond good and evil: prelude to a philosophy of the future*. New York, NY: Vintage Books.

OECD. (1996). *Ethics in the public sector: Current issues and practices*. Paris: OECD.

Pope, J. (2000). *Confronting corruption: The elements of a national integrity system (TI source book)*. Berlin: Transparency International.

Preston, N., & Sampford, C. (2002a). Institutionalising ethics. In C. Sampford, N. Preston, & C. Conners (Eds.), *Encouraging ethics and challenging corruption* (pp. 32–68). Annandale: Federation Press.

Preston, N., & Sampford, C. (Eds.). (2002b). *Encouraging ethics and challenging corruption.* Annandale: Federation Press.

Rahe, P. A. (2011). Montesquieu's anti-Machiavellian Machiavellianism. *History of European Ideas, 37*, 128–136.

Reginster, B. (1997). Nietzsche on ressentiment and valuation. *Philosophy and Phenomenological Research, 57*(2), 281–305.

Rozuel, C. (2011). The moral threat of compartmentalization: Self, roles and responsibility. *Journal of Business Ethics, 102*(4), 685–697.

Sampford, C. (2010). Adam Smith's dinner. In I. G. MacNeil & J. O'Brien (Eds.), *The future of financial regulation* (pp. 23–40). Oxford: Hart.

Sampford, C., Smith, R., & Brown, A. J. (2005). From Greek temple to bird's nest: Towards a theory of coherence and mutual accountability for national integrity systems. *Australian Journal of Public Administration, 64*(2), 96–108.

Scherkoske, G. (2010). Integrity and moral danger. *Canadian Journal of Philosophy, 40*(3), 335–358.

Scherkoske, G. (2012). Could integrity be an epistemic virtue? *International Journal of Philosophical Studies, 20*(2), 185–215.

Sullivan, V. B. (2006). Against the despotism of a republic: Montesquieu's correction of Machiavelli in the name of the security of the individual. *History of Political Thought, 27*(2), 263–289.

Vile, M. J. C. (1998). *Constitutionalism and the separation of powers* (2nd ed.). Indianapolis, IN: Liberty Fund.

Williams, B. (1973). Utilitarianism and integrity. In B. Williams & J. J. Smart (Eds.), *Utilitarianism: For and against.* London: Cambridge University Press.

Wueste, D. E. (2005). *We need to talk … about institutional integrity.* New York, NY: RIT Press.

Zuckert, M. (2012). On the separation of powers: Liberal and progressive constitutionalism. *Social Philosophy and Policy, 29*(2), 335–364.

THE IMPORTANCE OF THE ETHICS OF GOVERNANCE REGIME FOR THE CORPORATION AND THE CONNECTION TO CORPORATE GOVERNANCE PRACTICE

Timothy O'Shannassy

ABSTRACT

The purpose of this general review is to enhance understanding of the importance of a corporation's whole ethics of governance regime and the connection to governance practices. This connection is often missing from corporate governance discussion. There is need for better business community awareness of a well-developed ethics of governance regime guiding appropriate board structure and composition choices subject to firm age and size, understanding of how these choices evolve as the firm matures and grows, plus the benefits from more emphasis in this area for company director training and development. This paper synthesises the theoretical and empirical insight from the ethics and corporate govern-ance literatures to give guidance on best practice for large, medium size and small stock exchange listed companies. This synthesis of the

The Ethical Contribution of Organizations to Society
Research in Ethical Issues in Organizations, Volume 14, 41–55
ISSN: 1529-2096/doi:10.1108/S1529-209620150000014002

literature evidences that the preferred Australian Institute of Company Directors agency theory prescription for a corporate board is not always optimal. In terms of practical implications advice is given on sound choices on board composition, director selection, plus director training and development that will give the best probability of effective board decisions and strong firm performance – this is not 'one size fits all' corporations advice. Future research should focus on whole ethics of governance regimes and governance practices in place for companies that have succeeded compared with companies that have failed. This will improve understanding in this area. This is a substantial future research agenda item as deeper knowledge of this contrast may add significantly to understanding of corporate success and failure.

Keywords: Ethics of corporate governance; board composition; inside directors; grey directors; outside directors

INTRODUCTION

The global financial crisis (GFC) and the poor strategic and financial performance experienced by corporations large, medium size and small in many countries including the United States (e.g. The Bear Stearns Companies, Inc.) and United Kingdom (e.g. The Royal Bank of Scotland plc) give evidence of situations where board performance has not been as effective as it could be (Arjoon, 2005; Hambrick, Werder, & Zajac, 2008). Where board structure, director selection, director training and development, board decision-making and firm performance are not optimal there can be moments and circumstances where legal statutes and director's duties are not properly followed (Collier & Roberts, 2001; Harris, 2014; Krause, Semadeni, & Cannella, 2014). This can create a cycle of decline for the organization. A commitment to ethics of governance for the whole organization can help to avoid these circumstances (Wieland, 2001).

Ethics of governance refers to the ethics of the organization and the connection of this to the governance practices, management and control systems for the company (Collier & Roberts, 2001; Wieland, 2001). These matters are all inter-connected, helping to inform the manner in which a board goes about its choices on structure and composition, and the making of decisions (Wieland, 2001; Withers, Hillman, & Cannella, 2012). Directors on stock exchange listed company boards have a variety of substantial duties and responsibilities including compliance with the Corporations Act 2001, oversight of strategy, oversight of executive management, regulatory compliance, legal compliance, and audit compliance (Higgs, 2002; Kiel & Nicholson, 2003a). The ethics of the organization – the structural ethics – helps to provide values, a frame of reference and a decision-making framework to help economic actors (i.e. the employees) think through decisions and work in relation to these matters. Governance structures of corporations can differ in their capacity to facilitate business decisions with some arrangements, for example chief executive officer (CEO) duality (i.e. the same person appointed as chairperson and CEO to focus decision-making and executive power), effective for some businesses but a shortcoming and ineffective for others where separation (i.e. separate chairperson and CEO human resource appointments) of these roles is preferred (Krause et al., 2014).

A number of choices and issues need to go right for a board of directors to have the best probability of strong firm performance (Collier & Roberts, 2001; Krause et al., 2014). For the purpose of discussion firm performance here includes strategic, social and financial outcomes (Hart & Banbury, 1994). These choices range across a number of issues including the approach to ethics of governance, board composition, director selection, director training and development, this director training and development in relation to the ethics of governance, and the making of sound decisions on the board for a sustained period of time (Harris, 2014; Kroll, Walters, & Le, 2007; Wieland, 2001). When correct choices are made for a corporation in each of these areas the business has the best probability of delivering strong performance. The way the ethics of governance and the governance choices work together effectively varies between smaller, younger new ventures and older, more mature and larger corporations (Kroll et al., 2007).

The chairperson manages the board (Krause et al., 2014; O'Shannassy, 2010). The chairperson must effectively lead discussion with the owners and the executive on the best composition of the board for that organization (Kakabadse & Kakabadse, 2007). This is not necessarily a straight forward choice with the need to balance the management contribution and voting strength of the inside or executive directors with the contribution and voting power of the outside or non-executive directors (Kiel & Nicholson, 2003a). While Australian and United Kingdom research distinguishes between inside and outside directors, United States researchers have been interested in grey directors who might have had executive roles with the company in the past, or perhaps have an economic or family relationship, or have had prior business dealings or have worked as a consultant with the company (Hillman, Cannella, & Paetzold, 2000). It will be explained that these choices can vary between small and medium size

(SME) young stock exchange listed companies and larger, more mature stock exchange listed companies (Kroll et al., 2007).

Director selection is another important issue for the chairperson to manage. The human and social capital of a candidate for a board position determines selection and non-selection decisions; the human and social capital of the selected director working in a group of directors determines the effectiveness of the work of the board (Kim & Cannella, 2008; Tian, Haleblian, & Rajagopalan, 2011). The human capital of an individual director refers to that employee's knowledge, skill, training and experience. The social capital of an individual director refers to their interpersonal linkages to others both inside and outside the organization (Kim & Cannella, 2008). The human and social capital of a group of directors working together on a board is the sum of their knowledge, skill, training, experience, interpersonal linkages and the resources available to the firm as a result of these interpersonal linkages (Kim & Cannella, 2008). Larger more mature stock exchange listed companies can afford to pay higher remuneration to hire directors with more human and social capital than recently listed SMEs that do not have the same budget for the hiring and retention of directors (Kroll et al., 2007).

The training and development of the inside, grey and outside directors is an important responsibility of the chairperson to oversee as he or she goes about the management of the board (Harris, 2014). The training and development needs of inside directors with line management responsibility will differ from those with strategy responsibility or perhaps a top management team functional role such as chief financial officer. The relative experience levels of directors will also influence the timing, content and nature of the training and development opportunities they require to make an effective contribution to the board – this includes the vital contribution made by executive directors, especially the CEO responsible for development of strategy and the daily management of the executive management (O'Shannassy, 2010).

The research question that informs this discussion is: What is the interconnection of the ethics of governance of the corporation for the governance practices of that corporation? In building the answer to this research question the paper will first look at ethics of governance and board effectiveness. Second, theoretical perspectives on corporate governance relationships (i.e. agency theory, stewardship theory, resource-dependence theory) will be explained. Third, the connection of ethics of governance to structural corporate governance choices will be elaborated. A discussion and future research agenda and conclusion will then follow.

ETHICS OF GOVERNANCE AND BOARD EFFECTIVENESS

Professional bodies including the Australian Institute of Company Directors (AICD) and the Australian Institute of Management (AIM) have, in recent years, given more emphasis to the ethical training of their constituents, and the broader discussion of ethics. The values, conduct and decision-making of company directors has a critical influence on the sound management of business and also the well-being of business and society (Kiel & Nicholson, 2003a). The ethics of governance is an important component of this discussion (Wieland, 2001).

Earlier remarks note that the ethics of governance refers to the ethics of the organization and requirements in the governance, management and control systems for the company (Wieland, 2001). There is a difference between the moral values of the organization (governance ethics), the moral values of the individuals working in a particular role for the organization (management ethics) and the moral values of the individual working for the organization (value ethics) (Wieland, 2001). Understanding that these differences exist helps to inform development of insight into the various trade-offs, conflicts and challenges of these different levels of business ethics. The major point to make here in this paper is that there is only limited understanding of structural ethics and how this can and should be approached by the corporation (Wieland, 2001). A further consideration is the question of whether structural ethics should be approached differently by more mature, larger organizations compared with smaller, younger, more entrepreneurial organizations (Kroll et al., 2007).

For the purpose of this discussion and similar to Wieland (2001) the focus here will be limited to ethics of governance matters including the moral values of the organization and structural ethics. The organization is a contracted system of institutional behavioural constraints and enablers that give guidance on behaviour choices (Kiel & Nicholson, 2003a). Business ethics then can only be developed in the context of a comprehensive governance structure for the economic transactions of the corporation that constrains and enables the behavioural choices of the economic actors. This is because there is a *process* of organizing and a *form* within which this organizing takes place (Wieland, 2001). The *process* of organizing requires the individual employees to engage in formal employment contracts and take action to implement an agreed strategy documented and approved by the board and executive management in a strategic plan. In this context the virtues and possibly vices of the individual director's matter and can influence their decision-making in relation to development and execution of the strategic plan, and this can make a difference to firm performance (Hunter & O'Shannassy, 2007; Wieland, 2001). However, the *form* of organization or business firm is outside of the considerations of these virtues and vices, or ethical values, of the individuals as it has an infinite life separate to the human lifespan of the owners including major shareholders (Kiel & Nicholson, 2003a). The organization must then have its own ethics of governance with its own set of structures, informal constraints and formal constraints (Wieland, 2001). This leads to the notion that the moulding and shaping of business ethics has to take place on the basis of the firm that works as a governance structure with a constitutional contract or corporate charter (Kiel & Nicholson, 2003a; Wieland, 2001). The corporate charter for a corporation is:

> A written policy document that clearly defines the respective roles, responsibilities and authorities of the board of directors (both individually and collectively) and management in setting the direction, the management and the control of the organization. (Kiel & Nicholson, 2003a, p. 4)

The potential of the corporate charter in an ethics of governance regime is to focus the work and decision-making of inside, grey and outside directors in a collective way for the overall good of the corporation delivering appropriate outcomes for shareholders and stakeholders (e.g. employees, customers, suppliers, government, regulators, the general public) (Kiel & Nicholson, 2003a; Wieland, 2001).

Against this background the key internal stakeholders will be contracted to the organization usually in long term contractual employment arrangements whereby they agree to pursue the goals and objectives of the firm (Kiel & Nicholson, 2003a). The key internal stakeholders agree to constraints on their decision-making and behaviour in the interests of cooperation and teamwork for the wider benefit of the corporation. By doing this they agree to working in a particular *process* and *form* that is consistent with the corporate charter and agreed by the board of directors and top management team, including inside directors (Wieland, 2001).

A further ethics of governance consideration includes the motivations of the inside, grey and outside directors respectively and how they might organize for effective decision-making, power and influence (Kiel & Nicholson, 2003a; O'Shannassy, 2010). The core argument here based on empirical evidence is that this can and should be approached differently by more mature, larger organizations compared with smaller, younger, more entrepreneurial organizations (Kroll et al., 2007). Not approaching these important choices differently between corporations of different size and age risks weak firm performance and a loss of shareholder and stakeholder value.

THEORETICAL PERSPECTIVES ON CORPORATE GOVERNANCE RELATIONSHIPS

A multi-theoretic perspective is taken to explain corporate governance relationships in the development of this review. This approach helps to better understand the relations between the chairperson, CEO, inside directors, grey directors and outside directors. Agency theory, stewardship theory and resource-dependence theory are developed and applied here. These theories have different influences on the understanding of corporate governance choices for SMEs compared with large stock exchange listed companies. It is important to appreciate in this discussion that one theory is not more important than the other, but that a particular theory or theories helps to explain particular firm choices in particular circumstances (Johnson, Daily, & Ellstrand, 1996).

The dominant theory of corporate governance relations is agency theory (Krause et al., 2014). With greater size of the corporation there is separation of ownership from control (Shleifer & Vishny, 1997). This scale of the organization is often associated with more mature, successful stock exchange listed companies. Where there is separation of ownership from control there is a risk of the principal—agent problem emerging where priorities of the owners (the principals) may differ from management (the agents) including inside directors who may be motivated to act in their own interests (Kiel & Nicholson, 2003b). The assumption made is that the agents will be self-motivated and self-seeking (Hambrick et al., 2008). As a consequence monitoring systems, the structuring of performance and remuneration incentives and market discipline are considered the best means to keep the agents focused on the wider objectives of the organization (Johnson et al., 1996). Board of director structure including separation of the chairperson and CEO role with independent chairperson plus a voting majority of outside directors are preferred by agency theorists (Dalton & Dalton, 2011). Agency theorists do appreciate the value one or more inside directors can bring to board deliberations with an extra inside director providing a valuable alternative source of executive insight to the CEO (Johnson et al., 1996).

Stewardship theorists see the role of the director differently. In steward-ship theory a director is seen more as a trustee of the corporation (Kroll et al., 2007). This is because the steward or director will see the organiza-tion as more of a social institution with his or her interests closely tied to those of the business entity. The director will gain much social and profes-sional esteem from his or her association with the corporation, making a contribution to adding shareholder and/or stakeholder value (Johnson et al., 1996). What works at one time in the life and size of the corporation does not always work at a different time in the life and size of the corpora-tion. This type of company director who is a strong steward is associated in the empirical literature with younger, smaller, more entrepreneurial compa-nies. These types of companies will possess visionary, valuable and entre-preneurial human resource talent among the top management team who will also be a viable and cost effective source of inside director talent. In this scenario the agency theory prescription for board composition has been demonstrated in the empirical literature to be less relevant (Kroll et al., 2007).

Resource-dependence theory sees the board as being another source of the resources that need to be accessed to assist firm performance (Krause et al., 2014). Inside, grey and outside directors can all be a valuable source of strategic, legal, audit and functional resources (e.g. human resources, information technology, marketing). Board size, the ratio of outside direc-tors and the frequency and patterns of board interlocks are all choices that are influential for the corporation to have the right level and quality of resource access (Johnson et al., 1996). More well-connected directors increase the probability of wider resource access across the business com-munity. Through board of director interlocks the directors can provide access to valuable professional networks in other industries such as invest-ment banking and stockbroking. Investment banking and stockbroking are two important industries for access to professional networks given these linkages give access to capital (Johnson et al., 1996). More mature and suc-cessful corporations will have a bigger budget for board of director remu-neration giving access to directors with greater social and human capital than small and medium size entrepreneurial corporations with smaller remuneration budgets.

The emphasis within an organization on the application of these theories of corporate governance will have implications for the *process* and *form* that is consistent with the corporate charter and employment contracts agreed by the board of directors and top management team whether that corporation is large, medium size or small.

ETHICS OF GOVERNANCE AND IMPORTANT STRUCTURAL CORPORATE GOVERNANCE CHOICES

Building on the preceding discussion it is important that the *form* and *process* of the organization is suitable for the size of the organization and for the maturity of the organization. Not every firm is the same. It is notable that organizations such as the AICD have a preferred agency theory biased prescription for board of director structure but they do not distinguish between the needs of SMEs and large companies. This AICD prescription in essence includes separation of the chairperson and CEO role, an independent chairperson, and a voting majority of outside directors. However, the empirical literature raises questions as to the suitability of this governance structure for the making of sound business decisions (Kroll et al., 2007). As noted, there is empirical evidence that the agency theory prescription for board structure may not work as well for younger, more entrepreneurial corporations where a more stewardship-oriented approach to board structure can be more effective (Kroll et al., 2007). There is also some conjecture on the value of outside directors on large listed company boards in Australia with Kiel and Nicholson (2003b) finding a negative correlation between the proportion of outside directors and financial performance measured by three year average Tobin's Q.

The role of the independent chairperson is to manage the board; this is an agency theory application. In this role the chair determines board structure within the parameters of the corporate charter, hires the CEO, selects and determines the training requirements of the inside directors, and the selection and training of the directors. The costs and benefits associated with the practice of separation of the chairperson and CEO role or the alternative of duality has been the subject of much discussion over the past two decades (Krause et al., 2014). The practice of duality – which is an application of stewardship theory – gives the executive performing the dual chairperson and CEO roles considerable influence over firm strategy, daily management, performance of the board, director selection and board structure (Kakabadse & Kakabadse, 2007). Duality has been practised by up to 80 per cent of share market listed companies in the United States though this is now decreasing. Duality is preferred much less frequently in the United Kingdom and Australia (Fitzroy, Hulbert, & Ghobadian, 2012). Separation limits the capacity of the CEO to have a strong influence over all board and management matters (Fitzroy et al., 2012). Where there is separation the proper *process* is for the chairperson to be responsible for management of the board, with the CEO responsible for management. The role of the CEO in this *process* is to develop and then present strategy to the board; the board then has the task of assessing, criticizing, debating, supporting or seeking revision of the strategy presented (Kiel & Nicholson, 2003a). Empirical research indicates that a CEO selected from inside the corporation performs better than a CEO who is selected from outside; however, there are moments in a corporation's history (e.g. recent poor firm performance) when an outsider is the best selection (Zajac, 1990). There may also be circumstances in entrepreneurial stock exchange listed corporations where the founder has a desire to remain as Executive Chairperson, another application of stewardship theory. Where this Executive Chairperson wishes to remain in his or her role and is performing strongly it is in the best interests of that corporation for that founder to remain in the role.

Another key aspect of board structure choices is getting the balance right between inside directors, grey and outside directors (Coles, McWilliams, & Sen, 2001; Hillman et al., 2000). Many writers mainly in countries including Australia and the United Kingdom only distinguish between inside directors and outside directors (Kakabadse & Kakabadse, 2007). United States writers make a distinction between outside directors and grey directors (Hillman et al., 2000). Applying agency theory and resource-dependence theory best practice in structuring mature, large company boards requires a numerical and voting majority of independent, outside directors to aid decision-making, and compliance (Hillman et al., 2000; Walters, Kroll, & Wright, 2007). This allows the outside directors to perform their agency theory role of providing a check and balance to board matters prepared by the executive. Without a voting majority the influence of outside directors is reduced and can lead to circumstances where sound business decisions are not necessarily achieved. In an application of resource-dependence theory grey directors can be useful on the board with their knowledge of family history, commercial dealings, or consulting engagements; however, the numbers of grey directors in combination with inside directors should be less than the number of outside directors (Hillman et al., 2000).

Corporate boards often benefit from having one or more members of the top management team sitting on the board. In an application of stewardship theory these inside directors are a useful additional source of executive information and insight for the grey and outside directors other than the CEO (Kakabadse & Kakabadse, 2007; Westphal & Zajac, 1995). Agency theory, stewardship theory and resource-dependence theory come together in application here agreeing that the inclusion of inside directors and grey directors – in fewer numbers on the board than a voting majority of outside directors – can be helpful to the human and social capital of the board (Rutherford & Buchholtz, 2007; Westphal & Zajac, 1995).

Director selection is the responsibility of the chairperson with support from the corporation's human resource professionals and/or outside sourced human resource consultants. Boards with a number of well-trained, skilled and experienced inside, grey and outside directors in the right balance for the age, size and entrepreneurial orientation of the corporation can add value to board deliberations when able to work in a collegial environment (Kiel & Nicholson, 2003a). It is the role of the chairperson to identify, recruit and remunerate inside, grey and outside directors with individual human and social capital such that when they work together as a board a synergy arises from their collective knowledge, skills, experience, training and networks (Kim & Cannella, 2008). Where the chairperson is also the CEO then director selection provides an opportunity for the CEO to populate the board with preferred candidates, professional colleagues, family and/or members of his or her professional network (Westphal, 1999). Agency theory identifies that this may not be in the best interests of the corporation, especially over the long term with the risk of a decline in the quality of board discussion and deliberation and compromised voting behaviour (Johnson et al., 1996). Resource-dependence theory suggests that if this approach to director selection occurs and these directors bring important and useful human and social capital that the corporation that it is possible may benefit – so choices on director selection matters depending on the circumstances. In a further connection to resource-dependence theory board size reflects available human and social capital and is frequently used as a proxy for board expertise in empirical research (Johnson et al., 1996).

Director training and development is the responsibility of the chairperson to oversee with supporting input from human resource professionals and other consultants and/or professionals (e.g. the Company Secretary, General Counsel) as required (Harris, 2014). The training and development needs of grey and outside directors in large corporations with a stronger agency theory role may differ from training and development needs for grey and outside directors of SMEs with limited human and financial resources and an entrepreneurial orientation where these directors will be playing a resource dependence type role. The chairperson will be conscious of endeavouring to improve the human and social capital of the board whether the corporation is large or an SME (Harris, 2014; Tian et al., 2011). The training and development needs of inside directors will be twofold. First the chairperson will be conscious of their training and development for their director role (Kiel & Nicholson, 2003a). Second the chairperson will liaise with the CEO to identify areas of strategy, leadership, management and/or perhaps functional expertise which will enhance the performance of the inside director in their top management team role (Harris, 2014). Performance evaluation of individual directors will provide ongoing guidance on training and development needs (Kiel, Nicholson, & Barclay, 2005).

DISCUSSION

Company directors have tremendous corporate duties and responsibilities with important consequences for the wider community (Kiel & Nicholson, 2003a; O'Shannassy, 2010). The corporations they serve can account for annual turnover in the billions, employ thousands of employees, make substantial financial contributions to philanthropic causes, and make substantial contributions to taxation revenue. The global financial crisis evidences that poor performance in one financial institution (e.g. The Royal Bank of Scotland plc) can have major implications for the international banking system with serious adverse consequences for the international business community, governments and society. Symptoms of poor performing boards include poor strategy decisions, weak efforts at legal, regulatory and audit compliance, and/or the emergence of the principal–agent problem among top managers. These unfortunate circumstances can lead to deterioration in organization performance, leading to lost job opportunities, higher unemployment in communities, lost philanthropy opportunities, lost business development opportunities, and lower government tax receipts from a weak corporate sector. These are poor outcomes to consider for the wider community and circumstances to be avoided.

The over-arching message in this paper is that there is need for consistency in the ethics of governance regime for an organization and that consistency in approach can mean different things for SMEs compared with large corporations (Wieland, 2001). This disposition to sound governance and business practice in a firm is not something company directors can switch on an off – there is need for consistency, clear communication and role models (Tushman & O'Reilly, 1997). By adopting a clear ethics of governance approach that is communicated through the organization, and where this ethical approach is supported by governance practices board structure, director selection, director training and development, decision-making frameworks, decisions and firm performance the corporation is well positioned to adapt effectively to the business environment (Harris, 2014; Kiel & Nicholson, 2003a; Wieland, 2001).

Agency theory and resource dependence prescriptions will have a stronger role in larger, more mature stock exchange listed companies given the separation of ownership and control plus the availability of financial resources to employ more highly credentialed outside directors. The corporate charter should reflect this giving emphasis to the importance of the presence on the board of outside directors. Stewardship theory and resource-dependence theory will have a stronger role in small and medium size, younger, entrepreneurial stock exchange listed companies. The corporate charter for this type of corporation will highlight the value of inside directors on the board; this corporate charter may not necessarily stipulate a majority of outside directors on the board. In this environment the founder may also wish to stay on as chairperson (Krause et al., 2014); the SME may not be able to afford remuneration for highly credentialed outside directors. So the corporation will need to adapt its approach to governance practice to its circumstances (Kroll et al., 2007).

This paper set out to answer the following research question: What is the inter-connection of the ethics of governance of the corporation for the governance practices of that corporation? This general review including the discussion highlights the point that ethics of governance and related corporate governance choices is not a 'one size fits all' prescription. There is a range of contingencies and applications of theory and practical insight to consider for the corporation — whether that corporation is a large stock exchange listed entity or an SME. This is the major contribution here from the synthesis of theoretical and empirical insight presented.

Future Research

This paper is limited to a general review and does not provide new empirical evidence. Future empirical research should focus on whole ethics of governance regimes in place for companies that have succeeded compared with companies that have failed to better understand. This is a substantial future research agenda item as deeper knowledge of this contrast may add significantly to knowledge. Future research approaches can adopt a quantitative and/or qualitative approach to explore the connection between ethics of governance, corporate governance choices and organization performance. Key informant survey research targeting the chairperson of stock exchange listed companies will be informative given their key board role. In relation to qualitative methods options include the use of focus groups with chairpersons, then CEOs, then inside, grey and outside directors respectively to obtain multi-layered insights; interviews could be performed with five to ten interviewees in each director category. Another qualitative option is development of case studies on individual firms.

CONCLUSION

Sound ethical choices and practices are a key ingredient of success in business (Arjoon, 2005). Boards of directors are increasingly being required to consider a whole ethics of governance regime with implications for corporate governance practice. Such a board will be seeking to develop the right *process* and *form* for the organization to enable the best possible decisions on strategy, management, legal compliance, regulatory compliance and audit compliance. Such a company will seek best practice in board of director structure to maximize the probability of sound business practice and strong performance, delivering shareholder and stakeholder value which is a desirable situation for business and society.

REFERENCES

Arjoon, S. (2005). Corporate governance: An ethical perspective. *Journal of Business Ethics*, *61*, 343–352.

Coles, J., McWilliams, V., & Sen, N. (2001). An examination of the relationship of governance mechanisms to performance. *Journal of Management*, *27*, 23–50.

Collier, J., & Roberts, J. (2001). An ethic for corporate governance? *Business Ethics Quarterly*, *11*(1), 67–71.

Dalton, D., & Dalton, C. (2011). Integration of micro and macro studies in governance research: CEO duality, board composition, and financial performance. *Journal of Management*, *37*, 404–411.

Fitzroy, P., Hulbert, J., & Ghobadian, A. (2012). *Strategic management: The challenge of creating value*. Milton Park, UK: Routledge.

Hambrick, D., Werder, A., & Zajac, E. (2008). New directions in corporate governance research. *Organization Science*, *19*, 381–385.

Harris, H. (2014). Ethics training for corporate boards. *Research in Ethical Issues in Organizations*, *12*, 113–131.

Hart, S., & Banbury, C. (1994). How strategy making processes can make a difference. *Strategic Management Journal*, *15*, 251–269.

Higgs, D. (2002, June 7). Review of the role and effectiveness of non-executive directors. Consultation Paper. Department of Trade and Industry/HMSO, London, UK.

Hillman, A., Cannella, A., & Paetzold, R. (2000). The resource dependence role of corporate directors: Strategic adaption of board composition in response to environmental change. *Journal of Management Studies, 37*(2), 235−255.

Hunter, P., & O'Shannassy, T. (2007). Contemporary strategic management practice in Australia: "Back to the future" in the 2000s. *Singapore Management Review, 29*(2), 21−36.

Johnson, J., Daily, C., & Ellstrand, A. (1996). Board of directors: A review and research agenda. *Journal of Management, 22*, 409−438.

Kakabadse, N., & Kakabadse, A. (2007). Chairman of the board: Demographics effects on role pursuit. *Journal of Management Development, 26*, 169−192.

Kiel, G., & Nicholson, G. (2003a). *Boards that work*. North Ryde, Australia: McGraw-Hill.

Kiel, G., & Nicholson, G. (2003b). Board composition and corporate performance: How the Australian experience informs contrasting theories of corporate governance. *Corporate Governance: An International Review, 11*(3), 189−205.

Kiel, G. C., Nicholson, G., & Barclay, M. A. (2005). *Board, director and CEO evaluation*. North Ryde, Australia: McGraw-Hill Australia Pty Ltd.

Kim, Y., & Cannella, A. (2008). Toward a social capital theory of director selection. *Corporate Governance: An International Review, 16*(4), 282−293.

Krause, R., Semadeni, M., & Cannella, A. A. (2014). CEO duality: A review and research agenda. *Journal of Management, 40*(1), 256−286.

Kroll, M., Walters, B., & Le, S. (2007). The impact of board composition and top management team ownership structure on post-IPO performance in young entrepreneurial firms. *Academy of Management Journal, 50*(5), 1198−1216.

O'Shannassy, T. (2010). Board and CEO practice in modern strategy-making: How is strategy developed, who is the boss and in what circumstances? *Journal of Management & Organization, 16*(2), 280−298.

Rutherford, M., & Buchholtz, A. (2007). Investigating the relationship between board characteristics and board information. *Corporate Governance: An International Review, 15*(4), 576−584.

Shleifer, A., & Vishny, R. W. (1997). A survey of corporate governance. *Journal of Finance, 52*(2), 737−783.

Tian, J., Haleblian, J., & Rajagopalan, N. (2011). The effects of board human capital and social capital on investor reactions to new CEO selection. *Strategic Management Journal, 32*, 731−747.

Tushman, M., & O'Reilly III, C. (1997). *Winning through innovation*. Boston, MA: Harvard Business School Press.

Walters, B., Kroll, M., & Wright, P. (2007). CEO tenure, boards of directors, and acquisition performance. *Journal of Business Research, 60*, 331−338.

Westphal, J. (1999). Collaboration in the boardroom: Behavioural and performance consequences of CEO-board social ties. *Academy of Management Journal, 42*, 7−24.

Westphal, J., & Zajac, E. (1995). Who shall govern? CEO/Board power, demographic similarity, and new director selection. *Administrative Science Quarterly, 40*(1), 60−83.

Wieland, J. (2001). The ethics of governance. *Business Ethics Quarterly, 11*(1), 73−87.

Withers, M., Hillman, A., & Cannella, A. (2012). A multidisciplinary review of the director selection literature. *Journal of Management, 38*, 243−277.

Zajac, E. (1990). CEO selection, succession, compensation and firm performance: A theoretical integration and empirical analysis. *Strategic Management Journal, 11*, 217−230.

RETHINKING PETER DRUCKER'S 'PRUSSIAN ARMY'

Michael Schwartz

ABSTRACT

This paper considers the effects of the military organization upon the morality of the society within which that military organization exists. It initially considers Drucker's arguments as to the end of the Prussian Army which explores the significance of the military's role as an organization within a society. It then examines some dilemmas of military service and some of the harsher realities of military training. It concludes by considering those aspects with regard to a military reservist's account of his 18-year service in the military reserves where he remained loyal to his military unit whilst steadfastly opposed to much of what that military was helping to secure in part by his continued service in the military reserves.

Keywords: Military; military service; military training; Watzman

The Ethical Contribution of Organizations to Society
Research in Ethical Issues in Organizations, Volume 14, 57–69
Copyright © 2015 by Emerald Group Publishing Limited
ISSN: 1529-2096/doi:10.1108/S1529-209620150000014003

INTRODUCTION

The British philosopher, Heather Widdows, argues that the globalization of 'organizations beyond the traditional boundaries of the nation state' (2005, p. 166) caused numerous ethical dilemmas. So, though, have changes to organizations within the nation state. The renowned management thinker, Peter F. Drucker, who dismayed business ethicists with his harsh critique of their field (Drucker, 1985), and who lived in Germany when Hitler came to power, explored that phenomenon with regard to no less an organization than the Prussian Army.

Regardless of the fervent desire of some that the United States of America declare war on Nazi Germany, Hitler's declaration of war on America on the 11th of December, 1941 (Frater, 2011) was a development as unexpected as the 1939 Nazi–Soviet pact which Drucker (1939), perhaps alone, foresaw. But writing some months prior to Hitler's 1941 declaration of war on America, when an embattled Britain standing alone sought succour, Drucker explained that British officialdom was deluded in thinking that the Prussian Army could stop Hitler, although he conceded that their delusion was understandable as that army 'had been the basis of German political development' (Drucker, 1941, p. 1). Nonetheless, Drucker argued, that in 1941 that was irrelevant as by 1914 the Prussian Army had ceased to exist as a political force.

Drucker explained that the initial function of the Prussian Army was not military, but political and social, providing as far back as 1640 the very basis for a Prussian state. But by the nineteenth century much had changed. The emergence in Germany of a national consciousness along with an industrial society provided the basis for a unified German state. Those internal developments meant that the Prussian Army 'as a political force (had) ceased to exist' (Drucker, 1941, p. 1) and that 'the Prussian Army was no longer a living force' (Drucker, 1941, p. 1). Drucker therefore concluded that because of that terminal decline the Prussian Army could not do anything to oppose Hitler, and that consequently any such expectations by British officials that it would were 'an illusion' (Drucker, 1941, p. 1).

Drucker's, 1941 critique of the Prussian Army and his dispatch of it to such a moribund state might have been premature. After all, the most serious attempt to kill Hitler and overthrow the Nazi regime, was that carried out on the 20th July, 1944 by Count Claus von Stauffenberg, chief of staff of the German Home Army Command, assisted largely by a 'small group of young aristocratic officers' (Broszat, 1995, p. 32). Their failed attempt allowed Hitler to hang on meat hooks hundreds of German officers literally dispatching what remained of that Prussian Army which Hitler 'hated just as much as any German liberal ever did' (Drucker, 1941, p. 7).

Furthermore, Drucker presents the Prussian Army with a lengthy continuity which in reality never existed. In 1806 Napoleon's Army vanquished the Prussian Army. Geyer describes how that led to 'a cataclysmic transformation' (1990, p. 186) of the Prussian Army where its generals were court-martialled and its organization radically re-organized. Geyer writes that by the mid-1850s those 'modernizing efforts isolated the military from the mainstream of social life' (1990, p. 188). Arguably, it was both that isolation along with the conditions which Drucker describe as emerging in nineteenth century Germany, which ensured that by the outbreak of the First World War the Prussian Army had no other role within Germany then to be responsible for 'the social organization of violence' (Geyer, 1990, p. 189).

Nonetheless, regardless of the veracity of Drucker's claims as to the state of the Prussian Army in 1941, they do highlight the significance of the military as an organization within a society, and also that such an organization's role will impact upon the society in which it exists. This is germane to Australia where our future military necessities are currently being debated (McLean, 2015). Given that reality this paper explores, by considering the experiences of others, the two major conflicting impacts of the military organization upon a democracy such as Australia. The first is what the demands of military training means for the citizens of that state. The second is what the loyalty of enlisted citizens to their military units and regiments means regarding their loyalty to the state itself.

MILITARY SERVICE

Eliot Cohen argues that the ambivalence to conscription in countries such as Australia, Canada, New Zealand, the United Kingdom and the United States of America is due to 'Anglo-Saxon liberalism' (1985, p. 15) and the associated individual rights that it protects. As Cohen explains, 'considerations of domestic politics and justice strongly influence what systems of military service a state will choose' (1985, p. 33). Admittedly, he also argues that the geographical realities dominate as the system of military service in a county will be influenced by the length of its land borders with neighbouring states who are likely to be hostile, which is a situation none of those states face. He does though note that even within such states the demands of 'democratic egalitarianism' (1985, p. 15) may lead to the call for compulsory national conscription. This has, to a limited degree, been the case in Australia.

McCarthy has argued for compulsory national military service in Australia as it 'helps to break down social divisions and develop the trust vital to the operation of democracy' (2014, p. 2). As evidence of this he cites a report which attributes the 'highest level of social cohesion in the world' (2014, p. 2) in the Scandinavian countries due to their 'compulsory military service' (2014, p. 2). Such service will have consequences especially for those who experience it. McCarthy's arguments are most significant to my arguments as military training can break down those divisions but no one has ever suggested that such training is seen with joy by most who undertake it. Furthermore, McCarthy sees that training as facilitating democracy but some have questioned whether that is so. This paper explores both those aspects.

Cohen viewed 'military organizations as, first, fundamentally *political*; and, second, fundamentally *institutional*' (1985, p. 19, italics in the original) and, because they are, they have power. A large part of that power in the case of conscription is to press-gang or shanghai young men, and in some cases as in the case of Israel and no doubt others, young women, into military service. Doing so, and what in turn those young people will experience as a result of that experience, must raise numerous ethical concerns.

There have been recent scandals in the Australian military (Box, 2014). Those scandals cannot have been completely unexpected. They are after all similar to other such scandals in the larger Australian community (Perkins, 2015). Such instances reflect the view that 'it's not the army which shapes the nation, but rather the nation which shapes the army' (Oz, 1995, p. 53). However, some would argue that much more should be expected of the military. Those making that claim recognize that military conscription represents the ultimate demand which a society can impose: namely, that if called upon to do so the conscript will die for that community. Walzer (1971), however, suggests that it is not a case that they *will* die but that they *may* die. Following Walzer what binds individuals are that they 'are bound by their significant actions, not by their feelings or thoughts; action is the crucial language of moral commitment' (1971, p. 98). Regarding their actions he explains that 'soldiers normally are expected to surrender rather than be killed' (1971, p. 83) and also that the right exists 'under certain circumstances to run away' (1971, p. 85) but we know that in warfare soldiers are often placed in perilous circumstances where they have no option but to die. The besieged British garrison abandoned at Calais in 1940 was left there to die and the orders they received asked them 'to fight to the end' (Churchill quoted by Gilbert, 1983, p. 395).

In addition there have been arguments that the military cannot help but provide a type of moral education which 'must inculcate such virtues as loyalty, self sacrifice, and obedience to duly constituted authority' (Cohen, 1985, p. 33) and as such it not only protects the community but also make it morally stronger. Some countries such as Israel also view military service for many of its citizens as a form of further schooling and technical training (Senor & Singer, 2009).

Furthermore, history provides many examples of the benefits of universal military conscription to the larger society from which those conscripts came. One such example was when, before the First World War, Tsarist Russia created a conscript army to counter the growing threat of such armies in Germany and Austria. However, the very nature of such an army resulted in a consequence the Tsar's authorities had not envisaged. That was that they 'no longer possessed an army easily available to suppress a restive population' (Cohen, 1985, p. 34) as unlike the Tsar's earlier army the army now strongly identified with that population from which they came.

Tsarist Russia was an illiberal regime. When its population sought greater liberties and freedoms the conscripts now in the army could not but sympathize with the aspirations of their countrymen for a more liberal society. This is regardless of the fact that those aspirations were subsequently betrayed by the Bolsheviks (Johnson, 1985). However, the citizens of a liberal society when conscripted into its military face a different dilemma. The military is in many ways the very antithesis of a liberal society and 'the virtues and habits of thought and behavior that the armed forces must inculcate' (Cohen, 1985, p. 35) pose a challenge to those from a liberal society recruited into its military.

THE EXPERIENCE OF MILITARY TRAINING

Military historians argue that over the centuries little has changed regarding the essentials when it comes to educating soldiers. Van Creveld (2009) describes how throughout history recruits have been isolated from their societies. Once isolated, they have been humiliated, purposely, so that they understand their complete dependence on their superiors. Such humiliation is achieved partially through physical abuse so that 'individuality is eliminated ... and uniformity enforced' (2009, p. 49). But van Creveld stresses that is not its only objective. Recruits also have to learn specific skills and have self-confidence in their new found skills. For some to acquire that they must succeed in their training whilst watching others fail. Van Creveld provides approvingly the example of the German military in the period before Hitler came to power. Then, given the restrictions the Versailles Treaty imposed upon the German military, they had to secretly run the military colleges from which they were desperate for graduates to build up their military might. Nonetheless, they accepted a failure rate of two-thirds of those entering their colleges (Van Creveld, 2009). Needless to say those that graduated had outstanding skills.

Drucker (1999) once speculated that the unanswered question about Hitler's Germany was how in the six years, between Hitler coming to power and the outset of World War Two, Germany managed to create a well-trained army of close to two million men. That army when Hitler came to power was small. The Versailles Treaty limited Germany to an army of 100,000 men. There had been – as was discussed in the previous paragraph – attempts to circumvent the treaty but numerically this had not amounted to much. Drucker argues that the answer was that the German Army had successfully employed Taylor's Scientific Management techniques to train their troops and that 'enabled Hitler to create a superb fighting machine' (Drucker, 1999, p. 140). Nonetheless, there was something more. Chambers (1962) argued that when Hitler came to power the German Army *qualitatively* was the best in the world. That nucleus of quality enabled them to achieve that growth. And that nucleus existed because they had not sacrificed quality training during the Weimar period.

Such training has a dual objective. To be successful it must destroy those former ties that bound the recruits to the society from which they came. But simultaneously it must create new ties 'made up of discipline and comradeship' (Van Creveld, 2009, p. 53) which would enable them to function as an organized group 'even amid the chaos of battle' (Van Creveld, 2009, p. 54). Van Creveld argues that this can only be achieved if that training transmits a culture of war which is required as much by modern soldiers as those in the distant past as it helps 'counter the fear of death' (Van Creveld, 2009, p. 411).

Those are the dual dilemmas of military training. On the one hand recruits suffer the ignominy of it – the isolation from society, the humiliation, and the physical abuse – so as to learn how to function effectively as military units. And on the other hand by the time they are doing so they have exchanged one set of ties for another. But do these new ties within the

military — whose ideals embodies many values which are 'utterly repugnant' (Cohen, 1985, p. 35) to a liberal democracy — threaten the commitment of these recruits to the liberal democracies from which they are
recruited? The paper will explore that by considering the experiences of a
citizen soldier proud of the virtues of his military unit but simultaneously
concerned for the democratic viability of his country if it continues to pursue those policies which its military — of which he is a dedicated part —
makes possible.

COMPANY C

Haim Watzman is the author of *Company C: An American's Life as a
Citizen-Soldier in Israel*. Watzman discusses little in his book of his studies
at America's ivy-league Duke University other than that this led him to
migrate to Israel where he 'spends (his) life trying to keep (his) balance
between Jewish orthodoxy and Western humanism' (2005, p. 309).
Watzman also reveals next to nothing of his compulsory national service in
the Israeli army's Nachal Brigade: although the latter saw him fighting in
Beirut in 1982. Instead, his book contemplates only one specific month of a
year: and it does this for eighteen years. That one month, *and admittedly
sometimes more*, are those years, from 1984 until 2002, when he discharged
his — as we will discuss — debatably obligatory annual service as an army
reservist in the infantry unit Company C. This unit, under its previous
name as the Jerusalem Regiment, wrested the Old City of Jerusalem from
the Jordanian Army during the 1967 Six Day War (Oren, 2003).
Nevertheless, Watzman experiences for eighteen years what Cohen
describes as 'a militia system of military service' (1985, p. 27) in which he
undergoes ongoing military training and then each year after his training
returns to the larger society. His experiences in the militia therefore allow
us to consider both the effects of military training and — perhaps far more
importantly — the ties that training creates both in and out of the military.

Watzman explains that serving in the reserve was once mandatory for all
Israeli males. Indeed, that they needed to do so to both secure employment
and to exist in Israeli society. Others have made the very same argument
(Elon, 1983). However, Watzman argues that is no longer the case and that
currently the Israeli army does not bother pursuing those army reservists
intent on avoiding their annual service. Albeit, that some reservists do serve
at great personal cost: An example is given of a fellow Company C reservist

whose business went bankrupt due to his reserve duties. Nonetheless, human nature being what it is 'as more and more men wriggled out of reserve duty, it became more socially acceptable to do so, and as it became more acceptable, more men tried' (2005, p. 264). Watzman writes that by the 1990s of the Israeli Jewish male population between the ages of twenty-one and forty-five who should have been in the militia 'only about 4 percent served for twenty-six days or more' (2005, p. 265). Thus, for Watzman, those that actually serve in the reserves serve essentially as volunteers. This is most significant as it was as such a volunteer that Watzman served in areas of the Israeli occupied West Bank such as Hebron, Beit Sahour, Tubas and Jenin during the Palestinian *Intifada* or Uprising: And he did so whilst being strongly opposed to that occupation which he was voluntarily enforcing.

His antipathy to the occupation admittedly caused him whilst in the military to refuse certain assignments such as the 'command of the lockup at military government headquarters in Jenin' (2005, p. 151). Indeed, his opposition to the occupation of those territories, accompanied by his belief 'that the Palestinians had a legitimate claim to the same right the Jews demanded for themselves: self-determination' (2005, p. 230), led him as an Israeli civilian to demonstrate with the Israeli peace movement, Peace Now, against the occupation. Why he thus felt morally obligated to serve in such places in such times, even when he could have easily been discharged from such service on legitimate medical grounds after his toes were amputated, is what makes his book so fascinating. This highlights the very dilemmas of military training we discussed earlier. Watzman as a soldier has loyalties to his military unit which is engaged in maintaining an occupation which he as a civilian – regardless of those loyalties to his unit – is committed to ending.

Watzman explains his commitment to a two state solution to the Israeli/ Palestinian conflict. Furthermore, he opposes the view of a former Israeli prime minister, Ehud Barak, as to the necessity of such a separation as an end in itself, believing that such a two state solution will only work if the two states are bound by active social and economic ties. Watzman believes economic co-operation between Israeli's and Palestinian's can work. The example of such co-operation which he proffers is not legitimate, but perhaps the absence of any legitimacy ensures the equality of both the Israeli and the Palestinian contributors to this example of economic co-operation. This venture is the success of Israeli car thieves who deliver their stolen vehicles through Israeli-manned army roadblocks, protecting Israel proper from terrorist incursions, to Palestinian workshops in the occupied West

Bank. There these stolen vehicles become spare parts for those legitimate Israeli mechanics workshops in Israeli cities such as Tel Aviv and Haifa who do not mind utilizing such an ethically dubious supply chain.

Furthermore, Watzman supports the view of the assassinated Israeli Prime Minister, Yitzhak Rabin, that 'Israel must reach an accommodation with the Palestinians so that it could focus on the real military threats' (2005, p. 232). However, Watzman's ultimate reason for seeking such a two state solution is neither economic nor security related. Watzman, much like those Englishmen who argued that Britain should grant India independence not for the sake of the Indians, but for the sake of their fellow Englishmen (Embree & Carnes, 2006), believes the continued occupation of the Palestinian territories is morally corrosive for his fellow Jews. For him this would not least of all be because of what he sought from a Jewish state. Watzman describes in the synagogue of which he is president the objections to the messianic references in a prayer for Israel 'because it attached religious significance to the state, and that was dangerous. Sanctifying the state inevitably leads people to place the state above the law and to seek the state's territorial expansion' (2005, p. 312).

MUTUAL LOYALTY AND THE ABILITY TO FIGHT

Watzman's service as an Israeli reservist ended four years before the 2006 Israeli war against Hezbollah. However, that forthcoming conflict is already approaching lurking threateningly on the horizon in the pages of his book. In describing his annual reserve duty on Israel's northern border in 1994 he explains the ever-present ongoing threat of 'Hezbollah guerrillas just waiting for (their) chance' (2005, p. 262). Despite their presence and the rampant dangers thereof Watzman is happy to serve as an army reservist on that northern border as it is far 'away from the territories' (2005, p. 325) and their occupation which he desires an end to and of which he wishes no part. But there are things he experiences on the northern border which he is most unhappy with and his concerns relate to our earlier considerations as to the experience of military training.

Watzman complains bitterly about 'army budget cuts and efficiency measures' (2005, p. 262) resulting in their supplies being 'miserly, and our manpower inadequate' (2005, p. 262). He also describes their 'annual maneuvers' (2005, p. 263) being re-scheduled from one or two weeks to three or four days. Most importantly given our earlier arguments as to the necessity of creating ties 'made up of discipline and comradeship' (Van Creveld,

2009, p. 53) so that a military unit can indeed function, Watzman's major complaint is not with the new training regime per se, but that those efficiency measures meant that he and his fellow reservists 'had hardly any time to enjoy each other's company' (2005, p. 262). There is a specific reason for that complaint. This is his believe that 'only half of a unit's ability to fight depended on training and discipline. The other half hinged on the guys' mutual loyalty, fostered by the backgammon board and the coffeepot. ... (which) the army didn't seem to understand' (Watzman, 2005, p. 263): Although military historians such as Van Creveld (2009) most certainly do.

Furthermore, given our concerns as to those essential ties within the military unit but in turn also to one's society, what is of particular interest are those reasons why Watzman believes it is moral to serve as a reservist maintaining the occupation he as a civilian is committed to ending. Israel is a society under constant siege and requires its soldiers. Cohen reminds us that 'no army since the beginning of the nineteenth century has fought ... successfully without calling into service vast numbers of civilians' (1985, p. 37). Watzman differentiates between the status of the civilian and the soldier. As a civilian he can, like any other individual, campaign against his government. However, as a soldier he is not an individual 'but part of an army charged with carrying out the will of the country's elected civilian representatives' (2005, p. 379). And yet, Watzman has asserted that as such soldiers he and his fellow reservists are essentially volunteers, so why morally should he be volunteering to maintain a military occupation that he as an individual is actively opposed to?

Watzman answers this most clearly in his encounter with three conscientious objectors, one of whom 'had served time in a military prison' (2005, p. 375), and with the others facing similar prospects, because they believed 'that Israel's occupation of the territories was so fundamentally wrong that serving there was immoral' (2005, p. 375). They argued that Israel should withdraw from the areas it occupied in the Six Day War, return to the 1967 borders, and defend Israel from that border as 'defending ourselves was morally acceptable, while maintaining our rule over an alien population was not morally acceptable' (2005, p. 376). Watzman, however, whilst sympathetic to such thinking given his aspirations for his society, does because of his ties to his military unit see such thinking as fallacious as it 'assumed that there was a clear and obvious distinction between defensive and offensive actions. (And while) our moral choices would be much simpler if the world worked that way' (2005, p. 377) it did not with the offensive a part of the defensive.

Watzman considers that with such offensives the 'incursions into enemy territory are not necessarily more considerate of the lives of the civilians on the other side' (2005, p. 377). Rather, with regard to the safety of those civilians on the other side of the border 'such missions are much riskier (for those civilians) than raids conducted in territory that your army controls. You have less intelligence and must use more firepower to ensure your own soldiers' safety. In comparison, occupation may save lives and thus be the morally superior option — assuming that the occupation is temporary, pending the conclusion of a peace treaty' (2005, p. 377). Such thinking is instructive. It reflects those dual ties we explained above. Watzman could not hold such a position if he was not cognizant of the reality of the military of which he is a part. But whilst he is a part of that military he still has aspirations for the society to which he belongs and that is to end the occupation. Hence, when out of the military he joins others at Israeli Peace Now rallies calling for an end to the occupation and works in other ways to end the occupation.

Amos Oz, a founder of Israel's Peace Now movement, described how 'for seventy years now Israel has more or less lived out the experience of a collective Salman Rushdie' (1995, p. 107) and how that has affected the Israeli psyche. Regarding that psyche Israel's first Prime Minister, David Ben-Gurion, entrusted to the infant Israeli Army the very same nation building role that Drucker (1941) argued was the initial function of the Prussian Army. With hundreds of thousands of destitute Jewish refugees arriving from the Arab countries, and elsewhere, Ben-Gurion used the army to help absorb them and 'moved the army toward performing functions over and above purely military duties' (Herzog, 1996, p. 111). Those refugees like all other citizens were conscripted into the Israeli army and then served in the militia. In doing so they experienced the essentials of military training and all that involved. They also had to create new ties within the military but if those new ties did little to erode their prior ties to the larger society the military as an organization poses no ethical challenges to the society it protects.

Aronovitch has argued that 'effective soldiers are ethical soldiers, that good soldiers in the military sense are good soldiers in the moral sense' (2001, p. 13). Watzman (2005) presents nothing to dispute that. His experiences negate any concerns that Cohen (1985) contemplated regarding the dilemmas of military service. And because they do we can dare to hope that the effects of the military organization upon a democracy such as Australia will overall be beneficial, provided of course that we can succeed where Prussia failed and not 'isolate the military from the mainstream of social life' (Geyer, 1990, p. 188).

REFERENCES

Aronovitch, H. (2001). Good soldiers, a traditional approach. *Journal of Applied Philosophy*, *18*(1), 13–23.

Box, D. (2014). Military gets tough over email sex scandal. *The Australian*, August 7, p. 1. Retrieved from http://www.theaustralian.com.au/national-affairs/defence/military-gets-tough-over-email-sex-scandal/story-e6frg8yo-1227015837160.

Broszat, M. (1995). A social and historical typology of the German opposition to Hitler. In D. C. Large (Ed.), *Contending with Hitler: Varieties of German resistance in the third Reich*. Cambridge: Cambridge University Press.

Chambers, F. P. (1962). *This age of conflict*. New York, NY: Harcourt, Brace and World.

Cohen, E. A. (1985). *Citizens and soldiers: The dilemmas of military service*. Ithaca, NY: Cornell University Press.

Drucker, P. F. (1939). *The end of economic man: A study of the new totalitarianism*. London: Heinemann.

Drucker, P. F. (1941). What became of the Prussian Army? *Virginia Quarterly Review*, *17*(1), 1–7. Retrieved from http://www.vqronline.org/essay/what-became-prussian-army. Accessed on March 31, 2010.

Drucker, P. F. (1985). *The changing world of the executive*. New York, NY: Times Books.

Drucker, P. F. (1999). *Management challenges for the 21st century*. New York, NY: Harper Business.

Elon, A. (1983). *The Israelis: Founders and sons*. Ringwood, Australia: Penguin Books.

Embree, A. T., & Carnes, M. C. (2006). *Defining a nation: India on the eve of independence, 1945*. New York, NY: Pearson/Longman.

Frater, S. (2011). Hitler and arguably the most insane and pivotal decision in history, In *The history reader*. Retrieved from http://www.thehistoryreader.com/modern-history/december-111941-hitler-arguably-insane-pivotal-decision-history/. Accessed on December 11, 2014.

Geyer, M. (1990). The past as future: The German officer corps as profession. In G. Cocks & K. H. Jarausch (Eds.), *German professions 1800–1950* (pp. 183–212). Oxford: Oxford University Press.

Gilbert, M. (1983). *Finest hour: Winston S. Churchill 1939–1941*. London: Heinemann.

Herzog, C. (1996). *Living history: A memoir*. New York, NY: Pantheon Books.

Johnson, P. (1985). *A history of the modern world: From 1917 to the 1980s*. Johannesburg: Jonathan Ball Paperbacks.

McCarthy, G. (2014). Australians need a new common ground: Compulsory national service. *The Guardian*, pp. 1–3. Retrieved from http://www.theguardian.com/commentisfree/2014/jan/23/australians-need-a-new-common-ground-compulsory-national-service

McLean, M. (2015). Will Australia buy Japanese submarines? *The Interpreter*, p. 1. Retrieved from http://www.lowyinterpreter.org

Oren, M. B. (2003). *Six days of war: June 1967 and the making of the modern Middle East*. New York, NY: Ballantine Books.

Oz, A. (1995). *Israel, Palestine and peace*. San Diego, CA: Harcourt Brace & Company.

Perkins, M. (2015). Guru sex scandal at Mount Eliza yoga retreat. *The Age, January 20*, p. 1. Retrieved from http://www.theage.com.au/victoria/guru-sex-scandal-at-mount-eliza-yoga-retreat-20150120-12ugkk.html.

Senor, D., & Singer, S. (2009). *Start-up nation: The story of Israel's economic miracle.* New York, NY: Twelve.

Van Creveld, M. (2009). *The culture of war.* Gloucestershire: Spellmount.

Walzer, M. (1971). *Obligations: Essays on disobedience, war, and citizenship.* Cambridge, MA: Harvard University Press.

Watzman, H. (2005). *Company C: An American's life as a citizen-soldier in Israel.* New York, NY: Farrar, Straus and Giroux.

Widdows, H. (2005). *The moral vision of Iris Murdoch.* Aldershot: Ashgate.

A MORAL ARGUMENT FOR BENEFIT CORPORATIONS AS AN ALTERNATIVE TO GOVERNMENT SOCIAL SERVICES

Charles J. Coate and Mark C. Mitschow

ABSTRACT

Economic activity is typically provided by three distinct sectors. For-profit entities seek to maximize owner profit by providing various goods and services. The not-for-profit sector consists of private or quasi-public entities that provide goods and services without regard to making an explicit profit. Government entities extract resources from the economy and redistribute them to achieve certain public goods.

Recently a fourth or gray sector has developed that combines elements of the other three. As a corporate form that explicitly sacrifices profit maximization to advance some predetermined social good, benefit corporations are one example of this gray sector. Owners are aware of this dual mission but still invest as the social objectives are consistent with their personal goals. Thus, the benefit corporation can be viewed as a for-profit entity subject to an explicit social welfare constraint.

The Ethical Contribution of Organizations to Society
Research in Ethical Issues in Organizations, Volume 14, 71–92
Copyright © 2015 by Emerald Group Publishing Limited
ISSN: 1529-2096/doi:10.1108/S1529-209620150000014004

Since the late 1960s governments have spent trillions of dollars on a wide variety of social welfare programs. Nevertheless, poverty persists and government altruism may have made poverty more intractable in some respects. Economic logic suggests that providing social welfare transfer payments with few work or training requirements can make recipients dependent and enable dysfunctional behavior. Over time this may rob recipients of opportunities for labor and self-sufficiency.

Benefit corporations are typically viewed as a form of socially responsible investment that leverages the economic advantages of market-based systems. To date, however, little has been written about the benefit corporation's potential ethical dimensions. The purpose of this paper is to provide a moral argument based in Catholic Social Teaching to support the use of benefit corporations as a substitute for some government service programs. Our arguments are centered on the primary principle of Human Dignity *and will include, but not be limited to:* Work, Solidarity *and there role social and economic society as well as the* Role of Government *or* Subsidiarity *(including the* Welfare State*).*

Keywords: Benefit Corporation; Catholic social teaching; government transfer payments

INTRODUCTION

Economic activity within society has typically been driven by three sectors: for-profit, not-for-profit, and government. For-profit entities play a primary role in economic growth and societal wellbeing, generally operate in competitive markets, and seek to make a profit producing and selling goods and services to willing buyers. Many for-profit entities also receive tax incentives and other government benefits for certain activities. Not-for-profit entities (NFPs) provide goods and services without the goal of earning a profit from these activities. In addition, some NFPs provide goods and services to underprivileged individuals and communities (e.g., soup kitchens), while others (e.g., hospitals, universities) provide services to the wider community. Most NFPs rely on private donations and government grants for a significant portion of their revenue, though many also earn revenue by providing goods and services to the general public. Government generates revenue from taxes and fees and uses them for the common good (e.g., roads, schools) or as redistributions of wealth (e.g., supplemental food, housing or welfare payments) based on societal needs and political decisions. While a significant portion of government spending goes to government employee compensation, service contracts to for-profit and NFP entities, and activities such as national defense, most redistributed income provides social services to various groups.

Since at least the 1960s the government sector in developed economies has grown dramatically. In the United States, for example, between 1960 and 2004 real per capita federal expenditures increased by approximately 75% (Garrett & Rhine, 2006), and since 1964 the US federal government has spent approximately $12 trillion on the "War on Poverty." Currently over 100 federal programs spend a total of over $20,000 per poor person in America (Tanner, 2012).

Yet despite these huge expenditures, poverty in the United States remains intractable. The poverty rate declined from 22.4% in the late 1950s to a record low of 11.1% in 1973 (National Poverty Center, 2015), but rose steadily thereafter and is currently around 14.5% (Gongloff, 2014). Income inequality has also increased significantly since the early 1970s and the wealth gap between upper income earners and the rest of society is by some measures the greatest on record (Fry & Kochhar, 2014). Further, poverty is associated with many other social costs (e.g., family breakdown, crime, substance abuse, poor education).

How can the wealthiest society in world history spend so much fighting poverty to so little effect? While these and undoubtedly many factors that are beyond the scope of this paper, one reasonable possibility is that the money is not being invested properly. In short, the government redistribution model appears to be an ineffective means of addressing the root causes of poverty, social ills, and the resulting income inequality. If so, then devising better models for fighting poverty is a moral and economic imperative.

In the past decade a new corporate model has been developed that combines profit-making ventures with specific social objectives. Benefit corporations are a hybrid economic structure that consists of both a for-profit enterprise and a NFP "social good." Managers are explicitly required to sacrifice some level of profit in order to achieve the predetermined social objective. Thus, "the benefit corporation model provides a predetermined social benefit while also producing a profit for investors, thereby allowing socially conscious investors or customers a participation option in firms maximizing profit subject to a constraint defined by a specific social benefit" (Coate & Mitschow, 2015).

By their nature, benefit corporations seek to leverage the economic advantages of market-based systems to address poverty. Previous research has examined issues surrounding the structure of benefit corporations, the progress of state legislation, and whether benefit corporations will succeed in the market place. What has not been examined, however, are the benefit corporation's potential ethical advantages vis-à-vis government transfer payments. This manuscript presents a moral argument based in Catholic Social Teaching (CST) to posit that benefit corporations would be a superior tool than the existing government transfer payment model.

Section two will outline the means by which government welfare services are currently financed and provided. Section three will define benefit corporations and discuss how they can be used to promote economic opportunity, a crucial element of CST. Section four discusses CST, while section five argues its relevance to benefit corporations and their contributions to social welfare. Section six summarizes and concludes the paper.

CURRENT METHODS OF PROVIDING WELFARE SERVICES

Traditionally the private sector was viewed as the "engine of economic growth." Profit-making entities provided goods and services, employed workers, and invested in additional plant and equipment. Governments impose a series of revenue, income, and consumption taxes, the proceeds of which are used for multiple purposes. Governments must first incur administration and operating costs and then provide infrastructure (e.g., roads, schools) to meet basic common requirements. Government also directly and indirectly provides a variety of subsidies to people in need. These transfer payments might be considered a form of social charity. A number of NFP organizations also exist to provide private charity (e.g., Red Cross). The latter are generally supported by private donations from persons participating in the private sector and in some cases government grants.

Coate and Mitschow (2013) assert that the market provides a moral means of achieving economic growth in a society. However, Coate and Mitschow (2013) also recognize an efficient market-based economy will not adequately serve all members of society. For a variety of reasons, some persons or communities will be unable to fully contribute valued products or services in a market economy and consequently will not be adequately compensated by the market. By definition these communities are underserved by the market economy, resulting in areas of poverty. In the short run, such communities would typically be served by some form of public or private charity that is often funded (directly or indirectly) by government transfer payments.

For a variety of reasons beyond the scope of this paper, the size, scope, and nature of underserved areas receiving government benefits has significantly expanded since the 1960s. As social welfare programs expanded the government found itself increasingly unable to provide services that allowed for the effective development of economic self-sufficiency. Consequently, governments recognized the economic efficiency of the private sector and began "contracting out" certain social services by awarding grants to NFPs and for-profit entities that provide specific social services. This is arguably an element of the fourth or gray sector in that these are hybrid types of organizations.

"A basic tenet of economic theory is that competitive markets will result in cheaper and higher quality goods and services as consumers shop around for the best deal and suppliers work to provide the best products at the lowest cost" (Winston, Burwick, McConnell, & Roper, 2002). While state and federal governments still provide a number of services directly, according to the US Department of Health and Human Services at least 15% of government-funded social welfare services are actually provided by nongovernmental agencies (Winston et al, 2002). Government services that are commonly privatized include employment services, child support enforcement and child welfare services, as well as Temporary Assistance for Needy Families (TANF). Typical reasons for contracting out these services include cost savings, increased service quality, ability to acquire skilled staff, and greater flexibility. In addition, there is significant political support for privatization that cannot be ignored by government agencies (Winston et al, 2002).

While privatization appears to result in lower service costs (Cohen & Eimicke, 2001), the savings appear to be modest (Auger, 1999). The evidence regarding improved quality also appears to be mixed. Sanger (2003) determined that privatization resulted in higher quality services, but those results seem to depend on the type of services that are privatized (Nightingale & Pindus, 1997). There appears to be stronger evidence that non-governmental entities are better able to acquire skilled personnel and are more flexible than government entities. Reasons for this include easier access to private capital for hiring skilled workers, greater ability to transfer workers as needs change, and greater ability to discipline poor performing workers (Winston et al, 2002). Non-governmental service providers also appear to have greater access to technology (Government Accountability Office, 1996).

Efforts to privatize government services, while providing some increased efficiency, are still are primarily based in the transfer payment model. In some ways this represents putting "new wine in old wineskins," as poverty remains intractable despite both the enormous resources committed to fighting it and the privatization of certain specific programs. Benefit corporations offer another vehicle to address poverty. Could this new corporate model perhaps provide better a means to provide social welfare services? Before we can address the moral arguments for benefit corporations, there must be some economic justification for adding them to the mix of service providers. The following section explains the benefit corporation and examines its potential efficacy.

BENEFIT CORPORATIONS AND THEIR ECONOMICS ADVANTAGES

According to Andre (2012), "the organizational universe is comprised of the public sector, the private sector, the nonprofit sector (also termed "civil society"), and what has recently been called the 'fourth sector.'" Benefit corporations are a newly-legislated corporate form that permits management to sacrifice profit maximization to meet a specific social objective (Halsey, Tomkowicz, & Halsey, 2013) has emerged as a fourth sector organization. Consequently early research related to benefit corporation has been in the legal literature (e.g., Cummings, 2012; Reiser, 2011; Resor, 2012)

Benefit corporations, if they become viable, would fall into this fourth, or "gray," sector. The benefit corporation's "dual nature" could also be well-suited to advance various elements of corporate social responsibility (CSR), an "umbrella concept" used in a variety of fields to describe a company's responsibilities to all stakeholders. Benefit corporations have drawn attention in the professional financial literature (e.g., Gilbert, 2011; Glassman & Spahn, 2012; Mac Cormac & Haney, 2012); this literature has also suggested benefit corporations may be viewed as a capitalistic innovation (Shiller, 2013).

Equity investors in benefit corporations receive the usual rights accorded to shareholders (e.g., proportional rights to vote, share in profits, and receive any dividend) and the shares can be traded on public exchanges. In addition, shareholders also control a "social good" that they presumably care about in return for an explicit understanding that any benefit corporation profits will not derive solely to shareholders. Instead, profits will be used to provide a reasonable return to investors, subsidize the specific "social good" defined in the corporate charter, and support both the business and social enterprises going forward. "Thus, benefit corporation investors derive utility from the operations of the benefit corporation through a combination of profits (generating capital gains and dividends) as well as personal satisfaction from the social benefits" (Coate & Mitschow, 2015). Over half the states in the United States have enacted benefit corporation legislation, and more states are considering it, but it is currently too early to conclude whether this corporate form will be successful.

Benefit corporations could be especially useful in promoting economic opportunity. Vermont Law, as highlighted by Andre (2012, p 137) explicitly includes the elements below its definition of Public Benefit:

Providing low income or underserved individuals or communities with beneficial products or services, and

Promoting economic opportunity for individuals or communities beyond the creation of jobs in the normal course of business

Thus, our focus is on benefit corporations that serve individuals or communities that are underserved by a purely market based economic systems. By definition these are areas of poverty that are currently incapable of providing a market return to investors.

We view the benefit corporation model with a mission to invest in these underserved areas as a potential substitute to the government transfer payment model and hence a potentially superior privatization method. The benefit corporation attracts investors that are willing to sacrifice a market return on profit in exchange for providing economic opportunity in an underserved area. As a private sector "engine of economic growth," the benefit corporation would produce goods and services, employ workers, and invest in additional plant and equipment.

Benefit corporations have not existed long enough to draw conclusions regarding their economic efficacy. However, benefit corporations could provide advantages over current government transfer payment models. Potential economic advantages include directly providing employment opportunities, directly contributing goods and services, and increasing human capital in the underserved community. By its nature the benefit corporation's "social good" would derive most of its resources from nongovernmental sources (i.e., private investors and returns from the entity's for-profit operations), resulting in a reduction of governmental transfer payments and related administrative costs.

By definition, the benefit corporation would provide compensated employment. This compensation should exceed that of government transfer payments, thereby allowing for wealth accumulation in communities served by the benefit corporation in place of subsistence transfer payments. Further, because business produces products and services from the combination of investment and labor, society would have an increased level of output. This additional output may be available for distribution within the underserved community.

The most important advantage of benefit corporations could be the ability to develop human capital in underserved communities. The nature of employment suggests that benefit corporation employment would increase individual skill sets and expertise in the underserved area. As skill sets were developed in the context of a for profit business they would be transferable to the larger market-based economy.

Finally, we must consider the investor who forgoes a market return. In contrast to government transfer payment model, benefit corporation investment is voluntary. This means that the investor is personally made better off by the investment. Further, since benefit corporations are subject to market pressure the efficiency of a market-based system is imposed on the operations and performance of both parts of the benefit corporation.

We do not discount benefit corporations' economic advantages. Potential economic efficacy is a necessary but not sufficient condition for judging benefit corporations' suitability as a poverty fighting tool. However, the focus the manuscript is to provide a moral argument for benefit corporations model vis-à-vis the government transfer model. In the sections below we provide that argument in the context of Catholic Social Teaching (CST).

CATHOLIC SOCIAL TEACHING

CST is the Roman Catholic Church's moral framework, based in Judeo-Christian heritage, for outlining the relationship between individuals, society, and their Creator. This framework is designed to be universal and apply to all of humanity. In recent decades business ethics literature has recognized CST as having become more aware of and integrated with main stream economic theory. Notable examples include Williams (1993) and McCann (1997). Consequently, the business ethics literature includes significant contributions related to CST. Coate and Mitschow (2013) provide an overview of and references for this literature. Byron (1998) offered an educational and communicative perspective on CST by focusing on presentation in terms of Principles. He outlined CST in terms of principles to provide a framework for understanding and internalizing CST. Table 1 presents the Principles of CST taken from Catholic Charities (2012) and organized as they relate benefit corporations.

While CST has been developed over many centuries, Papal encyclicals of the past 125 years have been prepared to influence, enlighten, and enhance the ethical focus of business decision-making and influence public policy throughout the world. *Rerum Novorum* (Leo XIII, 1891) was motivated by the societal challenges of the industrial age and arguably provides

Table 1. Key Principles of CST.

Principles Most Relevant to the Benefit Corporation Model

Human dignity. Human life is sacred and that the dignity of the person is at the core of a moral vision for society. This is the foundation of all the principles or our social teaching.

Option for the poor (and vulnerable). A basic moral test of society is how the most vulnerable members are faring. Our tradition instructs us to put the *needs* or the poor and vulnerable first.

Dignity of work and rights of workers. The economy must serve people. If the dignity of work is to be protected, then the basic rights of workers must be respected: the right to productive work, to decent (living) and fair wages, to organize and join unions, to private property and economic initiative.

Role of government. Because we are human being the state is natural to the person. Therefore the state has a positive moral function. The functions of government should be performed at the lowest level possible.

Solidarity. We are our brothers' and sisters' keepers, wherever they live. We are one human family.

Rights and responsibilities. Human dignity can be protected and a healthy community achieved only if human rights are protected and responsibilities to one another, our family, the larger society are met.

Principles Relevant to the Benefit Corporation Model

Participation. All people have the right to participate in the economic, political and cultural life of society. It is a fundamental demand of justice and a requirement for human dignity that all people be assured a minimum level of participation in the community.

Community and the common good. How we organize our society, in economics, politics, law, and policy directly affects human dignity and the capacity of an individual to grow in the community. The role of institutions is to protect human life and human dignity and promote the common good.

Principles Less Relevant to the Benefit Corporation Model

Promotion of peace. "Peace is not just the absence of war. It involves mutual respect and confidence between peoples and nations. It involves collaboration and binding agreements" (John Paul II). Peace is the fruit of justice and is dependent upon the right order among human beings.

Stewardship of creation. We show our respect for the Creator by our stewardship of creation. We are called to protect people and the planet.

an important element of the basis for modern day businesses. Key concepts addressed were the relationship between labor and capital, the need for private property (in contrast with socialism), and the role of government. While these concepts have evolved over time (and have been further developed in a number of subsequent Papal encyclicals) these concepts are still relevant to the contemporary economic and business environments. Therefore, CST appears to be an appropriate, but not exclusive, tool to examine the moral issues surrounding benefit corporations as a social welfare provider.

CATHOLIC SOCIAL TEACHING AND BENEFIT CORPORATIONS

One economic argument suggests that benefit corporations focusing on underserved areas allow for a substitution effect of government transfer payments with private work opportunities. The benefit corporation replaces the need for some government welfare resources by creating work opportunities and supporting social welfare. The work produces goods and services (disproportionately in underserved areas) and increases the benefit corporation employees' human capital. This leads to the primarily utilitarian argument that an increase in both production and human capital leaves society better off. While we do not discount this argument we believe a deeper examination of CST can yield much stronger moral arguments for benefit corporations as a social welfare provider.

In the following sections we use CST to provide this moral argument for benefit corporations. While benefit corporations may include a variety of social missions within their corporate structure, we are particularly interested those social missions that provide economic opportunity in underserved areas. We will build our general argument using CST principles and then examine selected Papal encyclicals to extend our position in more specific terms.

The CST principles outlined in Table 1 were organized based on their importance to our moral argument. All of CST is focused on *Human Dignity*. This principle states that human life is sacred and that the dignity of the person is at the core of any moral vision for society. It is therefore the foundation of all other CST principles.

A transfer payment of the government model may allow a person to eat, but "man cannot live on bread alone" (Luke 4:4, Mathew 4:4, *Good News*

Bible, 1978). *Human Dignity* must be considered at the individual level. Thus, we build our arguments there rather than relying on a utilitarian society-based approach. This logic implicitly assumes that the human dignity of all is injured if the human dignity of one is diminished. Each person must be allowed to realize his or her human potential. In the following paragraphs we will argue how the benefit corporation enhances other CST principles, particularly *Human Dignity*.

A basic moral test of society is how the most vulnerable members are faring. CST instructs us to put the needs of the poor and vulnerable first, which means there must be an *Option for the Poor (and vulnerable)*. In a market based economic system the poor exist because the market does not sufficiently value their contributions. Simply put, the poor person's marginal contribution is less than the marginal cost of their employment. These persons or communities may thus be considered "underserved by the economy," which by definition leaves them vulnerable or marginalized.

A benefit corporation explicitly recognizes that at least some market-based profit or return on investment can be sacrificed to achieve a social good. Thus, benefit corporation investors are willing to sacrifice profit maximization and incur wage costs above the normal market equilibrium to allow a market-based employment option for the poor. A government transfer payment might also be considered an option for the poor in that a wealth transfer occurs. However, government transfer payments are a one sided transaction. A benefit corporation's employment opportunity or work also allows the individual to contribute to society as producer as well as consumer, thereby providing a powerful moral argument for benefit corporations vis-à-vis simple transfer models.

While *Human Dignity* is at the center of CST, the *Dignity of Work and Rights of Workers* is another significant part of our moral argument for benefit corporations relative to government transfer payments. The dignity of work requires the basic rights of workers be respected. Critical to our argument are the right to productive work, to fair wages, to private property and to economic initiative.

We first consider productive work and a fair wage. A benefit corporation operating in an underserved area offers work within a for-profit environment to people in that area. In contrast with a government transfer payment, the benefit corporation offers productive work that includes not only a wage but also the opportunity to produce goods and/or services within the underserved community. By virtue of the benefit corporation's mission, this wage is also above the worker's ordinary market (or "fair") wage.

Work is the first step in economic initiative and leads through saved wages to private property. Work allows the worker the ability to increase human capital via experience. This experience occurs in the context of for-profit organizations, the primary engine of economic growth. Hence, even an entry-level job with a benefit corporation offers a path to a "better" job as the worker's human capital increases. Transfer payments cannot offer the multiple benefits of work beyond a fixed wage. Further, work provides other non-economic benefits, including the ability to participate in and contribute to the common good (as discussed below).

Even if benefit corporations emerged to serve the economy a *Role of Government* would still exist. CST argues the state is natural to the person and has a positive moral function. Government should support both the society's markets and its underlying social system. However, government functions should be limited and performed at the lowest administrative level possible (e.g., local over national).

Government's role also includes providing short-term solutions to economic volatility. In contrast, benefit corporations are more focused on long run market-based means of developing a self-supporting society generally requiring fewer government structures and/or resources. Thus, governmental functions would still exist as the benefit corporation is addressing somewhat different issues.

Benefit corporation investments may thus be seen as a market-based form of (a broadly defined) charity that promotes *Human Dignity*. While discussions related to *Option for the Poor* and *Dignity of Work* focus on the worker or those providing human capital, benefit corporations serving economically underserved areas also provide an excellent example of *Solidarity*. *Solidarity* recognizes that we are our brothers' and sisters' keepers. The principle of *Solidarity* explicitly provides a role for benefit corporation investors (or those who provide other wealth capital). Investors experience the moral self-satisfaction of fulfilling a duty and providing for others. Society is able to enhance the individual's ability to experience *Solidarity* rather than be subordinated to the outside governmental processes. When contrasted with the benefit corporation model, government transfer payment models detract from the human dignity of all members of society, both workers and investors.

In the context of benefit corporations, *Rights and Responsibilities* are related to *Solidarity*. *Human Dignity* can be protected and a healthy community achieved only if human rights are protected and responsibilities to one another, to the family, and to the larger society are met. The benefit corporation model improves the larger society by enhancing the *Rights and Responsibility* of both workers and investors. The worker's right to meaningful employment is met through responsible investment in the benefit corporation. Investors meet their responsibility by using their wealth to provide employment, which in turn allows the employed workers to meet their responsibilities to family, community and the larger society.

CST holds that all people have the right to participate in the economic, political, and cultural life of society. *Participation* in the community is a fundamental demand of justice and a requirement for individual human dignity. Participation means the ability to "earn one's daily bread," not just to eat it. This implies that work, defined as the ability to exchange one's skill and human capital in return for a wage, is a necessary element of participation. Half of the work exchange allows for the purchases of goods and services in exchange for the wage and permits people to participate as consumers. The other half of the work exchange, which we argue is more important to human dignity, provides society with the product of one's work.

Full participation in society requires both halves of the work transaction. Unfortunately, government transfer payments only address the consumption portion. In contrast, the work provided by benefit corporations allows employees to both produce and consume, and is therefore a superior means of enhancing participation in society.

Participation also requires contributing to the *Community and the Common Good*. Society and its institutions must therefore promote the common good, which in turn implies that a person's actions benefit not only themselves but also others in society. Individuals cannot fully realize their value without the ability to contribute to others' wellbeing. In short, individuals must to have the opportunity to give (within the limits of their abilities).

The employment available through a benefit corporation allows workers to contribute to the common good by creating goods and services that are valued by other members of society. Investment in a benefit corporation also allows the investor to contribute to the common good with wealth. In contrast, government transfer payments deny recipients the ability to reciprocate because such transfers do not allow the person to create something that is valued by other members of society.

PAPAL ENCYCLICALS AND THE BENEFIT CORPORATION

In this section we consider the moral argument for benefit corporations vis-à-vis government transfer payments using specific Papal Encyclicals. Encyclicals apply the historical teaching foundations of the Catholic

Church to specific times and issues. To manage the scope of Papal writings we focus on four encyclicals; *Rerum Novorum* (Leo XIII, 1891), *Centesimus Annus* (Paul II, 1991), *Caritas in Veritate* (Benedict, 2009), and *Evangelii Gaudium* (Francis, 2013). We chose *Rerum Novarum (RN)* because it arguably provides the foundation of contemporary CST and it relates to business and economics. We chose *Centesimus Annus (CA)* as this was a 100-year update on the concepts from *RN*. We chose *Caritas in Veri*tate *(CV)* and *Evangelii Gaudium (EG)* as these are the relevant encyclicals of the two most recent Popes.

Leo XIII and Rerum Novorum

Rerum Novorum, or *Of Revolutionary Change*, was issued in 1891 by Leo XIII as the Catholic Church's response to the economic and political realities of the times, particularly in regards to the "condition of the working class" [2]. *RN* offered a definition of the rights and responsibility of rich and poor (e.g., wealthy and worker, or capital and labor) as well as addressing the concept of private property and a proper role for the state.

RN clearly stated the church's position in support of private property and rejected the socialist view of placing property in the hands of the state [4, 5]. The need for private property was not to protect the position of capital or the wealthy, but to provide the means for workers to obtain ownership and improve their position in life. *RN* cautioned against the transfer of wealth to the state, even for income redistribution, as this would deprive both capital and labor of economic autonomy. *RN* addressed the need for work [7, 8] as it gives people both the power to exercise choice and to provide for their own welfare. *RN* views the state's role as an agent to protect the individual rights in a community and to provide public aid in extreme cases. Consistent with *RN*, the benefit corporation offers work, self-reliance and the ability improve one's position in life. The government transfer model places the state rather than the individual (whose rights precede those of the state) in control of resources and their allocation.

RN [19] rejects the notion that there should be a hostile relationship between capital and labor (or the wealthy and workers). *RN* suggests that these two should be in harmony, as each need the other to prosper, and then specifies the duties that bind the owner and the worker. Working for gain, either as an owner or an employee, is honorable and allows people to earn a livelihood. However, to "misuse men as though they were things in pursuit of gain ... is truly shameful and inhuman." *RN* exhorts all to

"... bind the classes in friendliness and good feeling" [21]. *RN* calls for charity in "the right use of money" [22] and a duty for those with excess "... to give to the indigent" [22].

The benefit corporation offers a model of charity consistent with Leo XIII's teaching. The investment of capital in the benefit corporation with a return below the market rate binds the classes and allows people in underserved communities to earn their livelihood, acquire private property, and better their economic condition. In contrast, a constant transfer payment offers only future annuities that promote dependency on the state and an inability to realize the dignity of livelihood, property, and self-betterment.

John Paul II and Centesimus Annus

In *Centisimus Annus* John Paul II reasserts the concepts from *RN*, but also draws on his own earlier work *Laborem Exercens* (1981). Concepts addressed in *CA* that were drawn from *RN* include the *worker question* (or the conflict of labor and capital) [5], the need for private property [6], the relationship of state and citizen with a need for subsidiarity [10], and an option for the poor [12].

CA is highly critical of socialism's attempts to do away with private property and place the good of society above the good of individuals. *CA* also recognizes the principle of *Subsidiarity* (the limited role the state\government) [12–15] and supports mechanisms that "... deliver work from the mere condition of a "commodity" to guarantee its dignity" [19]. The benefit corporation is a mechanism that offers work and the resulting dignity, while government transfer payments promote dependency on the state.

By its nature, work is meant to unite peoples [27]. Work is critical for all people but especially for the poor. The poor need to be capable of making use of their ability to work and hence share and enjoy material goods. "The advancement of the poor constitutes a great opportunity for the moral, cultural and even economic growth of all humanity" [28]. To John Paul II the question was one of enhancing the dignity, creativity and choice of all peoples [29]. While these comments were made in the immediate aftermath of the Soviet empire's collapse, the message seems relevant to any society with economically marginalized people.

CA also recognizes that private property has an important social function in providing for the common good. In this context "property" referred not merely to physical property, but also to know-how and technical skill

[32]. Work is a means to create private property and is conducted both with and for others. Work, and use of private property generally, should be mindful of for whom the work is done [31].

While *CA* appreciates the numerous positive aspects of the modern economy [32], it also recognizes that many people lack the means to participate in this economy [33]. "They have no way of entering the network of knowledge ... (they have) no way to see their qualities appreciated and utilized. Thus if not exploited ... they are marginalized ..." [33]. *CA* further states that while a free market system is a highly efficient instrument for responding to market needs, there are human needs that fall outside of the market mechanism. Hence, society has the duty to help needy people acquire expertise to join the "circle of exchange" [34].

The benefit corporation model offers a means to unite the investor and the worker, to target the poor and provide the economic opportunity of work and with this work participation in society. Humanity advances due to the actions of both the individuals who invest and the individuals who work. In contrast with the transfer payment, work offers not only the ability to acquire physical property, but also technical skills, human capital. The benefit corporation is an example of *Solidarity*; work done both with and for others where both investor and worker contribute as they can to the corporation.

CA also outlines a solution to help those enter the "circle of exchange" and participate in society [35, 36] that is consistent with a benefit corporation. This solution rejects socialism (or excessive state control and influence over economy) in favor of a capitalism focused by society with the support of the state. Investment decisions such as those in benefit corporations reveal the human quality of the investor and worker. The investor offers capital and accepts a below market return while the worker accepts employment and offers product to society. *CA* suggests that business is a society of persons participating in different ways and with specific responsibilities to supply capital or labor to support a company's activities, all of which is consistent with a benefit corporation.

CA defines a limited role for the state with the primary duty being to support to the economic system. The state should work to create conditions (e.g., enable and support initiatives such as benefit corporations) to ensure job opportunities and minimize interventions (e.g., excessive and long term transfer payments) in the economic system. The state should guarantee individuals freedom and private property, thus providing security so those who work can enjoy their product [48].

Benedict XVI and Francis

The writings of Benedict XVI (*Caritas in Veritate*, 2009) and Francis (*Evangelii Gudium*, 2013) represent the more recent Papal thoughts regarding CST. We note that Benedict draws significantly from *Populorum Progressio* (Paul VI, 1967). While Francis and Benedict XVI are contrasted as different personalities, their writing reflects both some common concepts and a somewhat different perspective.

Both Benedict XVI, with *Caritas in Veritae*, and Francis, with *Evangelii Gaudium*, recognize a new harshness in contemporary economic and social systems. *CV* and *EG* view current unemployment as provoking a new form of marginalization. Benedict XVI [25] suggests that "being out of work on private or public assistance for prolonged periods of time undermines the freedom and creativity of the person and his family and social relationships causing psychological and spiritual suffering." Francis [53] expounds that "Exclusion ultimately has to do with what it means to be part of the society in which we live; those excluded are no longer society's underside or fringes – no longer even part of society. No longer 'exploited' but 'leftovers.'"

Both offer *Solidarity* and the need for charity or generosity as critical elements in efforts to avoid or reduce the new forms of marginalization. *CV* [6, 7] suggests persons should both offer and give what they have to those with need for the benefit of the common good. Further, this practice of charity should "correspond to vocation and degree of influence." Similarly, *EG* "exhorts (us) to share one's (our) wealth" [57] and reminds that the rich must help, respect and promote the poor [58].

These writings share the request for the more wealthy to support the marginalized, but with a charity that is designed to combat the *new* marginalization. The benefit corporation is designed to meet this need. The wealthy supply the capital or investment in an area underserved, or discarded, by society. The investor and the worker need each other to realize their common humanity, thereby advancing *Solidarity*.

The two Popes' encyclicals conflict vis-a-vis their views of the market. While Francis in *EG* [54] rejects a "naïve trust in the market and goodness of those wielding economic power," Benedict XVI in *CV* recognizes that a market governed solely by mutual exchanges limits the market's ability to produce social cohesion and "fulfill its proper economic function" [35]. Rather markets should be governed by the "logic of gift" [36].

Benedict XVI as the Patron of Benefit Corporations

In *CV* Benedict clearly sees the solution to social issues within the structure of the market economy, but recognizes that the market itself as neither good nor evil. Thus, the market cannot produce "social cohesion and fulfill its proper economic function" [35] on its own. To meet this function the doctrines of friendship, solidarity, and reciprocity must exist within the structure of the market. *CV* uses the phrase "the logic of gift" [36] as a strategy needed to guide normal economic activity.

The benefit corporation model is this logic. In a benefit corporation an exclusive profit motive is sacrificed in order to meet a social need. In this case the need is an investment in an underserved community with the investor's expectation of a below market return. This investment or gift is freely offered in solidarity by the investor. "Solidarity is first and foremost a sense of responsibility on the part of everyone with regard to everyone and it cannot be delegated to the State" [38]. *CV* all but explicitly calls for benefit corporations: "Alongside profit enterprises and various types of public enterprises there must be room for commercial entities to emerge based on mutual(ist) principles … one may expect hybrid forms of commercial behavior to emerge" [38].

The benefit corporation is by its very nature a hybrid commercial form. The benefit corporation combines the efficiency of the for profit firm, the ability to participate and grow in an economy, and the willingness of investors of all wealth levels to participate. The exchange of profit for social good is an example of human cooperation; a stark contrast to a transfer payment by the state.

In discussing the human family, *CV* recognizes economic isolation as a deep form of poverty that for some is a likely outcome of the market-based economy [53]. By definition underserved economic areas are those communities and person suffering with some degree of economic poverty or isolation. A benefit corporation offers economic inclusion by providing opportunity that would not exist in a pure market system.

The benefit corporation recognizes that all are capable of giving something and allows all to contribute to society. This is not the case of a state based transfer payment system. The benefit corporation, then, illustrates subsidiarity as a fraternal co-operation that no one group can accomplish on its own. This subsidiarity respect human dignity and recognizes that persons are capable of giving something to others [57]. *CV* states that reciprocity (as offered in the benefit corporation) is the heart of being human and subsidiarity is "... the most effective antidote against and form of all-encompassing welfare state [57].

CV closely links the principles of subsidiarity and solidarity calling for grass roots programs with increasing participation. *CV* cautions against social privatism and paternal social assistance which result from an imbalance of these two principles [58]. *CV* goes as far as to suggest a fiscal subsidiarity that allows citizens to allocate a portion of their paid taxes to social mission [60]. Favorable tax treatment for benefit corporation investment would meet this goal.

The benefit corporation model is separate from more conventional forms of charity and state programs. And while conventional charity is a necessary short run solution, the benefit corporation investments offer a long-term solution that provide human dignity at all elves of society. Benefit corporations are not only capital investments, but potentially also human investments where an owner or manager share knowledge of market based economic for profit systems. Thus, workers in the benefit corporation model increase human capital.

SUMMARY AND CONCLUSION

In the past 50 years market-based economies have grown and developed, offering increased wealth and improved quality of life to their societies. In this same time period the state has increasingly taxed this wealth to provide for greater social welfare spending. Despite the significant economic growth and the even more significant government wealth redistributions (transfer payments), poverty and related social ills persist and wealth disparity has increased. Attempts at privatization to increase operational efficiency for these transfer payments have offered only minimal improvements. These outcomes suggest an economic and moral imperative to find creative solutions to the economic processes and outcomes of society as individual citizens.

This paper offers benefit corporations as one possible solution. Benefit corporations are a new corporate form that combines profit making activities with an explicit "social good" and have an explicit mandate to sacrifice profit maximization to enhance that social good. We focus on cases where the benefit corporation's social good would be to support a community that is currently underserved by the economy, and thus by definition marginalized. Those investing in a benefit corporation would forgo a market return, but realize a benefit from providing the social good of economic opportunity in the economically underserved community. Benefit corporations, then, may provide a more efficient and effective means of delivering welfare service than current alternatives.

This paper offers a moral argument based in Catholic Social Teaching to support the benefit corporation model over the current State based transfer payment model. The central principle of CST is *Human dignity* so the argument is generally based on this principle. Specific arguments are based in the two principles of *Work* and *Solidarity*. Work is central to the human experience as it allows people to transform the earth, become self-sufficient, and participate in society as both producers and consumers. Solidarity is realized through the cooperation of capital and labor, in this case the investor in the benefit corporation and the workers drawn from the underserved area.

It is still too early to determine whether benefit corporations will be viable in the market. The success of the benefit corporation model relies on investors' willingness to accept returns below the market level and the efficient operations of benefit corporations to insure attracting these investors. Further, benefit corporations are more likely to succeed with state support, particularly in the areas of legislation and possible tax benefits. Assuming these conditions are met, however, benefit corporations may provide both an economically and morally superior solution to entrenched poverty and economic isolation.

REFERENCES

Andre, R. (2012). Assessing the accountability of the benefit corporation: Will this new gray sector organization enhance corporate social responsibility. *Journal of Business Ethics*, *110*, 122–150.

Auger, D. (1999). Privatization, contracting, and the states: Lessons from state government experience. *Public Productivity & Management Review*, *22*(4), 435–454.

Benedict XVI (2009). *Caritas in veritate* [*Charity and truth*].

Byron, W. (1998). Ten building blocks of catholic social teaching. *America*, *179*, 9–12.

Catholic Charities. (2012). *Key principle of Catholic social teaching*. St. Paul, MN: Office for Social Justice. Retrieved from www.osjspm.org/document.doc?id=13

Coate, C., & Mitschow, M. (2013). Free market economics supporting Catholic social teaching: A moral exemplar for business persons. *Research in Ethical Issues in Organizations*, *10*, 41–62.

Coate, C., & Mitschow, M. (2015). Benefit corporations as a socially responsible business model: The role of accounting. *Research on Professional Responsibility and Ethics in Accounting*, *19*, 129–147.

Cohen, S., & Eimicke, W. (2001, November 1–3). Obstacles to privatization: The art and craft of contracting. Presented at the 2001 Research Meeting of the Association of Policy Analysis and Management, Washington, DC.

Cummings, B. (2012). Benefit corporations: How to enforce a mandate to promote the public interest. *Columbia Law Review, 112*, 578–628.

Francis (2013). *Evangelii Gaudium (Joy of the Gospel)*.

Fry, R., & Kochhar, R. (2014). America's wealth gap between middle-income and upper-income families is the widest on record. *Fact-tank: News in the numbers*. Pew Research Center. Retrieved from http://www.pewresearch.org/fact-tank/2014/12/17/wealth-gap-upper-middle-income/. Accessed on December 17, 2014.

Garrett, T. A., & Rhine, R. M. (2006). On the size and scope of government. *Federal Reserve Bank of St. Louis Review*, (January–February), 13–30.

Gilbert, K. (2011). Sustainable investing in a benefit corporation. *Institutional Investor*, (April). Retrieved from http://www.institutionalinvestor.com/Article/2804775/sustainable-investing-in-a-benefit-corporation.html#.ViAePflViko

Glassman, D. M., & Spahn, K. (2012). Performance measurement for nonprofits. *Journal of Applied Corporate Finance, 24*, 72–77.

Gongloff, M. (2014). 45 Million Americans still stuck below the poverty line: Census. The Huffington Post, September 16.

Good News Bible. (1978). *American Bible Society*. New York, NY.

Government Accountability Office. (1996, December). *Child support enforcement: Early results on comparability of privatized and public offices*. Publication No. GAO/HEHS-97-4. Washington, DC: U.S. Government Accountability Office.

Halsey, B. J., Tomkowicz, S. M., & Halsey, J. (2013). Benefit corporation concerns for financial service professionals. *Journal of Financial Service Professionals.* 67(January), 74–82.

Leo XIII (1891). *Rerum novorum [Of revolutionary change]*

Mac Cormac, S., & Haney, H. (2012). New corporate forms: One viable solution to advancing environmental sustainability. *Journal of Applied Corporate Finance.* 24(Spring), 49–56.

McCann, D. (1997). Catholic social teaching in an era of economic globalization: A resource for business ethics. *Business Ethics Quarterly, 7*, 57–70.

National Poverty Center (2015). *Poverty in the United States: Frequently asked questions*, Gerald R. Ford School of Public Policy, University of Michigan. Retrieved from http://www.npc.umich.edu/poverty/#3

Nightingale, D. S., & Pindus, N. (1997, October 15). *Privatization of public social services: A background paper*. Prepared for the U.S. Department of Labor, Office of the Assistant Secretary for Policy. Washington, DC: The Urban Institute.

Paul VI. (1967). *Populorum progressio. [On the development of peoples]*.

Paul II, J. (1981). *Laborem exercens [Human work]*.

Paul II, J. (1991). *Centesimus annus [100 years]*.

Reiser, D. B. (2011). Benefit corporations: A sustainable form of organization? *Wake Forest Law Review, 46*, 591–625.

Resor, F. R. (2012). Benefit corporation legislation. *Wyoming Law Review, 12*, 91–113.

Sanger, M. B. (2003). *The Welfare Marketplace: Privatization and Reform*. Washington, DC: The Brookings Institution.

Shiller, R. J. (2013). Capitalism and financial innovation. *Financial Analysis Journal, 69*, 21–25.

Tanner, M. (2012, April 11). The American welfare state: How we spend nearly $1 trillion a year fighting poverty — and fail. *Policy Analysis, 294*. The Cato Institute, Washington, DC.

Williams, O. (1993). Catholic social teaching: A communitarian democratic capitalism for the new world order. *Journal of Business Ethics, 12*, 919–932.

Winston, P., Burwick, A., McConnell, S., & Roper, R. (2002). *Privatization of welfare services: A review of the literature*. Department of Health and Human Services, Office of the Assistant Secretary for Planning and Evaluation. Retrieved from http://aspe.hhs.gov/hsp/privatization02/

ETHICS ACROSS THE ORGANISATIONAL SPECTRUM

Peter Bowden

ABSTRACT

This paper explores the question of whether the identification of many wrongdoings in an organisation requires knowledge of the technical and operating mechanisms of that organisation. If such is the case, many ethical problems cannot be resolved by a generalist. They must be left to people with knowledge of that industry. In attempting to answer the question, the paper examines 11 different types of organisations. It then asks how the ethical issues in those organisations might be resolved. The organisations are veterinarians, pharmacies, media companies, engineering firms, doctors, general businesses, including two sub disciplines, marketing and accounting organisations, nursing institutions, political parties, scientific research organisations, legal firms and information technology companies. Each can be a small professional company, locally based, or a large organisation, possibly international. Each exhibits one or more ethical problems that are not easily resolved by accepted ethical theory. Accepted theory, as further defined in the text, is the mainline ethical theories that would be core components of most ethics texts or courses. The question arises then

The Ethical Contribution of Organizations to Society
Research in Ethical Issues in Organizations, Volume 14, 93–119
Copyright © 2015 by Emerald Group Publishing Limited
All rights of reproduction in any form reserved
ISSN: 1529-2096/doi:10.1108/S1529-209620150000014005

on how would ethics be taught if the ethical issues require specialised knowledge of that industry sector. After examining the 11 industries, the paper puts forth two views. One is that a number of wrongs can be identified in industries and organisations where the ethical problems are complex and difficult to resolve, and where the standard ethical theories are of little or no help. Resolving these issues requires action from the organisation, or from the industry association encompassing all companies within that sector. A further complication has developed in the near explosive growth in whistleblower protection systems. These systems, now introduced in close to 30 countries around the world, have their own lists of wrongdoings for which the whistleblower will receive administrative and legal support. These lists of wrongs are distinct from any moral theory One conclusion to be drawn is that new methods possibly need to be found for teaching the identification and resolution of ethical issues. A second is a consequence of the first — that the teacher of ethics in these courses has to be drawn from within the industry. Further questions then arise: One is whether this demand then requires that this industry specialist learn moral theory? A second is then how would generalist applied ethics causes be taught (in humanities departments for instance)? Alternate viewpoints on joint teaching by a moral specialist and an industry specialist have been put forward. The paper puts forward one possible approach for the industry courses — that the industry specialist has to present the course, with new methods and content, but that a theoretical content is taught by someone knowledgeable in ethical theory. For generalist courses, the moral theorist has to include a sufficiently wide sample of industry and organisational ethical issues to ensure that students are aware of the wide range of ethical concerns that can arise, as well as approaches to resolving them.

Keywords: Ethics; morality; ethical theories; moral philosophy; decision-making; institutional ethics

At times, many of us have wondered about what is the desirable answer to a complex ethical decision. In many issues in our work life, it is not always clear what is the most ethically acceptable course that we could adopt.

This paper is not about the obvious ethical wrongs evidenced by different types of organisations. A multitude of sins can be committed by doctors, business people, lawyers, etc., with which all of us are unfortunately quite familiar. I will outline only the ethical decisions that are unclear or uncertain, or that require technical knowledge to resolve.

The following paragraphs outline a number of difficult ethical concerns across several organisational settings. The 11 organisations have been chosen primarily as they were identified as exhibiting ethical issues that required knowledge of the industry to resolve. There are undoubtedly other industries that could be chosen, but 11 was believed to be a sufficient number to support the conclusions being reached by this paper.

Prior to that outline, however, it will be useful to remind ourselves of those principal ethical theories that are currently presented in ethics courses. The most common would be utilitarianism. It is a consequentialist theory, which argues for maximising the utility or preferences of those affected by the decision. It has four or five different versions. Avoiding the inflicting of harm, or creating happiness are argued as the overriding version (Bowden, 2012; Haidt, 2013). Immanuel Kant's deontological ethics or appeal to duty (drawn from the Greek, *deon* or duty) would be a second theory. Kant presents his categorical imperative in a number of ways but two principal versions would dominate. The two are: Do not use others for your own benefit, and: Make sure that all agree that the proposed action is universally acceptable, before taking that action.

The third theory is virtue ethics, which argues that we should act virtuously. Unfortunately with over 70 virtues having been identified (Fieser, 1998), many of which conflict, virtue does not provide a very practical guideline. It does have its adherents however. One proponent of this theory describes the earlier two, utility and deontology, as engaged in 'internecine warfare'. He then proceeds to advocate the benefits of virtue theory (Pence, 1993). This reference illustrates the conflict among the theories. Two other references note this lack of agreement in the theories. Vincent Punk points out:

> the lack of significant communication among philosophers as a major factor hindering the advance of philosophy as a humanly significantly enterprise. (1969, p. 1)

Also Richard Joyce in 'Moral fictionalism':

> The theories are plentiful, the convolutions byzantine, the in-fighting bitter, the spilt ink copious, and the progress astoundingly unimpressive. (2011)

A number of what could be called theories which advocate a combination of the mainline theories have been developed which attempt to overcome the conflict. Three of these, Gert's *Common Morality* (2007), Frankena's *Prima Facie Duties* (1973) and Beauchamp and Childress' *Principles of Biomedical Ethics* (2009) are outlined in Breakey (2012).

The approach put forward by a number of theorists of putting on two lecturers, one a theorist and the second an industry expert was examined in *Approaches to Ethics in Higher Education Learning and Teaching in Ethics across the Curriculum*, a report on the ETHICS Project, a one year initiative funded by the Learning and Teaching Support Network in the School of Theology and Religious Studies at the University of Leeds (Illingworth, 2004). The conclusion of that project argues for 'interdisciplinary collaboration between ethical theorists and those with expertise in its subject-specific application' (p. 7).

The report of that project also outlines 'three commonly used approaches or 'ways in' to (teach) Ethics'. The first pragmatic approach takes as its starting point the framework of rules and procedures defined by regulatory bodies charged with the task of raising or maintaining professional standards. In the second or embedded approach, students study ethics indirectly, by considering some broader conception of professional identity which has a significant ethical dimension. The third or theoretical approach begins with a study of moral theory, and considers real-life situations in terms of the application of that theory.

Each of these approaches needs a person with knowledge of the ethical issues faced by the organisation that have a technical or industry relevant implication.

This paper does reach a conclusion, however. That is that the examination of difficult ethical decisions across a wide number of occupations does give us insights into how we may resolve them. And how we might teach these methods in an industry specific or in a generalist ethics class. This question of resolving right and wrong across the organisational spectrum comes down to assigning some of the responsibility to the industry association or professional body. It also comes down to two other factors (i) deciding which of the several ethical theories are likely to resolve an ethical problem, and (ii) developing methods of resolving ethical difficulties when any theory appears irrelevant. These conclusions, if accepted as valid, could modify the teaching of some ethical courses.

The following paragraphs outline ethical issues across the 11 organisational settings. The overall intention is to describe a sufficiently wide spectrum of industries so that a degree of universality becomes evident. Each issue, therefore, is not described in depth.

VETERINARIANS AND YOUR PET

One issue with which many of us could be familiar is that of euthanising your pet Stephens brought up the issue of 'Sheba' the much loved pet of Rhonda, a recently separated woman (Stephens, 2012). Sheba, a nine-year old German Shepherd, was to have a laparotomy, as she appeared to have an enlarged liver. On the day of the operation, the vet rang with bad news, recommending that Sheba be put down. The liver was almost fully affected by cancer and there was no possibility of survival. The vet advised that Sheba should be euthanased without waking up from surgery.

Rhonda said no. She wanted to take her pet home and allow her to die at home with her. Sheba would be given painkillers as needed. Vets, however, are almost unanimous on this issue. Stephens argues that Sheba should have been 'euthanased on the operating table when the laparotomy revealed an inevitably fatal prognosis. The veterinarian should have insisted, even invoked animal welfare laws if the owner was intransigent to this suggestion' (Stephens, 2013, p. 224). It may seem to outsiders that the preferred alternative is to maximise the preferences and happiness of both parties taken jointly. Veterinarians, perhaps with information not known to us, would appear to differ: If society will not accept prolonged suffering in an animal for biomedical reasons (i.e. reasons that benefit humanity in general), it will surely condemn the owner who keeps a suffering animal alive for egotistic reasons because he or she cannot bear to let it go (Rollin, 2006).

Another issue is acupuncture for animals – a treatment that is very topical at the moment. Stephens quotes five research projects that show us that 'acupuncture has been shown to have no efficacy in animals and the effect in humans is most likely due to the placebo effect that cannot be replicated in animals' (p. 227).

So is it unethical for a vet to recommend, and charge for, an acupuncture? Especially when the client has asked for it? In veterinary practice as in medical practice, an overriding issue is that the patient, or in this case the owner speaking on behalf of the patient, has the dominant say.

The initial conclusion that can be drawn from this sector is that none of the three ethical guidelines clearly tell us what the desired ethical action is.

Deontology may in part tell us to do our duty. But that duty could only be that the veterinarian should follow the guidelines of a national or international animal ethics association. In teaching veterinary ethics, therefore, the teacher could possibly outline alternate options. He/she could then encourage students to discuss and resolve where their opinion would lie. In a generalist applied ethics course (one in a humanities teaching environment, not a discipline based or organisational environment such as the 11 discussed in this paper), the teacher could present a sample of organisational ethical decisions. The above veterinary ethics or any of several similar ethical decision-making questions in other types of organisations would be presented and discussed.

PHARMACIES

We have three issues to examine here.

1. A programme has recently been inaugurated by the Pharmacists Guild in Australia requiring pharmacists to report impaired colleagues, that is those affected by alcohol, illicit substances or mental illness would be reported (Chaar, 2012, p. 132). This recommendation is a concern. It seems somewhat like the Stasi (East German Security Police) at work. Or Orwell's Thought Police. But the effect would be to identify professional colleagues who could be unreliable. Shouldn't we have such a programme for all our professional colleagues? And our non-professional colleagues?

    It might be noted that staff at the Australian Customs and Border Protection Service were recently asked to 'dob-in co-workers' for similar misdemeanours (Swan, 2013). It is called the 'Immigration dob-in service' and it has its own website.
2. The new contraceptive pill is now freely obtainable. What then is the ethical obligation on pharmacists whose religious or personal beliefs preclude using contraception? If we try to utilise any of the three theories mentioned earlier, we find that none of them give us an answer. The Pharmacy Guild requires that the pharmacy provide a contraceptive pill if requested.
3. The request to provide a medicine late at night, needed to relieve the pain of an elderly patient, but who cannot find the required prescription. The dilemma is every pharmacist's concern. Should the pharmacist break the law?

The Pharmacy Guild is clear: the pharmacist should not act contrary the law. A survey of the current ethical theories, however, will provide different answers: Kantianism will say no, do your duty, which would be act as required by the industry association (in this case, the Pharmacy Guild), Gert will also say no (as obey the law is one of his ten guide- lines). Utility would say yes, as providing the medicine would maximise benefits to the patient. Virtue would give conflicting answers, depending on which virtue you utilised – sympathy empathy, honesty, or a law- abiding virtue.

This example may well be used to illustrate a second issue raised in the paper: deciding which of the several ethical theories are likely to resolve an ethical problem. Utilitarian theory is often described as providing the great- est good to the greatest number of people. Adopting this theory may guide the pharmacist to deny medication to an individual with no prescription because that decision provides the most utility. But that version of utility is derived from Jeremy Bentham's *A Fragment on Government* (1776). There are possibly six or seven versions of utilitarianism. The version used here follows J. S. Mill's requirement to maximise happiness, minimise harm (Mill, 1861, Ch. 2, para. 13): Utility includes not solely the pursuit of happiness, but the prevention or mitigation of unhappiness. It also follows Peter Singer's requirement to maximise the preference of the individual parties (Singer, 1993). The example illustrates the many conflicts in ethical theory, and the consequent need for the overriding industry association to decide the required reading. In this example it has. A pharmacist may decide to ignore this ruling and act in the patient's interests.

If the overriding guideline is to act according to the requirements of the industry association then these three issues have clear guidelines. The rea- son that Chaar has brought them up however, is that they would be issues which a newly graduating pharmacist will likely encounter on entering employment. They should therefore be included in ethics discussions and courses for student pharmacists.

Whether such industry specific ethical issues would be included in a gen- eralist ethics course would be a decision for the lecturer. It would appear necessary, however, that some coverage of these industry decisions would be desirable.

It should also be noted that of the 11 occupations examined in the paper, only the pharmacists profession has partially established a set of guidelines. In this case, it could well be argued that that the ethical theory could override the official guidelines. It is, however, not an either or propo- sition. Both industry guidelines and ethical theory are needed.

THE MEDIA AND JOURNALISTS

It can be argued that it is near impossible to regulate the ethical behaviour of journalists. Success — by journalists as well as editors and owners — is measured on who has more interesting story, and who got it first (Richards, 2005; Sykes, 2012).

These determinants of success have created, at minimum, exaggeration and hyperbole in media reports, but also the less than savoury practices we came across in the 2007 *News of the World* scandal. A related issue is the attacks on religions, one result of which were the Charlie Hebdo murders. These murders were a heinous crime, totally immoral in any language. But they do raise the question to what extent does the freedom to speak out allow us ethically to offend other religions. Different and opposing opinions have been put forward (Bowden, 2015).

The topic to discuss here is whether the media should have unfettered freedom? There are no controls at the moment (short of a ban on hate speech). Many of us are aware, however, of questionable issues that arise if there total freedom of speech. One is that children can access some unbelievably repulsive content on the web. Also, with multiple smart phones, tablets and computers in the house, it is near impossible to supervise a child's access to web content. Some form of content control would appear desirable. Or will freedom of speech be the ultimate decider?

Yet another ethical concern is partisanship on the part of the media. Fox News in the United States been accused by academics, media figures, political figures and watchdog groups of having various biases in their news coverage as well as more general views of a conservative bias. Fox News has publicly denied such charges, stating that the reporters in its newsrooms provide separate, neutral reporting. Several disagreements with Fox's own assessment are available (see Ackerman, 2001).

The dilemma then, is can we regulate the ethics of the media? The attempts by the Australian Minister for Communications, Stephen Conroy, and the subsequent condemnation by News Corporation (owner of *News of the World*), that likened him to Stalin and other dictators (Jones, 2013) suggest that the media is ungovernable. Conroy was accused of muzzling a fundamental human right — the right to free speech.

The sum of the issues in journalism then, is again, that news organisations do have their own set of ethical concerns, particular to their own profession. The industry does have codes of ethics at national and corporate levels which appear to be reasonably comprehensive. Sykes asserts that four components comprise the tenets of ethical journalism: (i) Accuracy and truth (ii) Public benefit (iii) Respect for sources, and (iv) Responsibility and accountability (Sykes, 2012). These guidelines cover problems encountered in incidents such as the News of the World, but at question then is whether these guidelines cover issues such as exaggeration, or unbalanced reporting. It would appear that they do not. The essence of the media discussion in these paragraphs is again that the ethical theories again give little or at best weak guidelines. The possible guideline here is if that of the no-harm version of utility – if media reporting is has the consequence of causing harm, then it is wrong.

The issues need to be discussed, in any case, within the industry and within ethics classes for journalists in training. Once again, at question is the extent to which generalist (or across the disciplines) classes in applied ethics should include this issue.

ENGINEERING

This occupation raises some interesting speculations. Engineers push the state of the art. That is the nature of the discipline. But what if they push too far? The construction – whatever it is – explodes, or collapses and people are killed. There are a number of examples – the Challenger disaster where seven astronauts died. This launch had doubts – uncertain warnings were raised beforehand about the sealing of the oxygen tanks. The seals leaked and the spaceship exploded. Was the engineering designer company, Morton Thiokol correct in taking the risk? Or NASA – the organisation that contracted the design and construction?

The Challenger disaster is a frequent case for discussion in ethics courses. A less discussed example is the Westgate Bridge in Melbourne, a state of the art box girder design, which collapsed during construction killing 35 workmen. The Royal Commission enquiring into the disaster said that the engineers did not check their design sufficiently (The Royal Commission, 1970). The engineers denied this accusation. Is it just the nature of engineering, or are there ethical issues here?

There are many ethical conundrums in engineering. Research on bid shopping has said about 94% of engineers believed that it was unethical. Bid shopping is searching around for successively lower price by the winning contractor. It is similar to reverse auctions – the sequential accepting of competitive bids, in reducing monetary value, from suppliers or subcontractors. Some 77% of engineers believe this practice is unethical (Bowden, 2012). Whether it is bid shopping or reverse auctions the majority of construction professionals believe the business is tainted by unethical behaviour (Electrical Construction and Maintenance, 2005). Both bidding methods are, nevertheless, methods for strengthening competition. Is either of them unethical?

The Hyatt Kansas walkway collapse was the largest engineering failure in the United States, with 114 dead. It occurred in 1981. It was a design failure, and caused the largest construction death toll in the country. The walkway design changes were initiated by the constructor, although it is unsure whether the supervising engineer gave approval or not. Regardless of actual responsibility, failure to check designs was responsible for the loss of life, and must be regarded as bordering on unethical practice. No engineering code of ethics makes this requirement. The US engineers involved lost their licence to practise in that state.

There are of course straightforward ethical failures in engineering. The collapse of the CTV building during the Christchurch earthquake is one-example of totally unethical engineering. A government inquiry into the building, which concluded in 2012, found that earlier modifications should not have been issued a building permit because the design failed to meet the building code of the time. In addition, inadequacies in the construction of the building also contributed to the inability of the building to withstand an earthquake (Craymer, 2012).

But strengthening design standards raises a conundrum. If national design or construction standards are raised, as happened in New Zealand prior to the Christchurch earthquake, does the responsible engineer have the obligation to check compliance on all his or her past work? As a teacher of engineering ethics, this author has raised this issue on a number of occasions. One such discussion was at a talk on engineering ethics at the head office for the designers of the Sydney Opera House. I said yes, the engineer had that obligation. A sizeable portion of the audience argued no, that there was no obligation to check past work when standards were altered. It would be difficult if not impossible to control, they asserted. It would be a government responsibility to ensure and pay for this retrograde back-checking, in any case. It is an issue that still needs resolution.

If we appeal to the ethical theories, we may find that no theory provides us with a clear cut answer. We may argue that utilitarianism, with its injunction against harming others, provides a guideline. But it would require technical assessment to decide whether a particular engineering practice did evidence the possibility of causing harm.

The answer is open. These issues in engineering would be best resolved by discussions in the professional engineering journals and the codes of ethics of the professional association in each country. Or, in the absence of an industry-wide resolution, by each individual engineering organisation. The teaching of engineering ethics would need to provide that information along with a sample of the ethical issues that the current students would likely be encountered on graduation.

MEDICINE

Medical organisations have some of the most difficult ethical questions of any discipline: informed consent; parental control over children's health care; and in particular, reproductive issues – abortion, stem cell research, as well as end-of-life issues, including euthanasia, are among them.

This paper does not canvass all these concerns. Two or three conundrums that can be found in the medical ethic literature are sufficient evidence to lend strength to the assertion that the profession and those organisations in it need to resolve their ethical dilemmas.

This issue and the next two were raised by Lipworth, Strong, and Kerridge (2012). A four-year old child, Shari, had a sudden attack that turned out to be a meningococcal infection. She went into emergency within hours, unconscious, and placed on a respirator in intensive care. Her parents were advised after some weeks on life support that she had suffered a major brain injury, would never regain consciousness, or lead an independent life, and that the respirator should be turned off. The parents refused. What to do?

Fifteen-year old Christina went to her local doctor for the first time without her mother. She was having a sexual relationship with her boyfriend and wanted a prescription for the oral pill. Again, what should the doctor do?

Ben, ten-year old son of Jehovah's Witnesses was hit by a car, suffering major abdominal and chest injuries. The hospital advised that he would need blood transfusions but the parents refused. What should the hospital do? The ethical theories do not provide usable answers in these cases.

This last mentioned problem, incidentally, was outdone by a recent Jehovah's Witness case in Australia where the patient, almost 18 (which is the age at which patients can decide for themselves), suffering from a lethal form of blood cancer, refused the transfusion. The NSW Supreme Court overruled the patient and his parents (*Sydney Morning Herald*, 18 April,

2013). It required a technical assessment, however, to decide that the young man was at medical risk.

Medical ethics also includes the ethics of reproduction and end-of-life issues — abortion, stem cell research, suicide and euthanasia primarily. These issues are sometimes taught under a topic titled under 'Bio-ethics' or 'Practical Ethics'. An example is when genetic testing before birth reveals a genetic defect — examples are CMT Charcot Marie Tooth disease or Thalassemia, a blood disease. The mother has the option of terminating the pregnancy. For many, abortion is a difficult decision. For several it is also an ethical decision.

The regular ethical theories do not provide an answer for these bioethical issues. The reason is that for a large part, these concerns are often raised by people with religious views, or with right-to-life values. Only some in the community regard them as ethical issues — Is abortion an ethical issue? Or euthanasia? The law is quite clear on both issues. The medical profession is in agreement with the law. Again, the issue is that these questions are best resolved by discussions in the professional journals, textbooks and the codes of ethics health organisations and of the medical associations. Two such examples of textbooks are Beauchamp and Childress (2009), and Kerridge, Lowe, and Stewart (2009). Each covers a wide range of ethical issues in the medical profession, including burgeoning practices in blowing the whistle on ethical wrongdoing in hospitals and nursing homes.

BUSINESS ORGANISATIONS

This section is not designed to identify the many wrongs with business — it is to set out some topics which are difficult to answer and then determine how they may be resolved. In particular, whether the existing ethical theories might provide sufficient answers to be the principal content of the general ethics or of business ethics literature. The ethical issues in business are almost without number. An investigation of ethical issues in this sector would list corporate social responsibility, issues of privacy and transparency, of justice, concerns of equity, of greed, and lack of compliance with the many business codes that have been established.

One question raises itself at an early stage — Corporate Social Responsibility (CSR) — very much a concern of growing importance. Howard (2012) defined it 'as accepting that business and society are intermingled and have mutual responsibilities'. Others define the prime role of business as making a profit (Friedman, 2007), provided the business acts within the law. Is there a conflict between Friedman and CSR? Was the recent campaign by the mining companies in Australia against a proposed excess profits mining tax, evidence of a lack of social responsibility? (Perkins, 2010).

Many of the ethical issues in business have no resolution – at least by applying the ethical theories. The reason is that the demands on the various stakeholders are in direct conflict. Shareholders wish to maximise their profits, management to maximise their incomes. Employees also hope to maximise their wages. They also want to ensure that they have safe working conditions, and fair employment contracts. Contractors and suppliers also wish to maximise their returns from the organisation. The multiplicity of demands is unanswerable. Younkins states 'stakeholder theory places corporate managers in the impossible position of balancing competing interests from multiple groups' (1997).

A major contribution to resolving these dilemmas is the work of R. Edward Freeman. His book *Strategic management: A stakeholder approach* (2010) is generally regarded as the originator of stakeholder theory (although the problems of balancing stakeholder demands had been recognised earlier). Nevertheless, there have been disagreements with Freeman (e.g. Miles, 2012). Freeman essentially treats the issue of the competing demands as a management concern, in which the requirements of the different stakeholders are identified, quantified where possible and then weighed one against the other. Freeman, to the extent that he draws on any moral theory, does so on Kant, where he states respect for persons is his guiding ethical principle. He directly contradicts the theories of Milton Friedman.

The issue at question in business ethics, relevant to the concerns of this paper, however, is that the competing demands of the various stakeholders do appear to be in conflict. Freeman's approach of quantifying the impact of each demand is a consequentialist assessment. Such an approach will assist but still will frequently requires judgement and technical knowledge on the part of the decision maker.

NURSING

Nursing raises several issues that can be repeated in other disciplines – the ethics of care for instance, or, as mentioned, the role and effectiveness of codes of ethics. Toiviainen (2012) also raises a concern that in fact is common to all types of organisation — to what extent should anybody in ethical educational and training programs, in this case nurses, be exposed to ethical concerns outside those of their discipline?

Toiviainen argued for human rights and global warming issues among others, as topics that nurses should include in their training (p. 122).The question here is should this practice be universal? For all disciplines? Should ethics courses in every discipline raise and discuss issues that are common to the wider society?

We can, as concerned academics, have our own opinion, but in reality, it will only be the professional societies which, in collaboration with the teaching institutions, can decide a universal answer to this question.

One issue in nursing is its code of ethics. The Code of Ethics for Nurses in Australia, last revised in 2011, sets out eight value statements:

1. Nurses value quality nursing care for all people.
2. Nurses value respect and kindness for self and others.
3. Nurses value the diversity of people.
4. Nurses value access to quality nursing and health care for all people.
5. Nurses value informed decision-making.
6. Nurses value a culture of safety in nursing and health care.
7. Nurses value ethical management of information.
8. Nurses value a socially, economically and ecologically sustainable environment promoting health and well-being.

As will be discussed in a subsequent section, a code, to be effective, should respond to the actual ethical issues faced by people in the respective organisations. The above values apply to almost all types of organisations.

An issue of concern to nurses, however, is whistleblowing, an issue discussed in greater depth in a subsequent section. The nurses code refers its reader to the Australian Nursing and Midwifery Federation, which says that the organisation should protect whistleblowers, although giving little information on the protections available. There are many examples of nurses revealing wrongdoing. Perhaps the issue with the greatest impact was the Mid Staffordshire Hospital inquiry into nurse whistleblowing in the British National Health service by Sir Robert Francis. It found poor care at the hospital could have led to the deaths of hundreds of patients as a result of maltreatment and neglect (BBC News, 2013). Toni Hoffman (Bowden, 2014) was an Australian example that generated much publicity. Yet we find ethics writers condemning the practice as akin to Nazi Germany or Stalinist Russia (Grace & Cohen, 2007, p. 222).

POLITICAL ORGANISATIONS

A proposition can be put forward that political life involves a special type of ethical decision to the extent that it is not appropriate to judge politicians by normal ethical standards. It is a claim with which many might agree. Political bodies can declare war, for instance, but the rest of us cannot. There are several other examples. Alan Tapper notes the allegiance to the party, versus the commitment to the common good, as a high ranking dilemma (Tapper, 2012, p. 179). The conflict between one side of the political spectrum and the opposing viewpoint where both sides will consider themselves ethically correct is the most common example. This issue is canvassed by Jonathon Haidt, who argues that both sides of the political spectrum regard their position as morally correct (Haidt, 2012). The political decision that will disadvantage one deserving need at the expense of an equally deserving need is a related issue. An example of both sides believing they are right is the controversy over the Obama health care programme. This programme is opposed by elements of the Republican Party. Each views its position as the ethically correct one. If we appeal to moral philosophers on this issue, we find controversy in the differing opinions and theories that they put forward. An example is Will Kymlicka (2002), who canvasses the various political and ethical theories, including those outlined above. He reaches the conclusion that there are differing theories, and some degree of controversy exists over which theory is the more applicable.

How then do politicians make such decisions? And is Tapper right when he says 'it will not be appropriate to judge politicians by the same standards as we judge everyday behaviour' (Tapper, 2012, p. 179)? The issue is not dissimilar to the ethical conflicts that arise in business, as discussed below.

To resolve such issues involves benefitting one section of the population at the expense of another. Such decisions have, at times, ethical implications. Complex decision-making systems that can assist are available. These include cost benefit and cost-effectiveness analyses (Garber & Phelps, 1997), ex-ante evaluations (e.g. European Commission, 2007–2013), programme budgeting techniques (Program Budgeting, n.d.) and zero based budgeting (Accounting Tools, 2015). These tools are applicable in both political budgeting decisions as well as organisational budgeting. It is not suggested that they need be part of an ethics course, but students need be aware of their availability in resolving conflicting investment and expenditure decisions that benefit one group to the detriment of another.

MARKETING

The reader will be aware of the many ethical issues that arise in marketing organisations. Schwartz (2012) raises some dilemmas of relevance to this paper. One is the not so new practice of undercover marketing – where those marketing the product disguise their intent. He uses the example of Natasha, an attractive woman who encourages men to buy Absolut Vodka, without divulging that she works for Absolut Vodka. Another example and perhaps one that is more common, is the appearance of a product in an everyday TV or magazine setting, but which is actually a paid advertisement. Schwarz quotes Pepsi Cola's sponsored teenage magazine where the models are drinking Pepsi.

Ethical? Should the marketing organisations or individual marketing companies establish guidelines for this practice? Or are they just another example of *caveat emptor* – where the consumer should be aware.

Schwartz's other example is consumer sovereignty – the now fading concept that the customer is always right. This concept is being replaced by postmodern concepts where the market predominates – that the market can decide is an ethical position often placed above all competing concepts. Is the marketing of human organs ethical, he asks? Then pointing out that a very poor man may willingly sell his kidney for the money it brings in and the opportunity to feed his family, and that maybe even provide him with a longer term income. The ethical answer, not clear under any of the theories, is still to be resolved (Marshall, Thomasma, & Daar, 1996).

ACCOUNTANCY

An issue in the accounting field is that of earnings management. Apparently a company can manipulate its earnings quite legitimately by adjusting its inventory write-offs. Good earnings, a better share price, and a subsequent increase in the value of the share price and options for owners and senior managers are the result.

The ethical concern then is how to ensure that a true statement of corporate earnings is made available for public use. Auditors face a strong conflict of interest – a conflict that was the cause of the demise of Arthur Andersen, Enron's auditor. Plummer (2012) advocates that public companies be required to purchase insurance on the accuracy of published figures. The auditor would be employed by the insurance company.

Answering the question of how do we best ensure that audited earnings figures reflect the performance of the organisation is a highly technical issue. It is not an issue that is amenable to moral theory, and so would not be possible in a generalist discussion. It again is a question for the professional association.

SCIENTISTS

Experiments on animals – is a question that looms large in many peoples' minds. 'Some kinds of research unavoidably involve killing animals without euthanasia' (Lamond & Lowe, 2012). Any research scientist trying to get approval for a new drug will verify this statement. Apparently such testing is required to determine the lethal dose. The question, incidentally, raises the interesting issue of the ethical value we place on a human life vis-à-vis that of a non-human animal.

Another related question is military weapons research, or biological and chemical warfare research. Should we support this type of research? Or trade in these items. Some condemn it – arguing that the scientist is being unethical. The contrary argument is that in the final analysis, we want our country to be able to outsmart some erratic dictator. Certainly, for our own well-being, we have an ethical obligation to keep up to date on weapons research. Where does each of us stand on these concerns? The issue is complex (Martin Susan & Daniel, 2013). Our ethical theories do not tell us what is the preferred answer.

LEGAL FIRMS

'There is a fundamental inconsistency in the lawyer's role between the task of upholding the law and the task of serving the client's interests' (Campbell & Holmes, 2012). We notice this legal inconsistency almost daily, as the media reports the defence counsel offering a somewhat implausible reason for their client behaving in a questionable manner.

The ethical question is whether a lawyer should use all the tricks of the trade to defend a guilty person? Legal people examining these issues have evidenced three points of view: (i) 'The duty to defend (in criminal cases) applies irrespective of any belief or opinion the lawyer may form as to whether the client is guilty or not'. (ii) 'A legal representative should not continue to represent a guilty client if that client insists on denying guilt.

And (iii) a lawyer, who is aware that his/her client is guilty, should not enter a plea (Asimow, 2006; Beasley, 2015; Portman, n.d.).

If we apply the three major ethical theories to these options, we find contradictions. Kant and duty would assert that the lawyer's role is to defend a client, even if s/he believes that the client is guilty. The other two options tend towards taking what might be called a virtuous position. They also favour a consequentialist outcome, although the consequences of the decision are not known. As such they could be classified as utilitarian.

Again, this question is an ethical issue for legal firms which has no resolution. It is again one that this writer would argue that necessarily needs to be discussed in ethics classes. It is also one that preferably be resolved in the code of ethics of individual organisations or in the codes of ethics for law societies.

IT ETHICS

This industry is no longer called IT, but ICT, Information and Communications Technology. The industry embraces a huge range of ethical issues. Burmeister (2012) points out many: illegal music downloads; piracy, in the form of copying software; computer abuse, such as intercepting and reading confidential emails; downloading pornography on the work computer (or even using the work computer for private purposes), doctoring photographs electronically; sending out spam; creating spyware; hacking; cyber-stalking; cyber-bullying; cyber-crime; or invasion of privacy.

These issues present a multitude of unanswered ethical questions. These paragraphs will present only one – the social media revolution. The new term ICT embraces the new technology that has landed on our doorstep – Facebook, Twitter, Linked In, etc. In themselves, they raise several ethical issues – cyber-bullying, and respect for privacy, and providing false information being among the more obvious.

An overriding question then is whose responsibility is it to determine what is ethical? As has been argued for the earlier organisations, such a determination could be through developing and following a code of ethics. But who would develop, and police that code – the industry, the company itself, or in this example, drawing on commonly accepted moral practices, the user? This writer believes that it is the responsibility of the industry behind the technology. Worldwide, that would be the Computer and Communications Industry Association. In Australia, it would be the Australian Computer Society. Burmeister has said no – it is the responsibility of the individual using the social media. Or at best it would be a joint responsibility (Burmeister, 2012, p. 252). Again, we have an unresolved ethical issue where the ethical theories provide little or no help. And in this case some disagreement on which organisation has responsibility for the decision.

POLICE ETHICS

Some new terminology arises in this examination: 'meat-eaters' and 'grass-eaters' emerges in a study of the ethics of policing. In describing dishonest police, Lauchs tells us (2012) that grass-eaters just happily accept the pay-offs that come through everyday policing — the offerings of normal citizens to avoid a speeding ticket or otherwise sort out their problems with the police. Meat-eaters aggressively seek pay-offs (p.168). For instance, offering a criminal who has just been arrested, a reduced charge in return for a share in the profits.

Many public sector jobs are open to corruption. They either involve a high degree of discretion (described as being 'wet'), or jobs which have no little or discretion, described as 'dry' (Heidenheimer & Johnston, 2002). Police work in general, is wet, providing many opportunities for deliberate corruption.

But corruption is not the only police activity that raises ethical concerns. Possibly the more noticeable are police killings while on duty. In the United States, the killings of black youths by white police in Ferguson and Berkeley in Missouri have raised widespread concerns (ABC News, 2015). Similar issues have surfaced in other countries. In the United Kingdom, police have shot dead 33 people since 1995, but only two officers have been named (Leake & Delgado, 2010). There have been very few criminal prosecutions of police who have killed members of the public in the line of duty (Ryley, 2014).

Lauchs focuses on the organisation itself 'as the source of core police culture' (Lauchs, 2012, p. 168):

> *A police officer can decide whether or not the law will be enforced. They have the discretion to provide a warning or to act. While this power is closely informed by policy and guidelines, there is no appeal mechanism. Consequently the power brings with it a substantial imbalance in favour of the police and requires a great deal of ethical awareness to avoid abuse.*

Policing raises an organisational issue not yet examined — that of the influence of organisational culture on ethical behaviour. A police person could be putting his/her life on the line when pulling over a motorist. Or when a hooded individual displays a knife. There is also the case of noble cause corruption — manufacturing evidence to convict a criminal that they are sure is guilty. Effective approaches for the handling of these issues are organisational issues — part of the training for police and within that, their ethics courses.

CONCLUSIONS SO FAR

The conclusions that can be drawn from the above paragraphs are, at this stage, only tentative. It would seem that there are three types of difficult ethical decision:

(i) Where the practices or guidelines for organisations within an industry are unclear or uncertain. Or at an extreme, where opinions on the issue are in conflict. Examples are seen in the conflicts in engineering over bidding practices, but several of the other organisational disciplines exhibit uncertainty — medical, nursing, politics and corporate ethics for example.

(ii) One option requires action that conflicts ethically with another, that is the chosen option may help one party but inflict harm on a second party. Examples are seen in political or corporate decisions which advantage one group to the detriment of another. Or some of the police decisions.

(iii) Where the ethical theories provide no or inadequate guidelines. The strongest evidence of this inadequacy is in the use of codes of ethics, or more recently in the near-exponential growth of whistleblowing support systems around the world, which have created their own listings of organisational wrongs, rather than rely on codes of ethics or ethical theory.

These last two factors mentioned will be discussed before attempting any further conclusions.

CODES OF ETHICS

Dealing initially with the first issue, codes of ethics, it would seem that the responsibility for clarifying uncertain or disputed ethical practices would lie with the industry association, at the national or even international level, or secondly, at the level of the organisation if the national association is quiet on the matter. Industry guidelines would be made publicly available through the industry association's policy documents and its code of ethics. Disputed practices that develop at an international level would be resolved internationally to the extent that an industry association is operative on a global basis, or by a collegiate determination by national associations. It is certainly possible to assert that ethical guidelines that respond to uncertain issues of the type documented above should be determined and set out for an organisation or for an industry sector in a relevant code.

At issue then is a determination of how useful is a code of ethics. A related question asks whether codes of ethics can ensure that its guidelines are observed.

Many observers decry the usefulness of a code.

It is doubtful, in fact, that codes of ethics can prevent unethical business conduct. There is substance in this rejection. Smythe (2012) provides extensive evidence of codes that are used as window dressing — to display to the public that the organisation is ethical. Haidt argues that this objective is the principle motivation behind ethical behaviour: The important thing for an ethical society is that 'everyone's reputation is on the line all the time' (Haidt, 2013, p. 86).

A second problem with codes is that they are primarily designed to stop actions that are detrimental to the organisation, such as stealing from an employer, or using its resources for an employee's benefit (Helin & Sandström, 2010; Smythe, 2012; Wood, 2000).

Nevertheless, at the level of the organisation, considerable evidence can be presented to support the argument that organisational codes should primarily address those ethical issues which are directly faced by staff (Kaptein, 2011; Kaptein & Wempe, 1998; Valentine et al., 2011). The Kaptein and Wempe's research reaches the conclusion that 'A good code corresponds into the concrete moral dilemmas which employees of the firm experience their duties' (Kaptein & Wempe, 1998, p. 863). If we follow this guideline, it will be possible to establish guidelines across a wide range of professional activities that are currently uncertain or in dispute.

Such findings, if implemented, will enable an organisation to reach a conclusion on what approach should be taken on a doubtful issue. That issue may be encountered in several organisations across that industry sector. Such an assertion sets out a much wider role, and likely a more effective role for industry-wide codes than has hitherto been the practice.

There is yet another role for industry associations and for their codes than has previously been mentioned. That is their role in blowing the whistle on wrongdoing.

WHISTLEBLOWING PRACTICES

Blowing the whistle is a rapidly growing sector in efforts to strengthen ethical behaviour in organisations. The reason is that whistleblowing has proven to be effective in stopping wrongdoing (Bowden, 2014; Tsahuridu, 2011). Close to 30 countries have now introduced legislation to protect whistleblowers against retaliation. The practice has 'overwhelming public support' (Vandekerckhove, 2012). Again, however, the problem of identifying the wrongs that could be committed by an organisation has forced those administrations that are developing whistleblower support systems to amplify and expand on established ethical theory. The United Kingdom's Public Interest Disclosure legislation lists six wrongs that qualify for investigation by anticorruption authorities. Whistleblowers are protected if they reveal any of the six. They are:

(a) that a criminal offence has been committed,
(b) that a person has failed, to comply with any legal obligation to which he is subject,
(c) that a miscarriage of justice has occurred,
(d) that the health or safety of any individual has been endangered,
(e) that the environment has been damaged or
(f) that information tending to show any matter falling within any one of the preceding paragraphs has been deliberately concealed.

Each of the paragraphs includes the proviso that if the action is being committed or is likely to be committed (fails, occur, endanger, etc.), the whistleblower is protected, and the allegation will be investigated. Each item also is a consequential outcome of the action itself, or of a failure to prevent a wrong. Whistleblowing could, therefore, be broadly classified as utilitarian.

The above six cover all wrongs in the private as well as the public sector.

In the United States, separate whistleblower support for the private sector has been developed under the appropriate legislative acts covering the entire economy, some 55 in total (transport, finance, the environment, etc.). In essence, the British support for blowing the whistle any criminal offence is contained in the United States in each relevant piece of legislation.

For government employees in the United States, the Whistleblower Protection Enhancement Act of 2012 is the most recent update. It covers seven wrongs — a violation of any law, rule, or regulation; gross mismanagement, a gross waste of funds, an abuse of authority, or a substantial and specific danger to the environment, public health or safety. Australia has effective legislation covering only the public sector. This legislation provides protection for twelve wrongs which, in essence, are a somewhat amplified version of the six British wrongs.

All whistleblower support programs clearly and unambiguously identify wrongs. None specify wrongs where the ethical response is uncertain, or unclear. As such, they have relevance to the issues in this paper. Some, however, require technical and discipline specific input to decide whether an issue is or is not a wrong. Examples are a gross waste of funds, or whether the health or safety of any individual or the environment has been endangered. Such questions can only be answered with technical knowledge.

Where whistleblowing issues also have relevance to this paper is the question of their place in the teaching of ethics. There would appear to be little doubt that whistleblowing needs to be a component of any ethics course. Assuming that the objective of any ethics programme is to strengthen ethical behaviour, the proven evidence that it does stop wrong doing, should ensure its inclusion in a course. Again, the question must be raised as to the relevance of teaching whistleblowing in an ethics course that is primarily based on ethical theory. Whistleblowing practices define their own wrongs, and would appear to have, therefore no need to identify the various ethical theories. As noted above and summarised in in the concluding paragraphs, however, this author's conclusion is that theory should be a strong component of all ethics courses.

WHO THEN SHOULD TEACH THE ETHICS COURSES IN THE DISCIPLINE?

The question of whether a course should be taught by a specialist in ethics or a specialist in the discipline or profession is a long standing one. We dismiss the arguments found in a number of journals that philosophy needs to be the dominant discipline, for example Klein (1998) argues that the necessary condition for a successful business ethics course: the teacher must be a philosopher. Her argument is that philosophers are the subject matter experts in ethics and that they therefore must teach ethics courses. Frederick (1998) disputes this assertion. He believes Klein's arguments are largely irrelevant, noting that if she is correct then in practice; two disciplines are needed to teach a course – a specialist in philosophical ethics and a second in the subject matter.

This paper joins with Frederick and others who question the philosophy argument. It bases its beliefs, however, on the questions raised presented in this paper. We have argued that four necessary elements, among others, of any ethics course must include: (a) structuring an organisation or an industry sector to resolve its own outstanding ethical issues (via an industry association, for instance, or directly by the organisation); (b) developing workable codes of ethics as the vehicle to achieve this objective; (c) managing public interest disclosures and (d) being aware of decision tools that can assist in ethically conflicting investment and budgeting decisions. Klein is correct in that philosophy is the subject matter expert. Should the philosopher argument be accepted then the philosopher has to move outside his or her discipline to embrace a number of additional skills. A teacher of an applied ethics course in a generalist discipline, such as philosophy, outside the applied disciplines examined in the above paragraphs, could decide to teach a sufficient number of examples of industry specific ethical issues (or bring into the classroom subject matter experts) to convey the concept that knowledge of the industry is a necessary condition for resolving some ethical issues in that sector.

Finally, this paper must resolve the question of what ethical theory or theories are best adopted to resolve the issues outlined in these paragraphs. The conclusion has to be drawn, however, that none appear entirely satisfactory, Utilitarianism, it could be argued, is the dominant philosophy behind the whistleblowing wrongs (which in turn are intended to cover the wrongdoing in all types of organisations). But utilitarianism does not necessarily provide universally applicable responses. Examples have been given in the above paragraphs of where a commitment to duty, or even virtue, have provided a satisfactory guideline. Despite this inconsistency, these pages would support a decision to teach the core ethical theories. They are theories that have evolved over the centuries, and as such they are part of the broader knowledge that should be imparted in an ethics course. It is a not dissimilar issue to the assertion made earlier in the paper that ethics courses should include social ethical issues outside the discipline Whether they are taught by a specialist in moral philosophy, or by a subject matter specialist, would appear to be immaterial.

REFERENCES

ABC News. (2015). *Protests over Missouri police shootings.* Retrieved from http://www.abc. net.au/news/2014-12-26/protests-over-missouri-police-shootings-die-down/5988994. Accessed on February 26, 2015.

Accounting Tools. (2015). Retrieved from http://www.accountingtools.com/zero-based-budgeting. Accessed on March 20, 2015.

Ackerman, S. (2001). The most biased name in news. FAIR Fairness and accuracy in reporting. Retrieved from http://fair.org/extra-online-articles/the-most-biased-name-in-news/. Accessed on February 26, 2015.

Asimow, M. (2006). *When the lawyer knows the client is guilty*. Retrieved from http://www.lsuc.on.ca/media/sith_colloquium_asimow_michael.pdf. Accessed on May 26, 2015.

BBC News. (2013, August 6). Retrieved from http://www.bbc.com/news/uk-england-stoke-staffordshire-23487863. Accessed on March 22, 2015.

Beasley, J. (2015). *What should a criminal defense attorney do if his client admits to him that he is guilty but wants to plead not guilty in court?* Retrieved from https://www.quora.com/. Accessed May 26, 2015.

Beauchamp, T. L., & Childress, J. (2009). *Principles of biomedical ethics* (6th ed.), New York, NY: Oxford University Press.

Bentham, J. (1776). *A fragment on government*. Retrieved from http://www.efm.bris.ac.uk/het/bentham/government.htm

Bowden, P. (2012). Harm to others. In M. Schwartz & H. Harris (Eds.), *Applied ethics: Remembering Patrick Primeau* (Vol. 8). Research in Ethical Issues in Organizations. Bingley, UK: Emerald Group Publishing Limited.

Bowden, P. (2014). *In the public interest: Protecting whistleblowers and those who speak out*. Melbourne, Australia: Tilde University Press.

Bowden, P. (2015). How do we decide if offending someone is unethical or not? *The Conversation*. Retrieved from https://theconversation.com/how-do-we-decide-if-offending-someone-is-unethical-or-not-36547. Accessed on January *29*, 2015.

Breakey, H. (2012). Moral pluralist approaches to ethics. In P. Bowden (Ed.), *Applied ethics*. Melbourne: Tilde University Press.

Burmeister, O. K. (2012). Ethics in information and communications technology. In P. Bowden (Ed.), *Applied ethics*. Melbourne: Tilde University Press.

Campbell, T., & Holmes, V. (2012). Applied ethics – For lawyers. In P. Bowden (Ed.), *Applied ethics*. Melbourne: Tilde University Press.

Chaar, B. B. (2012). Pharmacy ethics. In P. Bowden (Ed.), *Applied ethics*. Melbourne: Tilde University Press.

Craymer, L. (2012). New Zealand police deepen probe into CTV building collapse in quake. *Wall Street Journal*.

Electrical Construction and Maintenance. (2005). The construction industry's ethical dilemma. Retrieved from http://ecmweb.com/content/construction-industrys-ethical-dilemma. Accessed on February 15, 2015.

European Commission. (2007–2013). The new programming period 2007–2013. *Indicative guidelines on evaluation methods: Ex ante evaluation*. Directorate-General for regional policy.

Fieser, J. (1998). Hume's wide view of the virtues: An analysis of his early critics. *Hume Studies, 24*(2), 295–312.

Frankena, W. K. (1973). *Ethics* (2nd ed.), Englewood Cliffs, NJ: Prentice-Hall.

Frederick, W. C. (1998). One voice, or many? A response to Ellen Klein. *Business Ethics Quarterly, 8*(3), 575–579.

Freeman, R. E. (2010). *Strategic management: A stakeholder approach*. Cambridge: Cambridge University Press.

Friedman, M. (2007). The social responsibility of business is to increase its profits. *The New York Times Magazine*. Accessed on September 13, 1970.

Garber, A. M., & Phelps, C. E. (1997). Economic foundations of cost-effectiveness analysis. *Journal of Health Economics*, *16*(1), 1–31.

Grace, D. & Cohen, S. (Eds.). (2007). *Business ethics* (5th ed.), Melbourne: Oxford University Press.

Haidt, J. (2012). *The righteous mind*. New York, NY: Vintage Books.

Haidt, J. (2013). *The righteous mind, why good people are divided by politics and religion*. New York, NY: Vintage Books.

Heidenheimer, A., & Johnston, M. (2002). *Political corruption*. New York, NY: Transaction Books.

Helin, S., & Sandström, J. (2010). Resisting a corporate code of ethics and the reinforcement of management control. *Organization Studies*, *31*, 583–604.

Howard, H. (2012). Business ethics. In P. Bowden (Ed.), *Applied ethics*. Melbourne: Tilde University Press.

Illingworth, S. (2004). *Approaches to ethics in higher education: Learning and teaching in ethics across the curriculum*. A report on the ETHICS Project. Retrieved from http://www.basr.ac.uk/trs_resources/pubs_and_resources/projects/ethics/ethics_across_curriculum.pdf

Jones, G. (2013). Julia Gillard's henchman Stephen Conroy attacks freedom of the press. *Daily Telegraph*. Accessed on March 13, 2013.

Joyce, R. (2011). Moral fictionalism. *Philosophy Today*, *82*, p. 3.

Kaptein, M. (2011). Toward effective codes: Testing the relationship with unethical behavior. *Journal of Business Ethics*, *99*, 233–251.

Kaptein, M., & Wempe, J. (1998). Twelve Gordian knots when developing an organizational code of ethics. *Journal of Business Ethics*, *17*, 853–869.

Kerridge, I., Lowe, M., & Stewart, C. (2009). *Ethics and law for the health: Professions* (3rd ed.), Sydney: The Federation Press.

Klein, E. (1998). The necessary condition for a successful business ethics course: The teacher must be a philosopher. *Business Ethics Quarterly*, *8*(3), 561–567.

Kymlicka, W. (2002). *Contemporary political philosophy: An introduction* (2nd ed.), Oxford: Oxford University Press.

Lamond, J., & Lowe, K. (2012). Core issues in ethics for scientists. In P. Bowden (Ed.), *Applied ethics*. Melbourne: Tilde University Press.

Lauchs, M. (2012). Police ethics, In P. Bowden (Ed.), *Applied ethics*. Melbourne: Tilde University Press.

Leake, C., & Delgado, M. (2010, September 26). Police have shot dead 33 people since 1995. *The Mail on Sunday*.

Lipworth, W., Strong, K., & Kerridge, I. (2012). In P. Bowden (Ed.), *Applied ethics*. Melbourne: Tilde University Press.

Marshall, P., Thomasma, D., & Daar, A. (1996). Marketing human organs: The autonomy paradox. *Theoretical Medicine*, *17*(1), 1–18.

Martin Susan, S., Daniel, T. D. (2013). Chemical weapons and trade: Preventing the next Syria. *The Conversation*. Retrieved from theconversation.com/au. Accessed on November 9, 2013.

Miles, S. (2012). Stakeholders: Essentially contested or just confused? *Journal of Business Ethics*, *108*(3), 285–298.

Mill, J. S. (1861). *Utilitarianism*. Retrieved from www.utilitarianism.com/mill1.htm.

Pence, G. (1993). Virtue theory. In P. Singer (Ed.), *A companion to ethics* (p. 249). Oxford: Blackwell Publishers.

Perkins, J. (2010). Fear campaign on resources tax is a furphy. *The Age*. May 21.

Plummer, K. (2012). Accounting ethics. In P. Bowden (Ed.), *Applied ethics*. Melbourne: Tilde University Press.

Program Budgeting. (n.d.). Retrieved from http://www-personal.umich.edu/~steiss/page24. html. Accessed on March 3, 2013.

Punk, V. (1969). *Reflective naturalism an introduction to moral philosophy*. New York, NY: Macmillan Company.

Richards, I. (2005). *Quagmires and quandaries: Exploring journalism ethics*. Sydney, Australia: UNSW Press.

Rollin, B. E. (2006). *An introduction to veterinary medical ethics, theory and cases* (2nd ed.). New Jersey, US: Blackwell Publishing.

Ryley, S. (2014). In 179 fatalities involving on-duty NYPD cops in 15 years, only 3 cases led to indictments — and just 1 conviction. *New York Daily News*. Accessed on December 8, 2014.

Singer, P. (1993). *Practical ethics* (p. 95). Cambridge: Cambridge University Press.

Smythe, V. (2012). Codes of ethics. In P. Bowden (Ed.), *Applied ethics*. Melbourne: Tilde University Press.

Stephens, T. (2012). Veterinary ethics. In P. Bowden (Ed.), *Applied ethics*. Melbourne: Tilde University Press.

Swan, J. (2013). Customs staff asked to DOB on co-workers. *The Age*, February 15.

Sykes, J. (2012). Ethical journalism. In P. Bowden (Ed.), *Applied ethics*. Melbourne: Tilde University Press.

Tapper, A. (2012). Ethics in politics. In P. Bowden (Ed.), *Applied ethics*. Melbourne: Tilde University Press.

The Royal Commission. (1970). *Report of the royal commission into the failure of the West Gate Bridge*. Melbourne, Australia: Government Printer.

Tsahuridu, E. (2011). Whistleblowing management is risk management. In D. Lewis & W. Vandekerckhove (Eds.), *Whistleblowing and democratic values*. UK: The International Whistleblowing Research Network, Middlesex University.

Valentine, S., Godkin, L., Fleischman, G., & Kidwell, R. (2011). Corporate ethical values, group creativity, job satisfaction and turnover intention: The impact of work context on work response. *Journal of Business Ethics*, 98, 353–372.

Vandekerckhove, W. (2012). *Public attitudes to whistleblowing*. Retrieved from http://gala.gre. ac.uk/10298/1/UK_Public_Attitudes_to_WB_Press_Release_and_Report_20121115.pdf

Wood, G. (2000). A cross cultural comparison of codes of ethics: USA, Canada and Australia. *Journal of Business Ethics*, 25(4), 287–298.

EQUATOR PRINCIPLES – NOW AND THEN

Manuel Wörsdörfer

ABSTRACT

The Equator Principles are a transnational corporate social responsibility initiative in the project finance sector. In 2013, the Equator Principles Association celebrated the tenth anniversary of its principles and at the same time the formal launch of the latest generation of the Equator Principles (EP III). The paper describes the historic development of the Equator Principles – from the initial drafting process in the early 2000s up to the latest review process which led to the third generation of the Equator Principles. The paper also analyzes the current state of affairs of the Equator Principles (Association) and gives a brief outlook on potential lines of (future) development. In particular, the paper deals with the following questions: What are the main characteristics of the Equator Principles framework? What are the relevant actors involved in the drafting and reviewing process? Why are the EPs and other organizational and associational codes of conduct in the finance sector so important? What has been achieved so far by the Equator Principles (Association) and the participating (financial) institutions and what remains to be done?

The Ethical Contribution of Organizations to Society
Research in Ethical Issues in Organizations, Volume 14, 121–160
Copyright © 2015 by Emerald Group Publishing Limited
ISSN: 1529-2096/doi:10.1108/S1529-209620150000014006

Keywords: Equator Principles/EP III; Equator Principles financial institutions; Equator Principles association; international finance corporation; project finance

INTRODUCTORY REMARKS

The last years (and decades) saw a series of corporate (governance) scandals in the finance sector. Banks and other financial institutions have in several cases been involved in scandals of money laundering, fraud, and the manipulation of key interest rates (e.g., Libor and Euribor). Furthermore, several finance organizations have been embroiled in morally dubious lending practices – for example, speculative investments and subprime lending leading toward the global financial market crisis of 2007ff. – and other forms of ethical malpractices, such as the funding of "dirty projects" and "dodgy deals" (i.e., corporate complicity in human rights violations).

As a consequence, nowadays, financial institutions in general face a far-reaching trust and legitimacy crisis, especially in North America and Western Europe: The public perception and reputation of banks and other financial organizations has decreased tremendously in these (and other) countries. Some (major) financial market players seem to be aware of the current situation and its inherent risks for doing business – a type of business which is essentially based on informal norms such as trust and trustworthiness (the term "credit," for example, stems from the Latin word "credere" which simply means "to believe" or "to trust"). Their aim is to provide a cultural change inside their own organization and within the financial sector as a whole. What is in particular needed in this regard is to put adequate governance mechanisms (i.e., enforcement, monitoring and sanctioning institutions) in place which ensure that financial organizations (and their clients) do indeed behave (more) ethically. Of special importance are the adoption and adherence to organizational and/or associational codes of conduct and ethics. The Equator Principles (for a general overview see Baumast, 2013; Gonzales Napolitano, 2011; Wörsdörfer, 2013), a voluntary Corporate Social Responsibility (CSR) standard in the project finance sector which got established in 2003 and revised in 2006 and 2013, can be regarded as one such example that might help – given that certain reform measures are adopted (see below) – to restore trust in the finance sector. Two years ago, the Equator Principles Association celebrated the formal launch of the third generation of the Equator Principles (EP III) and at the same time the tenth anniversary of the Equator Principles framework — enough reasons for critically assessing this transnational CSR initiative from a historiographic and organizational-institutional perspective.

The paper describes the historic development of the Equator Principles, from the initial drafting process in the early 2000s up to the latest review process and the third generation of the Equator Principles, as well as the current state of affairs of this CSR agenda, including a brief outlook on potential lines of (future) development. In particular, the paper deals with the following questions: What are the main characteristics of the Equator Principles framework? What are the relevant actors involved in the drafting and reviewing process? Why are the EPs and other organizational and associational codes of ethics in the finance sector so important? What has been achieved so far by the Equator Principles (Association) and the participating (financial) institutions and what remains to be done?

The remainder of the paper is structured as follows: The second section gives a general overview of the Equator Principles framework and introduces the keywords related to this transnational CSR initiative. The third section summarizes the main features of the latest generation of the Equator Principles (EP III). The fourth section analyzes the special role of project finance within the Equator Principles framework. Section five gives an overview of the history of the Equator Principles. The sixth section discusses the main "stakeholders" behind the Equator Principles initiative. The paper concludes with a summary of the main findings as well as a brief outlook on likely developments.

GENERAL OVERVIEW

The Equator Principles are officially described as a voluntary and self-regulatory finance industry benchmark in the international project finance sector.[1] In particular, they are a finance industry standard for environmental and social risk management or as it is often referred to a "credit risk management framework for determining, assessing, and managing environmental and social risk in Project Finance transactions" (Equator Principles Association, 2015). The Equator Principles Association refers to the principles as the "gold standard" (Lazarus & Feldbaum, 2011, p. i) and best practice example in environmental and social risk management for project finance.

The term "Equator" represents the balance between industrialized (OECD) countries, "developing countries" and emerging markets, a balance between the southern and the northern hemispheres and between east and west. Furthermore, it indicates that the Equator Principles apply globally on both sides of the Equator to the following four financial market products:

1. Project finance, where total project capital costs exceed US$ 10 million;
2. Advisory services related to project finance;
3. Project-related corporate loans; and
4. Bridge loans.

The Equator Principles are adopted by so-called Equator Principles Financial Institutions (EPFIs), that is, banks and other financial institutions which are active in project finance, project finance advisory services and project-related corporate loans. The EPFIs commit themselves to not providing loans and credits to projects where the borrower is not able (or willing) to comply with the respective social and environmental standards and guidelines.

As of May 2015, 80 financial institutions from 36 countries and 6 continents have adopted the Equator Principles. According to official data provided by the Equator Principles Association, the Equator Principles cover over 70% of international project finance debt in emerging markets.

The Equator Principles are based on the *Performance Standards on Environmental and Social Sustainability*[2] of the International Finance Corporation (IFC) – that is, the private sector lending arm of the World Bank Group – as well as on the World Bank Group's *Environmental, Health, and Safety Guidelines* (EHS Guidelines).[3] Typically, a revision of the IFC Performance Standards precedes a revision of the Equator Principles.

The overall aim of the Equator Principles is the promotion of environmental (i.e., protection of project-affected ecosystems) and social stewardship (i.e., CSR and corporate citizenship[4] in the form of respect for human rights) in the (project) finance industry. An illustrative list of potential socio-environmental issues tackled by the involved EPFIs and their clients includes the following topics:

• Protection and conservation of biodiversity (i.e., protection of endangered species, sensitive ecosystems, and critical habitats);
• Sustainable resource management and use of renewable natural resources;

- Responsible management and use of dangerous substances;
- Chemical waste management;
- Efficient production, delivery and use of energy;
- Pollution prevention and waste minimization;
- Respect of human rights (i.e., prevention and mitigation of adverse human rights impacts);
- Awareness of labor issues and occupational health and safety;
- Participation and consultation of project-affected stakeholders in the design, review and implementation of the project; and
- Management and reduction of adverse socio-economic impacts – especially impacts on project-affected communities and disadvantaged or vulnerable groups; for example, impacts on indigenous peoples, and their unique cultural systems and values, including avoidance of land acquisition and involuntary resettlement as well as protection of cultural property and heritage. (Equator Principles Association, 2013, p. 20).

To promote socio-environmental stewardship in the project finance industry, the Equator Principles impose obligations on both lenders (EPFIs) and borrowers (clients), in particular with regard to:

- Review and categorization;
- Environmental and social impact assessment;
- Environmental and social management systems and action plans;
- Stakeholder engagement;
- Grievance mechanism; and
- Monitoring and reporting.

While the participating EPFIs have adopted the Equator Principles and help enforcing and monitoring them[5], it is in fact the client or borrower that is expected to fulfill and adhere to the requirements laid down by the Equator Principles. These obligations are imposed by the lender upon the borrower and they get formalized as covenants, which are part of the loan documentation or investment agreement between the financial institution and the project developer.

EQUATOR PRINCIPLES: THE THIRD GENERATION

The third generation of the Equator Principles (EP III) consists of 10 principles. The first principle (*Review and Categorization*) requires the EPFIs to categorize each proposed project "based on the magnitude of its potential environmental and social risks and impacts" (Equator Principles Association, 2013, p. 5).[6] The screening process is based on the environmental and social categorization process of the IFC (IFC, 2012a, 2012b). According to that, three project categories are to be distinguished:

- Category A projects are "Projects with potential significant adverse environmental and social risks and/or impacts that are diverse, [cumulative,] irreversible or unprecedented" (Equator Principles Association, 2013, p. 5);
- Category B projects are "Projects with potential limited adverse environmental and social risks and/or impacts that are few in number, generally site-specific, largely reversible and readily addressed through mitigation measures" (*ibid.*, p. 5);
- Category C contains "Projects with minimal or no adverse environmental and social risks and/or impacts" (*ibid.*, p. 5).

The categorization process is crucial since it determines which environmental and social standards and procedures are subsequently applied. The following Equator Principles apply to Category A and B projects only. Category C projects do not fall into the Equator Principles framework since they are regarded as socially and environmentally inoffensive; they can be classified as safe from an environmental, social, and human rights perspective.

Principle 2 (*Environmental and Social (Impact) Assessment*) requires the client to conduct for all Category A and B projects an environmental and social assessment process to address all relevant environmental and social risks and impacts of the proposed project. The Environmental and Social Assessment Documentation should include "measures to minimize, mitigate, and offset adverse impacts" (*ibid.*, p. 5). It should also include an Environmental and Social Impact Assessment and an Alternatives Analysis for projects emitting more than 100,000 tons of CO_2 equivalents annually.[7] For these projects, an alternatives analysis has to be conducted to evaluate less Greenhouse Gas (GHG)-intensive technologies and procedures.

Which environmental and social standards are applicable depends also on the location of the particular project. In "designated countries" – that is, mainly industrial and (high income) OECD countries – compliance with host country laws, regulations and permits pertaining to environmental and social issues is required. In emerging markets and developing countries (the so-called "non-designated countries"), however, compliance is also required with the IFC Performance Standards on Environmental and Social Sustainability and the World Bank Group's Environmental, Health and Safety Guidelines (Principle 3: *Applicable Environmental and Social Standards*).

Principle 4 – *Environmental and Social Management System and Equator Principles Action Plan* – demands that the client develops and maintains an Environmental and Social Management System as well as an Environmental and Social Management Plan (for more information on Environmental (and Social) Management Systems see Wood, 2003a, 2003b and Wood & Johannson, 2008). The overall aim is to comply with the applicable environmental and social standards. In case that the applicable standards are not met, the client and the EPFI(s) will develop a joint Equator Principles Action Plan.

Principle 5 asks for an encompassing and constant *stakeholder engagement* process. Project-affected communities and other stakeholder groups must have rights to information, consultation and influence. Of particular importance is the "Informed Consultation and Participation" (ICP) process, a process which ideally takes place in a "culturally appropriate manner" (Equator Principles Association, 2013, p. 7). Information has to be made readily and publicly available to the affected communities in their local languages. The disclosure of information (e.g., assessment documentation) should occur as early as possible in the assessment process – ideally within the planning stage and before construction commences – and on an ongoing basis. Moreover, project-affected communities have to have the right to participate in decision-making (i.e., notion of *Teilhabe* and inclusion – for more information on the notions of inclusion and *Teilhabe* and their connection to the EPs see Wörsdörfer, 2014). Their voices have to be heard, and the interests and needs of disadvantaged and vulnerable groups shall be taken into consideration. The whole stakeholder engagement process should be free from external manipulation, interference, coercion, and intimidation. Projects with adverse impacts on indigenous or aboriginal peoples even require their "Free, Prior and Informed Consent" (FPIC).

The client is, furthermore, required by Principle 6 to establish a (project level and worker) *grievance mechanism*– as part of the Environmental and Social Management System –, which is "designed to receive and facilitate resolution of concerns and grievances about the Project's environmental and social performance. [...] It will seek to resolve concerns promptly, using an understandable and transparent consultative process that is culturally appropriate, readily accessible, at no cost, and without retribution to the party that originated the issue or concern" (Equator Principles Association, 2013, p. 8).

To assess compliance with the principles, independent monitoring, reporting, and reviewing is required. Principles 7 and 9 deal with these issues: Principle 7 requires that an *independent review* of the Assessment Documentation – including Environmental and Social Management Plan and System and the stakeholder engagement process – is conducted by an independent environmental and social expert or consultant who is not directly linked with the client. Moreover, the consultant can propose a suitable action plan for the projects that are not in compliance with the Equator Principles. Projects which contain potential adverse impacts on indigenous peoples, critical habitat and cultural heritage impacts and large-scale resettlements are the most sensitive ones.

Principle 9 is devoted to *independent monitoring and reporting*. Here, an independent consultant or a "qualified and experienced external expert" (*ibid.*, p. 10) is required to assess project compliance with the Equator Principles. The consultant or expert is responsible to verify monitoring and reporting information after financial close and over the life of the loan.

The *Covenants*-Principle 8 also deals with compliance: It requires the client to "covenant in the financing documentation to comply with all relevant host country environmental and social laws, regulations and permits" (*ibid.*, p. 9). Furthermore, the client has to covenant to comply with the Environmental and Social Management Plan and Equator Principles Action Plan, to report publicly in an appropriate format and to decommission facilities where applicable. Finally, "[w]here a client is not in compliance with its environmental and social covenants, the EPFI will work with the client on remedial actions to bring the Project back into compliance to the extent feasible. If the client fails to re-establish compliance within an agreed grace period, the EPFI reserves the right to exercise remedies, as considered appropriate" (*ibid.*, p. 9).[8]

The final principle 10 deals with accountability in the form of *reporting and transparency* requirements both for clients and EPFIs: The client should ensure that a summary of the Environmental and Social Impact Assessment is publicly available and readily accessible, for example, via online disclosure. Principle 10 also requires the client to publicly report on GHG-emission levels for projects emitting more than 100,000 tons of CO_2 equivalents annually.[9] The EPFI, on the other hand, is required to report publicly on an at least annual basis on "transactions that have reached Financial Close and on its Equator Principles implementation processes and experience, taking into account appropriate confidentiality considerations" (*ibid.*, p. 10f.). The EPFI is further requested to provide additional information on the total number of deals financed under the Equator

Principles, the number of Category A, B, and C projects, the sector, region and country of financed projects as well as information with regard to Equator Principles implementation (i.e., credit and risk management policies), independent review, role of senior management, internal preparation and (ongoing) staff training, etc. Project names are conveyed to the Equator Principles Association. Given the client's approval, this information might be made public on the Equator Principles website in the future.

The Governance Rules as well as the legal *Disclaimer* state that "the Equator Principles do not create any rights in, or liability to, any person, public or private" (*ibid.*, p. 11). That is, EPFIs adopt and implement the Equator Principles on a voluntary, legally non-binding basis. The Equator Principles framework is therefore voluntary in use relying purely on self-enforcement and the goodwill of EPFIs, that is, no mandatory obligations or direct punitive actions can arise from the principles themselves (i.e., exclusion of liability) (Andrew, 2009, p. 306).

ON THE SPECIAL ROLE OF PROJECT FINANCE

The Equator Principles apply (mainly) to the project finance sector (Haack, Schoeneborn, & Wickert, 2010; Kleimeier & Versteeg, 2010; Marco, 2011, p. 456; Wright & Rwabizambuga, 2006, p. 96). This finance industry sector funds the design, construction and operation of large industrial and infrastructure projects especially in emerging markets and developing countries. Examples include:

- Dams;
- Mines (gold, silver, copper, etc.);
- Mountaintop removal;
- Oil and gas projects (e.g., oil pipelines);
- Hydraulic fracturing (fracking);
- Tar and oil sands;
- (Coal and nuclear) power plants;
- Chemical processing plants;
- Manufacturing plants; and
- Transportation and telecommunication infrastructures.

These large infrastructure and industrial projects can have substantially large ecological and social footprints (i.e., impact on natural resources and local communities). Moreover, they are technically complex (a), capital-intensive (b) and involve significant financial and non-financial risks (c). Thus, they are usually conducted by short-term joint ventures most often in the form of special purpose vehicles. On the financiers' side, these kinds of projects are typically financed jointly by syndicates that involve several financial institutions. The reason is that the failure of a project may result in a near-complete loss of investments. In addition, significant politico-economic risks are involved. Sources of risk include the following:

- *Market* and/or *financial risks*: that is., interest rate risk, credit risk, off-balance-sheet risk, foreign exchange risk and risk of currency devaluation, liquidity risk, insolvency risk, and operational risk;
- *Environmental and social risks:* that is, financial institution's direct liability for environmental and social damage caused by its borrowing clients;
- *Political risks*: that is, risk of political interference and confiscation, expropriation risk, risk of governmental nationalization, risk of political turmoil, social unrest and civil war; and
- *Reputational risks*: that is, risks to the bank's reputation and negative publicity (i.e., public naming and shaming campaigns and boycott movements) from environmental, social and corporate governance (ESG) issues (Jeucken, 2001/2002, p. 118; Lozinski, 2012; Nwete, 2005).

Typically, the lender's loan is secured by the different project assets and repaid mainly from the cash flows of the project and the value of the facilities. What makes the project finance sector so attractive is the fact that it is a (potentially) high margin business with large revenue streams – given that the project runs successfully.[10]

The market itself is shaped by a few market players. The major lenders in project finance are the World Bank Group – and in particular the IFC – export credit agencies, development banks, and large private commercial banks. Noteworthy is the fact that project finance is a rather small segment of major financial institutions. It commonly accounts for up to 5% of the overall turnover of financial institutions. As such, the Equator Principles apply only to a small fraction of multinational bank's total activities (Haack et al., 2010, p. 17).

Project finance is often the preferred financial tool in countries with high political risk and poor political, administrative, and corporate governance. It is regarded as a substitute for underdeveloped financial markets and a lack of local or regional institutional and financial development. In other words: Project finance as a complement for foreign direct investments can compensate for a lack of managerial capabilities and poor corporate and political governance. The public sector in developing countries is often not capable to design, construct, and operate such complex projects due to politico-economic inefficiencies and lack of management know-how. Project finance thus transfers the development, construction, and management to the private sector and its (often) superior technical and managerial expertise.

In addition, project finance is able to stimulate economic growth: Newly acquired telecommunication and transportation infrastructures, for example, can lead to improved economic growth in developing countries and emerging markets — so-called "finance-growth nexus" (Kleimeier & Versteeg, 2010). With its growth-enhancing properties, project finance might be regarded as a main driver of economic growth in low-income (developing) countries and emerging markets.[11]

A BRIEF HISTORY OF THE EQUATOR PRINCIPLES

The first informal gathering of the later "Equator banks" took place in October 2002 when a meeting was convened with the IFC in London, United Kingdom. The main purpose of this meeting was to discuss socio-environmental risk issues in the project finance sector. The gathering was triggered by the growing reputational pressure from civil society groups and Non-Governmental Organizations (NGOs), such as BankTrack, Bankwatch, Friends of the Earth, Greenpeace, Human Rights Watch, International Rivers Network, Rainforest Action Network, and World Wide Fund for Nature.

In January 2003, the *Collevecchio Declaration on Financial Institutions and Sustainability* (Missbach, 2004, p. 81; O'Sullivan & O'Dwyer, 2009, p. 563; Richardson, 2005, p. 288; Wright, 2012) was launched at the World Economic Forum in Davos, Switzerland. Its aim was to coordinate NGO-finance sector campaigning. The declaration laid the foundation of the NGO BankTrack and was endorsed by more than 100 civil society organizations. In the center of the declaration were the following six principles:

- *Commitment to Sustainability*: Financial Institutions "must expand their missions from ones that prioritize profit maximization to a vision of social and environmental sustainability. [...] [They must] integrate the consideration of ecological limits, social equity and economic justice into corporate strategies and core business areas [...], [and] put sustainability objectives on an equal footing to shareholder maximization ...";
- *Commitment to "Do not harm"*: "Financial institutions should commit to do no harm by preventing and minimizing the environmentally and/or

socially detrimental impacts of their portfolios and their operations. Financial institutions should create policies, procedures, and standards based on the Precautionary Principle to minimize environmental and social harm";

- *Commitment to Responsibility*: "Financial institutions should bear full responsibility for the environmental and social impacts of their transactions" including the "social and environmental costs that are borne by communities";
- *Commitment to Accountability*: "Financial institutions must be accountable to their stakeholders, particularly those that are affected by the companies and activities they finance";
- *Commitment to Transparency*: "Financial institutions must be transparent to stakeholders, not only through robust, regular and standardized disclosure, but also by being responsive to stakeholder needs for specialized information on financial institutions' policies, procedures and transactions. Commercial confidentiality should not be used as an excuse to deny stakeholders information"; and
- *Commitment to Sustainable Markets and Governance*: "Financial institutions should ensure that markets are more capable of fostering sustainability by actively supporting public policy, regulatory and/or market mechanisms ..." (Collevecchio Declaration, 2003, p. 3ff).

The Collevecchio Declaration had a tremendous impact on the Equator Principles drafting process and accelerated the dynamic interactions between EPFIs, NGOs, civil society organizations, and other affected stakeholder groups.

On June 4th 2003, the first generation of the Equator Principles (EP I) was launched and adopted by the first 10 financial institutions. Among the founding members were: ABN AMRO, Barclays, Citigroup, Credit Lyonnais, Credit Suisse, HVB, Rabobank, Royal Bank of Scotland, WestLB, and Westpac.

Beginning of 2006, the first strategic review and update process took place. Several NGOs, civil society organizations, export credit agencies, and industry associations participated in this first engagement and review process. The aim was to revise the Equator Principles and to incorporate the various changes in the IFC Performance Standards, which came into effect in April 2006.

A few months later, on July 6th 2006, the second generation of the Equator Principles (EP II) was launched. Key changes (EP I vs. EP II) include the following aspects:

- Lowering of the financial threshold from US$ 50 million to US$ 10 million;
- Extension of scope and inclusion of project-related advisory services in the scope of the Equator Principles (i.e., the Equator Principles were now applied at an earlier stage, namely the advisory stage of project planning);
- Inclusion of stronger socio-environmental standards as outlined in the IFC Performance Standards, for example, environmental *plus* social assessment, and enhanced consultation requirements (i.e., prior and informed consultation), covenanting requirements, labor standards, and project-level grievance mechanisms; and
- Increased transparency by requiring each EPFI to report publicly on the Equator Principles implementation on an at least annual basis (i.e., newly added Principle 10).

In April 2008, the Equator Principles Secretariat got established followed by the formal establishment of the Equator Principles Association and the launch of the Governance Rules in July 2010. Both steps contributed immensely to the (enhanced) formalization and institutionalization of the Equator Principles and their public visibility.[12]

From October 2010 until May 2011, the Equator Principles Association launched a Strategic Review Process followed by an official Update Process starting in July 2011. This update and review process reflected ongoing learning, implementation experiences, and emerging good business practices. Moreover, the process reflected the changing financial landscape as well as the changing public perception of the role of financial institutions. Not least the financial crisis of 2007 and 2008 had contributed to a legitimacy crisis and a loss of public trust in finance industry institutions. The Equator Principles can thus be seen as an attempt of restoring trust in the banking sector via implementing and adhering to organizational and associational codes of conduct.

Key thematic areas during the second update and review process were the extension of scope of the Equator Principles as well as reporting, transparency and governance issues (including stakeholder engagement and membership criteria), the fight against climate change and the respect for human rights in the finance industry.

In the first phase, an internal consultation process yielded a first draft of EP III. The second phase, the stakeholder consultation and public comment period, gave stakeholder groups the chance to comment on the initial draft and to make suggestions for further improvement (although not all recommendations were taken into account by the Equator Principles Association and included in the final draft). In the third phase, the third generation of the Equator Principles was finalized and launched – taking into considerations the newly revised IFC Performance Standards which came into effect on January 1st 2012.

June 4th 2013 marked the formal Launch of EP III as well as the tenth anniversary of the Equator Principles. Until the end of 2013, a transition period applied to give EPFIs as well as clients the chance to implement EP III for all products in the newly extended scope. From January 1st 2014, EP III is now applied to all new transactions.

EP III is characterized by three major innovations:

I. With the introduction of EP III the scope of the Equator Principles is extended to cover not only project finance and project-related advisory services, as it was the case under EP II, but also project-related corporate loans and bridge loans. This implies that more projects are assessed under a strengthened and broadened environmental and social risk management framework.[13]

II. An even more important fact is that the EP III framework takes into account climate change, human rights, and stakeholder engagement issues – although major deficiencies in terms of the Equator Principles' governance mechanisms (including enforcement, monitoring, and sanctioning) still exist (Wörsdörfer, 2014, forthcoming).

With regards to global warming, EP III requires an Alternatives Analysis for high CO_2 emitting projects.[14] Projects emitting more than 100,000 tons CO_2 equivalents should consider alternative technologies and procedures requiring less carbon intensive fuel or energy sources. These resource-saving technologies have to be technically and financially feasible and cost-effective. The overall aim of the Equator Principles is to reduce project-related GHG emissions during the design, construction, and operation phases of the particular project. The alternatives analysis should include a comparison to other viable and feasible technologies and procedures used in the same country, region, or industry sector. High carbon intensity sectors include thermal power, cement and lime manufacturing, steel mills, metal smelting and refining and foundries. Moreover, borrowers have to report publicly on GHG emissions (Equator Principles Association, 2013, p. 12).

III. With regards to stakeholder engagement and human rights issues, EP III introduces the term human rights into the Equator Principles framework for the first time. EP III also acknowledges John Ruggie's

"Protect, Respect and Remedy" Framework as well as the U.N. "Guiding Principles on Business and Human Rights" which both stress the importance of human rights due diligence processes.

In addition, the previous Consultation and Disclosure procedure is replaced by the current Stakeholder Engagement process: The latter requires a dialogue with project-affected communities (and other stake-holders) either in the form of the "Informed Consultation and Participation" (ICP) paradigm or in the form of the "Free, Prior and Informed Consent" (FPIC) paradigm − given that indigenous peoples are involved. This consent, however, does not entail any veto rights nor does it require unanimity − a majority decision suffices (for more information see IFC Performance Standard No. 7 (on Indigenous Peoples) (IFC, 2012a, p. 3) as well as IFC Guidance Note No. 7 (IFC, 2012b, pp. 7, 9); see also Ong, 2010, p. 64).

The year 2013 also saw the publication of a very important working paper: The so-called Thun Group of Banks, consisting of seven leading international banks (Barclays, BBVA, Credit Suisse, ING Bank, RBS Group, UBS, and UniCredit), published a paper draft on banks and human rights (Thun Group of Banks, 2013). The paper is the result of two years of deliberations among the Thun Group members and provides a (first) guide to the banking sector for operationalizing the U.N. Guiding Principles on Business and Human Rights. The paper recognizes that the Guiding Principles apply to all parts of a bank's business segments, including asset management, corporate and investment banking. The paper has been welcomed by the NGO BankTrack as a significant step toward recognizing the relevance of human rights to banks' core business (BankTrack, 2013; de Felice, 2014). Yet the paper has also been criticized for its limited scope: the main problem is that it focuses solely on principles 16−21 of the Guiding Principles (which are related to the corporate responsibility to respect human rights) while leaving aside the foundational principles 11−15 as well as all those principles devoted to operational-level grievance, complaint and remedy mechanisms (e.g., principles 22 and 29 of the Guiding Principles).

THE MAIN STAKEHOLDER GROUPS

The Equator Principles framework can be described as a "multi-stakeholder initiative" in the wider sense.[15] Several actors have been involved in the drafting and reviewing process of the principles and/or have been directly or indirectly affected by the principles themselves. The main stakeholder groups "behind" the Equator Principles are the following ones:

- Equator Principles Financial Institutions (EPFIs);
- Equator Principles Association (EPA);
- International Finance Corporation (IFC) and World Bank Group;
- Non-Governmental Organizations (NGOs); and
- Project-affected communities and in particular indigenous peoples.

Equator Principles Financial Institutions

EPFIs are financial institutions that have adopted the Equator Principles and are active in project finance or advisory services related to project finance (Equator Principles Association, 2010/2013, p. 2). As of May 2015, the Equator Principles have been adopted by 80 EPFIs from 36 countries. Major EPFIs include ABN Amro, Banco Santander, Bank of America, Barclays, BNP Paribas, Citigroup, Credit Suisse, Crédit Agricole, HSBC, ING Bank, JPMorgan, Rabobank Group, Royal Bank of Scotland, Société Générale, UniCredit, and Wells Fargo. A full list of all current EPFIs can be found in the appendix of this paper and on the website of the Equator Principles Association (Equator Principles Association, 2015).

When taking a closer look at the current rankings of the top banks in the world by total assets as well as market capitalization (see appendix), it becomes clear that not all big banks are part of the Equator Principles initiative. Only 9 respectively 10 out of the top 15 banks are members of the Equator Principles initiative. Major global players are still missing, for example, Deutsche Bank, Morgan Stanley, and UBS. Of particular importance are the missing Chinese banks Agricultural Bank of China, Bank of China, China Construction Bank, and Industrial and Commercial Bank of China (ICBC) since all of them belong to the top 10 banks in the world either according to total assets or market capitalization. Other Asian players are also missing, for instance, the Industrial Credit and Investment Corporation of India (ICICI) Bank, the Russian Sberbank, and the State Bank of India.

In general, several big banks from the BRICS countries (Brazil, Russia, India, China, and South Africa) are still not yet a member of the Equator Principles Association. So far, only one Chinese (Industrial Bank Co.) and one Indian bank (IDFC Ltd.) have joined the Equator Principles initiative; yet there is no Russian bank being a member of the Equator Principles framework – Otkritie, the only Russian member so far, left the Equator Principles Association shortly after becoming a member of the Equator Principles.

Especially the missing (South-East) Asian banks represent a great draw-back for the Equator Principles initiative since those banks belong to the big-gest banks in the world (as is the case for the Chinese banks) or are among the biggest mandated project arrangers (as is the case for the Chinese, Indian, and Korean (development) banks) (cp. appendix). Given the fact that most projects get financed and constructed in the BRICS countries and that several BRICS banks are not yet a member of the Equator Principles framework the Equator Principles in their current version are not able to guarantee a worldwide application of minimum environmental, social and human rights standards. Due to major players still missing in this initiative, the "playing field" is not completely leveled.[16]

Equator Principles Association – Governance and Management

The Equator Principles Association is the unincorporated association of EPFIs.[17] Its objective is the management, administration and further devel-opment of the Equator Principles. The association got established on July 1st 2010. It is governed by a set of Governance Rules which is accessible on the website of the Equator Principles Association. Two governance levels have to be distinguished: the administration level and the management level.

The *management level* consists of the Steering Committee which is responsible for the coordination of the administration, management and further advancement of the Equator Principles on behalf of EPFIs. The Steering Committee can set up permanent or temporary working groups fostering the inclusion of stakeholder groups. One of the main tasks of these working groups is to discuss governance and implementation issues and to provide guidance to EPFIs with regards to the further advancement of the Equator Principles. Currently, nine working groups exist, for exam-ple, on external relations (i.e., communication with external stakeholders such as NGOs and civil society organizations), consistency, regional out-reach, biodiversity, climate change and social risk.

As of May 2015, 15 members are part of the Steering Committee (the Governance Rules state that the Steering Committee should consist of no fewer than seven members and no more than 15 members). EPFIs become members of the Steering Committee on the basis of a rotation principle for a maximum of three years (a re-election is under certain conditions possible). Among the members of the Steering Committee, one EPFI gets elected by at least 50.1% of all current committee members as Chair of the Steering Committee. The chair functions as the speaker and provides coordination across the Steering Committee, the other member institutions and the working groups. Members of the Steering Committee hold the chair for a term of approximately one year – with the maximum of two consecutive terms – on the basis of a rotation principle as well. Currently, the Japanese Mizuho Bank holds the Chair of the Equator Principles Association Steering Committee. This is remarkable since it is the first time for an Asian bank to become the Chair of the Equator Principles Association Steering Committee.

The second level of the Equator Principles Association is the *administration level* consisting of the Equator Principles Secretariat. The Secretariat manages the everyday running of the Equator Principles Association. In particular, the Secretariat is responsible for the Equator Principles website, internal and external communications, public relations, advice and assistance with regards to adopting and implementing the Equator Principles and the management of financial affairs.

Decision-making within the Equator Principles Association aims at consensus-seeking. The following decision rule applies for associational decision-making: Each EPFI has one vote; proposals are typically adopted when at least 50% of all EPFIs cast votes – so-called quorum of half – and when 66.7% of them vote in favor of a particular proposal.[18] This consensus-seeking approach gets increasingly difficult the more EPFIs coming from heterogeneous backgrounds and having conflicting interests adopt the Equator Principles. In the recent past, decision-making was slowed down by the de facto veto rights granted to each EPFI. Moreover, in several occasions, only the lowest common denominator could be found which inhibited the further advancement of the Equator Principles initiative. As a result, the recent review and update process took much longer than expected (it took in total almost two years to update the Equator Principles framework).

The annual fee for the financial year 1 July 2014–30 June 2015 is GBP £3,265.00. The fee supposedly covers all of the costs incurred in the administration, management and further advancement of the Equator Principles. However, due to the relatively low membership fee, the Equator Principles Association is de facto under-staffed and under-funded (Lazarus & Feldbaum, 2011). A properly functioning monitoring (of Equator Principles compliance) and sanctioning system is – under these conditions – hard to achieve, given the inadequate financial and personal resources of the association. This in turn might inhibit the proper implementation of the

Equator Principles on the ground and might, in the long run, damage the reputation and "brand value" of the Equator Principles initiative.

International Finance Corporation and World Bank Group

The International Finance Corporation, established in 1956, is a public financial institution affiliated with the World Bank Group. It is often described as the private sector lending arm of the World Bank Group. As such, it is a separate legal entity with its own operational mandate, professional staff and financial resources. Its main aim is to encourage private sector growth and investment in developing countries and emerging markets. In fact, the IFC is one of the largest providers of multilateral finance in those countries. Its activities supplement the work of the World Bank (Group) that exclusively lends to member state governments. It has a commercial orientation and its loan syndications program includes private multinational banks. The IFC also functions as a meeting facilitator and technical advisor. In this respect, the IFC is well-known for its expertise in environmental and social risk management. It has formed partnerships with the U.N. Global Compact and the United Nations Environment Program Finance Initiative (UNEP FI). As such, the IFC is often regarded as a de facto standard-setter in the finance industry sector. For instance, the Equator Principles use the IFC's environmental and social safeguard policy framework as a blueprint. In fact, a revision of the IFC Performance Standards typically precedes an update of the Equator Principles. (for more information on the IFC see Wright (2009, p. 52) and Torrance (2012)).

Non-Governmental Organizations

In general, NGOs function as "watchdogs" and quasi-political counterweights, that is, they challenge the moral and organizational legitimacy of businesses in general and financial institutions in particular (for foundation see Baur, 2011). For instance, NGOs monitor the business activities of EPFIs and their clients[19] and check whether they adhere to the respective CSR standards. They check whether EPFIs and their clients' ethical and socio-environmental commitments and promises have been met or whether they just pay lip service to CSR. In short, they hold financial institutions and their clients "accountable for perceived deficiencies in recognizing and reporting credibly on their social and environmental responsibilities"

(O'Sullivan & O'Dwyer, 2009, p. 558). In case of apparent non-compliance (i.e., adverse socio-environmental impacts, human rights violations and various types of corporate governance scandals), NGOs might start public "naming, blaming and shaming campaigns," customer boycotts and civil disobedience or protest movements. These protesting campaigns often catch media attention and cause negative publicity for the involved EPFIs and their clients. As a consequence, the reputational pressure increases, while the reputational capital of the EPFI and its client(s) decreases. "Public scrutiny of bank activity can be extremely detrimental to a bank's reputation, leading to a devaluation of a bank's brand and potentially a decrease in the stock price.[20] To avoid the negative publicity, private banks began to incorporate into their financial agreements environmental [and social] standards that go above and beyond the standards of the country where the project is being constructed" (Hardenbrook, 2007, p. 206).

To put it differently: Non-CSR behavior might backfire in the sense that it may cause media-driven scandalization, which in turn might directly and negatively affect the reputational capital and stock market value of a company. For instance, if the project developer – the bank's client – performs in a socially and environmentally irresponsible manner, this may cause legal and other financial costs and reduce revenues due to NGO pressure and reputational damage. Thus a direct link between the reputational capital of a company (e.g., a financial institution's client) and its ability to repay loans and/or to generate future revenues exists. Adopting and implementing CSR guidelines and corporate codes of conduct like the Equator Principles – being part of the general (reputation) risk management framework – might provide (some) defense against potential customer boycott and NGO criticism. That is, CSR strategies – properly implemented – might be beneficial since they (ideally) help in enhancing a company's (i.e., a bank's and its client's) reputation (Macve & Chen, 2010, p. 894).

In fact, NGO activism has played a huge (catalyzing) role in developing and adopting the Equator Principles. Almost all of the founding members of the Equator Principles have been targeted in one way or the other by NGO criticism and civil society organizations' advocacy campaigns. This is in particular true for ABN AMRO, Barclays, Citigroup and WestLB.

Prominent examples causing public outcry include:

• Three Gorges Dam project on the Yangtze River in the Peoples Republic of China;
• Baku–Tbilisi–Ceyhan oil pipeline project;

- Sakhalin II oil and gas project in Russia; and
- Orion Paper-Pulp Mill case in Uruguay.

Current controversies include for example:

- Fracking and tar and oil sands mining in Canada and the USA (which has potential negative impacts on the (North American) ecosystem and on climate change[21]);
- Bristol Bay controversy in Alaska (in which the interests of salmon fisheries and indigenous peoples compete, and partially conflict, with those of the copper and gold mining companies);
- Keystone XL oil pipeline from Alberta/Canada to the Gulf of Mexico/USA;
- Enbridge Northern Gateway Pipelines Project (a pipeline proposal connecting the Athabasca oil and tar sands in Alberta/Canada with the Pacific Ocean);
- Belo Monte Dam in the Brazilian Amazon;
- Nicaragua Grand Canal and Development Project (a shipping route currently under construction which will connect the Atlantic Ocean with the Pacific Ocean);
- Marlin mining project in Guatemala (involving the Canadian mining company Glamis Gold/Goldcorp);
- Fenix mining project in Guatemala (involving the Canadian mining company Skye Resources/HudBay Minerals); and
- Pascua Lama mining project[22] in Argentina and Chile (involving the Toronto-based mining company Barrick Gold) (Hardenbrook, 2007, p. 215; Imai, Maheandiran, & Crystal, 2012; Imai, Mehranvar, & Sander, 2007; Lee, 2008; Meyerstein, 2012/2015; Wright, 2012, p. 65).

One of the most important NGOs in the field of project finance is BankTrack. BankTrack is a worldwide operating network and consortium of various NGOs and civil society organizations. It was founded in January 2004 as a side-product of the drafting and standardization process of the Collevecchio Declaration. Currently, 38 member organizations such as Greenpeace, Rainforest Action Network, (local sections of) Friends of the Earth and Facing Finance are part of the "umbrella organization" named BankTrack. BankTrack functions as a watchdog of the activities of global financial institutions and their impact on people and the planet. The organization has played an important role in reviewing and updating the Equator Principles as well as in channeling civil society pressure on the EPFIs. BankTrack's website, for instance, provides a database on current Equator

Principles projects, the respective project sponsors and developers as well as the particular environmental and social risks and impacts. Furthermore, BankTrack publishes regular reports on the Equator Principles' implementation process and EPFIs' business practices. Among its most important publications on the Equator Principles are "The Outside Job" (2011) and "Tiny Steps Forward" (2012).

Project-Affected Communities: Indigenous Peoples

Indigenous peoples[23] are defined as social and cultural groups which possess the following characteristics:

- Self-identification;
- Traditional life styles;
- Socio-cultural distinctiveness from populations in national societies, for example, customary, cultural, socio-economic and political organizations and institutions, and distinct language (much of them facing distinction);
- Collective attachment to geographically distinct habitats or ancestral territories;
- Living in historical continuity in a certain area, or before others "invaded" or came to the area; and
- Experience of subjugation, dispossession, alienation, marginalization, discrimination and exclusion (Amazon Watch, 2011; Anaya, 2004; IFC, 2012a; Performance Standard No. 7, p. 2; Oxfam Australia, 2010; Rumler, 2011).[24]

It is estimated that there are around 370 million indigenous peoples spreading across 90 countries (Labeau, 2012, p. 266). Most indigenous peoples live in remote areas famous for their wilderness and unique ecosystems. Their lives, survival and well-being are intimately entwined with the natural ecosystem, that is, an intimate relationship between indigenous peoples and their land, territory and natural resources exist. In addition, many indigenous peoples do not live as settled agriculturalists. Instead, their farming systems are often based on rotational agriculture that is spread across vast and extensive areas and they live nomad-like lives.

The problem is that many extractive or infrastructure development projects take place in exactly these sensitive ecosystems of high biodiversity and cultural diversity, that is, areas which are extremely vulnerable to the adverse socio-environmental impacts of project finance. Furthermore, several countries, where indigenous peoples live, lack adequate and effective socio-economic and political institutions and governance mechanisms, which are needed to ensure that projects do not negatively affect local communities and the environment. To the contrary, several of these countries even enhance the problems of exclusion and marginalization of indigenous peoples due to a lack of democratic legitimacy and accountability as well as a lack of the rule of law (see also the ILO Convention No. 169 on Indigenous and Tribal Peoples (International Labor Organization, 1989) and the U.N. Declaration on the Rights of Indigenous Peoples (United Nations, 2007)).

THE EQUATOR PRINCIPLES — A STORY OF SUCCESS?

Since their emergence, the Equator Principles have seen a rapid and widespread adoption rate, both in terms of quantity and (regional) diversification. This can be seen — among others — in Fig. 1 which displays the yearly rate of adoption of the Equator Principles since 2003.

Several of the most important banks, that are currently engaged in project finance, have adopted the Equator Principles framework, including Barclays, BNP Paribas, Citigroup, Credit Suisse, Royal Bank of Scotland and ING, to name a few (Equator Principles Association, 2015; for more information about the Equator Principles "diffusion process" see Haack et al., 2010).

Noteworthy is the high rate of adoption between 2003 and 2009 and in particular in the years 2003 (the year of foundation of the Equator Principles initiative), 2007 (the year after the launch of the newly revised IFC Performance Standards as well as EP II) and 2009 (the year after the establishment of the Equator Principles Secretariat).

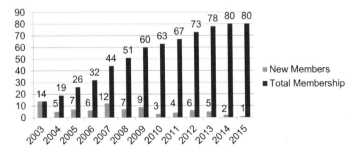

Fig. 1. Adoption of the Equator Principles since 2003. *Source*: M.W. (based on data published by the Equator Principles Association, 2015).

It is also obvious from Fig. 1 that the rapid adoption rate of the early years (2003–2009) has slowed down in the years following the recent financial market crisis, especially after 2009. It has given way to a nearly stagnation or saturation phase – in terms of absolute numbers – in the last few periods: From 2010 to 2014, on average, only four financial institutions joined the Equator Principles per year. A new absolute low-point was reached in 2014 when only two financial institutions – the Commonwealth Bank of Australia and Eksportkreditt Norway – joined the Equator Principles initiative (please note: in the first five months of 2015, only one financial institution – the Taiwanese Cathay United Bank – became a member of the Equator Principles Association; Equator Principles Association, 2015).

Since financial institutions are free to leave the Equator Principles initiative at any time (as has been the case with WestLB/Portigon and Otkritie, the first Russian bank that had adopted the Equator Principles), the total number of EPFIs has fluctuated between 78 and 80 Equator banks in the last few years (*ibid.*).

Taken together, these empirical facts might be interpreted as a sign that the Equator Principles framework has already lost some of its appeal and attraction to potential new candidates and that a slow down might already be under way. To prevent this, a new orientation and realignment strategy seems promising – which is going to be discussed further in part III of this section (see below).

Beside the yearly adoption rate, valuable insights can also be gained by taking a closer look at the regional distribution of signatories of the Equator Principles. Fig. 2 displays the adoption of the Equator Principles by geographical regions.

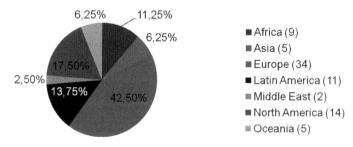

Fig. 2. Adoption of EPs by region. *Source*: M.W. (based on data published by the Equator Principles Association, 2015).

A closer look at the regional distribution of signatories of the Equator Principles reveals that most of the Equator banks have their headquarters either in North America or in (Western) Europe. One reason might be that especially Western European and North American financial institutions face strong reputational pressure to become "green" and to behave socially responsible.[25]

Furthermore, what becomes obvious is that several BRICS countries' banks are not yet a member of the Equator Principles Association (see also the full list of all current EPFIs in the appendix). Particularly the new economic powerhouses, China and India, are underrepresented. As of May 2015, only one Chinese and one Indian bank have joined the Equator Principles Association, while the major Asian players (e.g., Agricultural Bank of China, Bank of China, China Construction Bank, ICBC, ICICI Bank, Sberbank, and State Bank of India) are still missing (Equator Principles Association, 2015). Especially the fact that the major Chinese (global) players are missing is a great drawback for the Equator Principles (Association) since China is a major cross-border lender even larger than the World Bank Group (Meyerstein, 2012/2015, p. 20).

In total, only six Asian banks – three Japanese banks, one Taiwanese bank (Cathay United Bank (member since March 2015)) plus the already mentioned Chinese Industrial Bank Co. and the Indian bank IDFC Ltd. – are members of the Equator Principles Association. Asian banks thus represent only a tiny fraction of all EPFIs (around 6%).[26]

In addition, Equator banks from emerging markets represent around 25–35% of EPFIs – depending on the definition of emerging markets – while there is still a high number of Western European, North American and Australian EPFIs within the Equator Principles Association accounting for up to 60% of all EPFIs.[27] In sum, around 50 out of the current 80 EPFIs are from industrialized countries – a heavy contrast with the regional distribution of project finance markets and the tremendous growth of project finance transactions in Asia (Equator Principles Association, 2015).

The global project finance market has changed tremendously in the aftermath of the recent financial market crisis. While the European and North American shares have dropped significantly – due to limited liquidity, constrained risk appetite, and closed project finance business due to mergers and acquisitions by governments – project finance activity has grown in emerging markets and in particular in Asia. Asian investments account nowadays for up to 45% of the market in 2012 (Lazarus, 2014; Thomson Reuters, 2013).

By 2012 and 2013, the top five banks in the project finance sector were all Asian. However, two of them were not members of the Equator Principles (Association) (i.e., State Bank of India (2012/2013) and Korea Development Bank (2012), respectively, China Development Bank (2013)). This of course threatens the impact of the Equator Principles in the global project finance community since global coverage is missing (i.e., geographical limitations of the Equator Principles). With some major project finance lenders not being an EPFI, the playing field is not completely leveled. Thus, the Equator Principles in their current version cannot guarantee the worldwide application of (minimum) socio-environmental and human rights standards.

What follows from the analyses above is that the Equator Principles Association – together with the EPFIs – should develop a realignment strategy which focuses on two aspects: (1) broadening the regional scope of the Equator Principles and (2) deepening the Equator Principles framework, especially with regards to human rights protection.

Ad 1: The Equator Principles Association must make it a priority to promote the adoption of the Equator Principles in China and India, that is, those countries where most of the project finance activities is taking place (i.e., extension of regional scope). In other words: An outreach and geographical diversification strategy to the BRICS countries is required with the aim to (completely) level the playing field and to guarantee worldwide applicable socio-environmental and human rights standards.

This will be one of the major tasks of the Japanese Mizuho Bank which in March 2014 has been announced as new Equator Principles Association Steering Committee Chair. It was the first time that an Asian bank has been appointed as Equator Principles Association Chair. It remains to be seen whether Mizuho Bank will be successful in promoting the Equator Principles in other areas of the world and in particular in the emerging markets China and India.

Ad 2: The Equator Principles also need a (qualitative) realignment strategy to win over those financial institutions that are not yet a member and/ or dissatisfied with the current strategic focus of the Equator Principles framework. To prevent the risk of losing attraction and popularity, a major (qualitative) overhaul is required, one which also takes into consideration the most recent developments in the business and human rights realm, such as Ruggie's "Protect, Respect and Remedy" framework and the U.N. Guiding Principles on Business and Human Rights (the already mentioned working paper of the Thun Group of Banks on banks and human rights has to be regarded as a first step in the right direction).

Thus, it makes perfect (business) sense for the Equator Principles Association to develop a deepening (and strengthening) strategy — beside the already mentioned broadening strategy. Such a strategy should focus on the question of how to harden the soft law CSR approach (e.g., in terms of human rights protection) and how to establish more mandatory and legally binding governance rules (including formalized enforcement, monitoring, and sanctioning mechanisms) to increase the on-the-ground effectiveness of the Equator Principles (this, in turn, would also increase the reputation and brand value of the Equator Principles — which, in the end, would also benefit the respective member institutions).[28]

At first glance, both strategies — the deepening and the broadening strategies — seem to be mutually incompatible. Yet there is a way to bridge the gap between the broadening (ad 1) and the deepening considerations (ad 2). For example, both aims could be achieved via a structural reform of the Equator Principles Association: A two-tiered Equator Principles Association membership structure (Lazarus & Feldbaum, 2011) reflecting different aspirations would allow EPFIs to voluntarily apply the spirit of the Equator Principles to fields other than project finance, thus moving beyond the rather small project finance sector. This European Union-like "two speeds" or "clubs within the club" structure would allow EPFIs to proactively respond to ethical and environmental issues and to meet the demands of multiple stakeholder groups. EPFIs would have the strategic opportunity to "over-comply" (Kulkarni, 2010), to go beyond what is formally legally and informally required and gain first-mover advantages. They might boost their credibility and as a consequence gain (additional) reputational capital that directly adds to their brand value. In case that the "essence of the Equator Principles" is internalized and embedded throughout the whole organization, this could also trigger a cultural change within banks and other financial institutions (this cultural change could then help to overcome the currently prevailing trust and legitimacy crisis in the banking sector).

While a tiered membership structure once established would allow EPFIs to voluntarily comply with additional and strengthened environmental, social, and human rights standards that go beyond the IFC Performance Standards, it would at the same time take into consideration that some EPFIs are not willing or able to comply with the respective strengthened standards and to bear additional implementation and compliance costs. Nevertheless, these EPFIs would still be part of the Equator Principles Association. This would ensure that at least minimum socio-environmental standards are met and that the human rights of project-affected stakeholder groups are respected (which is not yet the case under the current Equator Principles regime; see Hennig & Wörsdörfer, 2015).

NOTES

1. The Equator Principles are thus a *transnational* self-governing code of conduct. Since this code of ethics binds both the financial organization (and its clients) as well as the respective members of the association it can be classified both as an *intra-organizational* and *associational* code of conduct (cp. Wright & Rwabizambuga, 2006; see for more information on codes of ethics in general: Webb, 2004a, 2004b, 2012; Webb & Morrison, 2004).

2. The *IFC Performance Standards* include the following guidelines: Assessment and Management of Environmental and Social Risks and Impacts; Labor and Working Conditions; Resource Efficiency and Pollution Prevention; Community Health, Safety and Security; Land Acquisition and Involuntary Resettlement; Biodiversity Conservation and Sustainable Management of Living Natural Resources; Indigenous Peoples; and Cultural Heritage (International Finance Corporation, 2012a, 2012b; see also Torrance, 2012).

3. The *EHS Guidelines* are technical reference documents containing examples of good international industry practices. Two sets of guidelines are essential: the *General Environmental, Health and Safety Guidelines* (which contain information and data on cross-cutting environmental, health, and safety issues applicable to all industry sectors; they are divided into sections entitled: Environmental (e.g., air emissions and air quality; energy conservation; water conservation; wastewater; hazardous materials management; waste management; noise pollution); Occupational Health and Safety (e.g., physical, chemical, biological and radiological hazards); Community Health and Safety (e.g., life and fire safety; traffic safety; disease prevention; emergency preparedness); Construction; and Decommissioning) and the *Industry Sector Guidelines* (which contain sector-specific recommendations) (International Finance Corporation/World Bank Group, 2007).

4. Properly implemented and realized Equator Principles can be seen as being part of a conception of good corporate citizenship (Crane & Matten, 2004/2010; Matten & Crane, 2005; Moon, Crane, & Matten, 2005; Néron & Norman, 2008): Financial organizations and their clients form an integral part of society. As such, they have rights and corresponding responsibilities. One of these duties as a good citizen is to contribute to the common good, for example, in the sense of respect for human rights and/or provision of public and social goods (Scherer & Palazzo, 2007, 2008; Scherer, Palazzo, & Baumann, 2006; Scherer, Palazzo & Matten, 2009, 2014).

5. I.e., lenders are held accountable to implement responsible and sustainable lending practices. They are held liable for negative social and environmental externalities of their clients' operations

6. The following quotes refer to the third generation of the Equator Principles (EP III): cp. Equator Principles Association (2013).

7. This includes Scope 1 and Scope 2 emissions: Scope 1 emissions are direct GHG emissions from the facilities themselves while Scope 2 emissions refer to the indirect GHG emissions associated with the off-site production of energy used by the infrastructure or industry project (Equator Principles Association, 2013, p. 19).

8. "... EP 8 requires that the obligations imposed by the project lenders upon the project developers get formalized as covenants in the loan documentation between the bank syndicate and the project developer. By making these requirements covenants, the bank lenders can condition project financing upon their adequate fulfillment and can use their non-fulfillment as conditions of material default, that is, a basis for calling for repayment of the loan ..." (Meyerstein, 2012/2015, p. 26).

9. Interestingly, the new IFC Performance Standards require annual reports for projects emitting over 25,000 (and not 100,000) tons of CO_2 equivalents annually. This implies that the Equator Principles threshold is much higher than the one of the IFC Performance Standards. Thus, the Equator Principles fall behind the commitments made by the IFC. "EP III does not contain any commitments on issues that are beyond what is included in the IFC Performance Standards. In some cases the commitment in EP III is even below what is required in the IFC Performance Standards (such as reporting requirements on CO_2 emissions)" (BankTrack, 2012, p. 8). The Equator Principles should ideally go beyond the Performance Standards of the IFC and not fall behind.

10. Especially projects that circumvent socio-environmental and human rights standards cause the most adverse environmental and social impacts. Yet they also happen to generate the most (corporate) revenue — at least in the short run — due to lower regulation and implementation costs.

11. Project finance is often undertaken as part of a national growth strategy. "It remains particularly popular in emerging markets: in the aftermath of the financial crisis, India developed a $475 billion infrastructure stimulus plan and Brazil has plans to build 24 dams in the Amazon this decade at a cost of roughly $100 billion (the nation already gets 80% of its power from dams but wants to boost its capacity by 60% by 2019 to keep-up with its economy)" (Meyerstein, 2012/2015, p. 9). The need for project finance and in particular infrastructure projects stems also from the fact that developing countries have to meet population growth needs and thus increasing energy and food supply needs.

12. The Governance Rules got updated and revised in 2013 (Equator Principles Association, 2010/2013).

13. EP III also aims at greater consistency in the implementation of the Equator Principles and enhanced transparency through extended reporting requirements.

14. EP III focuses (solely) on carbon dioxide (CO_2) emissions, while other greenhouse gases such as methane (CH_4), nitrous oxide (N_2O), ozone (O_3), and chlorofluorocarbon (CFC) are mainly neglected. In addition, EP III concentrates on fossil fuel burning, while other sources of the greenhouse effect such as deforestation and logging only play a minor role. Moreover, new technologies such as fracking, oil, and tar sands or deep-water drilling raise complex socio-environmental issues such as groundwater contamination, depletion of water reserves, methane leakage, contamination from spills, and related health effects. The question that comes up in light of these new technologies is whether EP III is readily equipped to deal with these rather new technological challenges — which at least partially threaten the overall goal to fight climate change due to their (partial) increase in GHG emissions. As it looks, the Equator Principles as well as the IFC Performance Standards and EHS Guidelines in their current versions provide only limited guidance related to these new technologies (cp. Lazarus, 2014).

15. The business and society relationships between EPFIs, their clients and other stakeholder groups can also be analyzed from a stakeholder theory perspective

(Donaldson & Preston, 1995; Freeman, 1984; Melé, 2008/2013). According to this theory, Equator banks and their clients have certain responsibilities toward their stakeholders (including project-affected communities and the local environment and have to balance and coordinate the (partially) conflicting claims of multiple stakeholder groups.

16. Noteworthy exceptions among the BRICS countries are Brazil with four EPFIs and South Africa with three EPFIs (Equator Principles Association, 2015).

17. For more information see the website of the Equator Principles Association (2015) and in particular: www.equator-principles.com/index.php/about-ep/governance-and-management; www.equator-principles.com/index.php/best-practice-resources/working-groups; www.equator-principles.com/index.php/about-ep/ep-secretariat; and www.equator-principles.com/index.php/adoption/annual-fee.

18. The basic rule for decision-making is valid for Steering Committee decision-making as well as general associational decision-making that materially alters the principles in a major way, as determined by the Steering Committee. Proposals that would change the principles in a minor way require only an absolute majority (50.1%), instead of a two-thirds majority (cp. Equator Principles Association, 2010/2013, p. 13f).

19. Due to the great visibility of most of the financed projects within project finance, socio-environmental and ethical malpractices are highly exposed to external stakeholder pressure, which in turn might cause reputational damage for the companies involved (cp. Wright/Rwabizambuga, 2006, p. 109).

20. Empirical research has shown that properly addressed environmental, social and corporate governance issues positively affect corporate reputation and in the end long-term shareholder value, pointing towards the link between environmental, social and financial performances (cp. Jones & Murrell, 2001; Kulkarni, 2010, p. 474: i.e., corporate social performance as a heuristics and signaling device has positive impacts on the firm's stock price).

21. For example, fracking for shale oil and gas (may) lead to an increase in overall carbon emissions − due to a higher release of methane. In addition, it (might) cause water contamination, pollution from (toxic) wastewater and increased water stress (and a decreased water security). Higher GHG emissions are also expected from oil and tar sands. In sum, fracking, oil, and tar sands seem to have a worse socio-ecological footprint compared to conventional fossil fuels since the extraction process is very energy intensive and (might) cause high carbon impacts (Facing Finance, 2014, p. 68f.).

22. It is noteworthy that two Equator Banks, Ex-Im Bank and Export Development Canada, decided to not finance the project due to NGO pressure and the clear violations of the Equator Principles, including serious human rights violations committed on the Diaguita indigenous community. In October 2013, Barrick Gold has decided to temporarily suspend construction activities at Pascua Lama. This case illustrates that the Equator Principles have the potential to make a difference on the ground. Yet not all EPFIs make use of their leverage over their clients and the Equator Principles still lack proper governance mechanisms, including adequate enforcement, monitoring and sanctioning institutions, that could help to prevent these kinds of dodgy deals.

23. In what follows, the terms indigenous peoples, tribal peoples and aboriginals are used synonymously, since a single, universally accepted definition, which could be applied globally, is lacking. The term "First Nations," however, only refers to aboriginal peoples living in Canada which are neither Inuit nor Métis.

24. In fact, indigenous peoples are often among the most marginalized, disadvantaged and vulnerable groups in society due to a lack of political representation, participation and inclusion, a lack of access to education, healthcare and other social services, and a far-reaching exclusion from power and socio-economic and political decision-making.

25. Scholtens and Dam (2007), for example, found that institutions that adopt the Equator Principles are significantly larger in size than those that do not. The reason is that reputation appears to be more important for large financial institutions since they experience more pressure from NGOs. CSR issues are thus essential for large, multinational banks in the spotlight — which is especially the case in "Western" countries (Kulkarni, 2010, p. 475; Scholtens & Dam, 2007).

26. The BRICS countries are also underrepresented in terms of the Equator Principles Association Steering Committee. Here, only two out of the fifteen representatives come from emerging market institutions (Equator Principles Association, 2015).

27. Most of the member institutions are from high-income OECD countries such as Australia (5 EPFIs), Canada (7), France (4), Germany (4), Spain (5), the Netherlands (6), the United Kingdom (5), and the United States (5) (cp. Equator Principles Association, 2015).

28. A good starting point for further discussions on the societal role of banks in a global political economy could be the working paper of the Thun Group of Banks (2013). The paper provides a first guide to the banking sector for operationalizing the U.N. Guiding Principles on Business and Human Rights. Despite its various shortcomings, the paper nevertheless touches upon the very important topic of the politico-economic role of banks with regards to human rights protection. As recent academic research has shown (cp. Wörsdörfer, forthcoming), the EPFIs are equipped with a considerable leverage over their clients. This leverage could be used to exert considerable pressure on their clients to change their business practices on the ground and to promote socio-environmental and human rights stewardship. In the end, this leverage-based responsibility could make a fundamental difference in reality for project-affected communities and other stakeholder groups (and it could also help to boost the credibility and attractiveness of the entire CSR initiative).

ACKNOWLEDGMENTS

The author would like to thank one anonymous reviewer for his/her constructive comments. They helped to improve the paper significantly. The usual caveats apply.

REFERENCES

Amazon Watch. (2011). *The right to decide: The importance of respecting free, prior and informed consent.* Retrieved from http://amazonwatch.org/assets/files/fpic-the-right-to-decide.pdf. Accessed on July 31, 2014.

Anaya, S. J. (2004). International human rights and indigenous peoples: The move towards the multicultural state. *Arizona Journal of International and Comparative Law, 21*(1), 13–61.

Andrew, J. (2009). Responsible financing? The Equator Principles and bank disclosures. *Journal of American Academy Business, 14*, 302–307.

BankTrack. (2011). *The Outside Job: Turning the Equator Principles towards people and planet.* Retrieved from www.banktrack.org/show/pages/equator_principles. Accessed on July 11, 2014.

BankTrack. (2012). *Tiny steps forward on the Outside Job: Comments on the Equator Principles III official first draft.* Retrieved from www.banktrack.org/show/pages/equator_principles#tab_pages_documents. Accessed on December 18, 2014.

BankTrack. (2013). *BankTrack on the Thun group paper on banks and human rights.* Retrieved from www.banktrack.org/download/banktrack_on_the_thun_group_paper_on_banks_and_human_rights/banktrack_thun_group_paper_131119_0.pdf. Accessed on January 9, 2015.

Baumast, A. (2013). Equator principles. In S. O. Idowu, N. Capaldi, L. Zu & A. Das Gupta (Eds.), *Encyclopedia of corporate social responsibility* (pp. 1045–1051). Dordrecht: Springer.

Baur, D. (2011). *NGOs as legitimate partners of corporations: A political conceptualization.* Dordrecht: Springer.

Collevecchio Declaration. (2003). *The role and responsibility of financial institutions.* Retrieved from www.banktrack.org/download/collevechio_declaration/030401_collevecchio_declaration_with_signatories.pdf. Accessed on December 18, 2014.

Crane, A., & Matten, D. (2004/2010). *Business ethics: Managing corporate citizenship and sustainability in the age of globalization.* Oxford: Oxford University Press.

de Felice, D. (2014). *Banks and human rights: The Thun Group and the UN guiding principles on business and human rights.* Retrieved from http://papers.ssrn.com/sol3/papers.cfm?abstract_id=2477126. Accessed on January 12, 2015.

Donaldson, T., & Preston, L. E. (1995). The stakeholder theory for the corporation; concepts, evidence, implications. *Academy of Management Review, 20*(1), 65–91.

Equator Principles Association. (2010/2013). *Governance rules 2010/2013.* Retrieved from http://equator-principles.com/resources/ep_governance_rules_december_2013.pdf. Accessed on December 18, 2014.

Equator Principles Association. (2013). *The Equator Principles.* Retrieved from http://equator-principles.com/resources/equator_principles_III.pdf. Accessed on December 18, 2014.

Equator Principles Association. (2015). *Equator Principles website.* Retrieved from http://equator-principles.com/index.php/about-ep/about-ep. Accessed on January 10, 2015.

Facing Finance. (2014). Dirty profits III: Report on companies and financial institutions benefiting from violations of human rights. Retrieved from www.facing-finance.org/files/2014/12/Facing-Finance_Dirty-Profits-3_2014_EN_online.pdf. Accessed on January 12, 2015.

Freeman, R. E. (1984). *Strategic management: A stakeholder approach.* Boston, MA: Pitman.

Gonzales Napolitano, S. S. (2011). Equator principles. In *Max Planck encyclopedia of public international law*. Retrieved from http://opil.ouplaw.com/view/10.1093/law:epil/ 9780199231690/law-9780199231690-e1038?rskey=85Alyt&result=1&prd=EPIL. Accessed on December 18, 2014.

Haack, P., Schoeneborn, D., & Wickert, C. (2010). *Exploring the constitutive conditions for a self-energizing effect of CSR standards: The case of the "Equator Principles"*. Working Paper Series, No. 115. Institute of Organization and Administrative Science, University of Zurich, Zurich.

Hardenbrook, A. (2007). The Equator Principles: The private financial sector's attempt at environmental responsibility. *Vanderbilt Journal of Transnational Law, 40*, 197–232.

Hennig, A., & Wörsdörfer, M. (2015). *Challenging voluntary CSR-initiatives: A case study on the effectiveness of the Equator Principles*. Working Paper, Goethe University, Frankfurt.

Imai, S., Maheandiran, B., & Crystal, V. (2012). *Accountability across borders: Mining in Guatemala and the Canadian justice system*. Osgoode CLPE Research Paper 26/2012.

Imai, S., Mehranvar, L., & Sander, J. (2007). Breaching indigenous law: Canadian mining in Guatemala. *Indigenous Law Journal, 6*(1), 101–139.

International Finance Corporation. (2012a). *Performance standards on environmental and social sustainability*. Retrieved from www.ifc.org/wps/wcm/connect/115482804a0255db96fbff d1a5d13d27/PS_English_2012_Full-Document.pdf?MOD=AJPERES. Accessed on December 18, 2014.

International Finance Corporation. (2012b). *Guidance notes: Performance standards on environmental and social sustainability*. Retrieved from www.ifc.org/wps/wcm/connect/ e280ef804a0256609709ffd1a5d13d27/GN_English_2012_Full-Document.pdf?MOD= AJPERES. Accessed on January 10, 2015.

International Finance Corporation/World Bank Group. (2007). *Environmental, health and safety guidelines*. Retrieved from www.ifc.org/wps/wcm/connect/554e8d80488658e4b7 6af76a6515bb18/Final%2B-%2BGeneral%2BEHS%2BGuidelines.pdf?MOD=AJPERES. Accessed on December 18, 2014.

International Labor Organization. (1989). *The Indigenous and tribal peoples convention*. No. 169. Retrieved from www.ilo.org/indigenous/Conventions/no169/lang–en/index.htm. Accessed on April 13, 2015.

Jeucken, M. (2001/2002). *Sustainable finance and banking: The financial sector and the future of the planet*. London: Earthscan.

Jones, R., & Murrell, A. J. (2001). Signaling positive corporate social performance: An event study of family-friendly firms. *Business and Society, 40*(1), 59–78.

Kleimeier, S., & Versteeg, R. (2010). Project finance as a driver of economic growth in low-income countries. *Review of Financial Economics, 19*(2), 49–59.

Kulkarni, P. (2010). Pushing lenders to over-comply with environmental regulations: A developing country perspective. *Journal of International Development, 22*, 470–482.

Labeau, P.-C. (2012). Performance standard seven: Indigenous peoples. In M. Torrance (Ed.), *IFC performance standards on environmental and social sustainability: A guidebook* (pp. 261–294). Markham: LexisNexis.

Lazarus, S. (2014). The equator principles at ten years. *Transnational Legal Theory, 5*(3), 417–441.

Lazarus, S., & Feldbaum, A. (2011). *Equator Principles strategic review: Final report*. Retrieved from www.equator-principles.com/resources/exec-summary_appendix_strategic_review_report.pdf. Accessed on December 18, 2014.

Lee, V. (2008). Enforcing the Equator Principles: An NGO's principled effort to stop the financing of a paper pulp mill in Uruguay. *Northwestern Journal of International Human Rights*, 6(2), 354–373.

Lozinski, A. (2012). The Equator Principles: Evaluating the exposure of commercial lenders to socio-environmental risk. *German Law Journal*, 13(12), 1487–1507.

Macve, R., & Chen, X. (2010). The "equator principles": A success for voluntary codes? *Accounting, Auditing & Accountability Journal*, 23(7), 890–919.

Marco, M. (2011). Accountability in international project finance: The Equator principles and the creation of third-party-beneficiary status for project-affected communities. *Fordham International Law Journal*, 34(3), 452–503.

Matten, D., & Crane, A. (2005). Corporate citizenship: Towards an extended theoretical conceptualization. *Academy of Management Review*, 30(1), 166–179.

Melé, D. (2008/2013). Corporate social responsibility theories. In A. Crane, D. Matten, A. McWilliams, J. Moon & D. S. Siegel (Eds.), *The Oxford handbook of corporate social responsibility* (pp. 47–82). Oxford: Oxford University Press.

Meyerstein, A. (2012/2015). Global private regulation in development finance: The Equator Principles and the transnationalization of public contracting. In M. Audit & S. Schill (Eds.), *The internationalization of public contracts* (pp. 1–41). Brussels: Bruylant.

Missbach, A. (2004). The Equator Principles: Drawing the line for socially responsible banks? An interim review from an NGO perspective. *Development*, 47(3), 78–84.

Moon, J., Crane, A., & Matten, D. (2005). Can corporations be citizens? Corporate citizenship as a metaphor for business participation in society. *Business Ethics Quarterly*, 15(3), 429–453.

Néron, P.-Y., & Norman, W. (2008). Citizenship Inc: Do we really want businesses to be good corporate citizens? *Business Ethics Quarterly*, 18(1), 1–26.

Nwete, B. O. N. (2005). The Equator Principles: How far will it affect project financing? *International Business Law Journal*, 2, 173–188.

Ong, D. M. (2010). From 'international' to 'transnational' environmental law? A legal assessment of the contribution of the 'Equator Principles' to international environmental law. *Nordic Journal of International Law*, 79(1), 35–74.

O'Sullivan, N., & O'Dwyer, B. (2009). Stakeholder perspectives on a financial sector legitimation process: The case of NGOs and the Equator Principles. *Accounting, Auditing & Accountability Journal*, 22(4), 553–587.

Oxfam Australia. (2010). *Guide to free, prior and informed consent*. Retrieved from www.culturalsurvival.org/files/GuideToFreePriorInformedConsent.pdf. Accessed on July 31, 2014.

Richardson, B. J. (2005). The Equator Principles: The voluntary approach to environmentally sustainable finance. *European Environmental Law Review*, 14(11), 280–290.

Rumler, M. (2011). *Free, prior and informed consent: A review of free, prior and informed consent in Australia*. Retrieved from http://resources.oxfam.org.au/pages/view.php?ref=671&k=. Accessed on July 31, 2014.

Scherer, A. G., & Palazzo, G. (2007). Toward a political conception of corporate responsibility: Business and society seen from a Habermasian perspective. *Academy of Management Review*, 32(4), 1096–1120.

Scherer, A. G., & Palazzo, G. (2008). Globalization and corporate social responsibility. In A. Crane, D. Matten, A. McWilliams, J. Moon & D. S. Siegel (Eds.), *The Oxford handbook of corporate social responsibility* (pp. 413–431). Oxford: Oxford University Press.

Scherer, A. G., Palazzo, G., & Baumann, D. (2006). Global rules and private actors: Toward a new role of the transnational corporation in global governance. *Business Ethics Quarterly, 16*(4), 505–532.

Scherer, A. G., Palazzo, G., & Matten, D. (2009). Introduction to the special issue: Globalization as a challenge for business responsibilities. *Business Ethics Quarterly, 19*(3), 327–347.

Scherer, A. G., Palazzo, G., & Matten, D. (2014). The business firm as a political actor: A new theory of the firm for a globalized world. *Business and Society, 53*(2), 143–156.

Scholtens, B., & Dam, L. (2007). Banking on the equator: Are banks that adopted the Equator Principles different from non-adopters. *World Development, 35*(8), 1307–1328.

Thomson Reuters. (2013). *Project finance review full year 2012*. Retrieved from http://dmi.thomsonreuters.com/Content/Files/Q42012_Project_Finance_Review.pdf. Accessed on January 11, 2015.

Thomson Reuters. (2014). Global project finance review: First nine months 2014. Retrieved from http://dmi.thomsonreuters.com/Content/Files/3Q2014_Global_Project_Finance_Review.pdf. Accessed on January 11, 2015.

Thun Group of Banks. (2013). *UN guiding principles on business and human rights*. Discussion Paper for Banks on Implications of Principles 16-21. Retrieved from www.csrandthelaw.com/wp-content/uploads/2013/10/thun_group_discussion_paper.pdf. Accessed on January 9, 2014.

Torrance, M. (Ed.). (2012). *IFC performance standards on environmental and social sustainability: A guidebook*. Markham: LexisNexis Canada.

United Nations. (2007). *Declaration on the rights of indigenous peoples*. Retrieved from http://www.un.org/esa/socdev/unpfii/documents/DRIPS_en.pdf. Accessed on April 13, 2015.

Webb, K. (2004a). Understanding the voluntary codes phenomenon. In K. Webb (Ed.), *Voluntary codes: Private governance, the public interest and innovation* (pp. 3–31). Ottawa: Carleton Research Unit for Innovation, Science and Environment.

Webb, K. (2004b). Voluntary codes: Where to from here? In K. Webb (Ed.), *Voluntary codes: Private governance, the public interest and innovation* (pp. 379–402). Ottawa: Carleton Research Unit for Innovation, Science and Environment.

Webb, K. (2012). *From de-responsibilization to re-responsibilization: The global institutionalization of the social responsibility norm — Exploring the key role of non-state actors and rule instruments in regulating multinational companies*. Retrieved from www.crsdd.uqam.ca/pages/docs/04-2012.pdf. Accessed on April 15, 2015.

Webb, K., & Morrison, A. (2004). The law and voluntary codes: Examining the "tangled web". In K. Webb (Ed.), *Voluntary codes. Private governance, the public interest and innovation* (pp. 97–174). Ottawa: Carleton Research Unit for Innovation, Science and Environment.

Wood, S. (2003a). Environmental management systems and public authorities in Canada: Rethinking environmental governance. *Buffalo Environmental Law Journal, 10*, 129–210.

Wood, S. (2003b). Green revolution or greenwash? Voluntary environmental standards, public law and private authority in Canada. In Law Commission of Canada (Ed.), *New perspectives on the public-private divide* (pp. 123–165). Vancouver, University of British Columbia Press.

Wood, S., & Johannson, L. (2008). Six principles for integrating non-governmental environmental standards into smart regulation. *Osgoode Hall Law Journal, 46*(2), 345–395.

Wörsdörfer, M. (2013). *10 years 'Equator Principles': A critical economic-ethical analysis.* Comparative Research in Law & Political Economy (CLPE) Research Paper Series, Research Paper No. 54/2013. Osgoode Hall Law School.

Wörsdörfer, M. (2014). 'Free, prior and informed consent' and inclusion: Nussbaum, Ostrom, Sen and the Equator Principles framework. *Transnational Legal Theory, 5*(3), 464–488.

Wörsdörfer, M. (forthcoming). The Equator Principles and the 'business and human rights debate': Hype or hope? In R. Tomasic & A. De Jonge (Eds.), *Research handbook on transnational corporations.* Cheltenham: Edward Elgar.

Wright, C. (2009). Setting standards for responsible banking: Examining the role of the international finance corporation in the emergence of the equator principles. In F. Biermann, B. Siebenhüner & A. Schreyrogg (Eds.), *International organizations and global environmental governance* (pp. 51–70). London: Routledge.

Wright, C. (2012). Global banks, the environment, and human rights: The impact of the Equator Principles on lending policies and practices. *Global Environmental Politics, 12*(1), 56–77.

Wright, C., & Rwabizambuga, A. (2006). Institutional pressure, corporate reputation, and voluntary codes of conduct: An examination of the Equator Principles. *Business and Society Review, 111*(1), 89–117.

APPENDIX

Full List of EPFIs (as of May 2015)

ABN Amro; Access Bank; Ahli United Bank; ANZ; Arab African International Bank; ASN Bank NV; Banco Bilbao Vizcaya Argentaria; Banco Bradesco; Banco de Crédito; Banco de Galicia y Buenos Aires; Banco de la República Oriental del Uruguay; Banco do Brasil; Banco Espírito Santo; Banco Mercantil del Norte; Banco Popular Español; Banco Sabadell; Banco Santander; Bancolombia; Bank Muscat; Bank of America Corporation; Bank of Montreal; Bank of Nova Scotia; Bank of Tokyo-Mitsubishi UFJ; Barclays; BMCE Bank; BNP Paribas; CAIXA Economica Federal; CaixaBank; Canadian Imperial Bank of Commerce; Cathay United Bank Co.; CIBanco; CIFI; Citigroup; Commonwealth Bank of Australia; CORPBANCA; Credit Suisse Group; Crédit Agricole Corporate and Investment Bank; Deka Bank; DNB; DZ Bank; Ecobank Transnational; Efic; Eksport Kredit Fonden; Eksportkreditt Norway; Ex-Im Bank; Export Development Canada; Fidelity Bank; FirstRand; FMO; HSBC; IDFC; Industrial Bank; ING Bank; Intesa Sanpaolo; Itaú Unibanco; JPMorgan; KBC Group; KfW IPEX-Bank; Lloyds Banking Group; Manulife Financial; Mauritius Commercial Bank; Mizuho Bank; National Australia Bank; Natixis; Nedbank; NIBC Bank; Nordea Bank; Rabobank Group; Royal Bank of Canada; Royal Bank of Scotland; Skandinaviska Enskilda Banken; Société Générale; Standard Bank; Standard Chartered; Sumitomo Mitsui Banking Corporation; TD Bank Financial Group; U.K. Green Investment Bank; UniCredit Bank; Wells Fargo Bank; Westpac Banking Corporation.

Source: www.equator-principles.com/index.php/members-reporting.

Table A1. Top Banks in the World by Total Assets (US$ billion/March 2014; Bold: Equator Bank).

1.	Industrial & Commercial Bank of China (ICBC)	3,181.882
2.	**HSBC Holdings**	**2,758.453**
3.	China Construction Bank Corporation	2,602.544
4.	**BNP Paribas**	**2,589.195**
5.	**Mitsubishi UFJ Financial Group**	**2,508.846**
6.	**JPMorgan Chase**	**2,476.997**
7.	Agricultural Bank of China	2,470.438
8.	Bank of China	2,435.499
9.	**Crédit Agricole**	**2,346.5610**
10.	**Barclays**	**2,266.8211**
11.	Deutsche Bank	2,250.6412
12.	**Bank of America**	**2,149.8513**
13.	Japan Post Bank	1,968.2714
14.	**Citigroup**	**1,894.7415**
15.	**Société Générale**	**1,740.7516**

Source: www.relbanks.com/worlds-top-banks/assets

Table A2. Top Banks in the World by Market Capitalization (US$ billion/March 2014; Bold: Equator Bank).

1.	**Wells Fargo**	**261.722**
2.	**JPMorgan Chase**	**229.903**
3.	ICBC	196.214
4.	**HSBC**	**191.435**
5.	**Bank of America**	**181.776**
6.	China Construction Bank	160.837
7.	**Citigroup**	**144.638**
8.	Agricultural Bank of China	126.419
9.	Bank of China	115.9210
10.	**Commonwealth Bank of Australia**	**115.3511**
11.	**Banco Santander**	**110.5712**
12.	Allied Irish Banks plc	104.8113
13.	**Westpac**	**99.2214**
14.	**BNP Paribas**	**96.0315**
15.	**Royal Bank of Canada**	**95.1816**

Source: www.relbanks.com/worlds-top-banks/market-cap

Table A3.   Biggest Mandated Project Arrangers 2013/2014 (Bold: Non-Equator Bank; Bold and Italics: Asian Non-EPFI).

Financial Institution	Rank in 2014 (QI-QIII)	Rank in 2013
Sumitomo Mutsui Financial Group (Japan)	1	4
Mitsubishi UFJ Financial Group (Japan)	2	2
BNP Paribas SA (France)	3	16
Mizuho Financial Group (Japan)	4	5
Crédit Agricole CIB (France)	5	7
ING (The Netherlands)	6	11
Commonwealth Bank of Australia (Australia)	7	22
HSBC Holdings PLC (U.K.)	8	9
Société Générale (France)	9	15
Natixis (France)	10	12
ANZ Banking Corp (Australia)	11	23
National Australia Bank	12	18
Santander (Spain)	13	43
RBC Capital Markets (Canada)	14	14
State Bank of India (India)	*15*	*1*
Westpac (Australia)	16	34
KfW IPEX-Bank GmbH (Germany)	17	31
Deutsche Bank (Germany)	18	8
CIBC World Markets Inc.	19	25
Bank of America Merrill Lynch (USA)	20	17
Standard Chartered PLC (U.K.)	21	10
Scotiabank (Canada)	22	44
Citi (USA)	23	20
China Development Bank (China)	*24*	*3*
Barclays (U.K.)	25	6

Source: Thomson Reuters (2014, p. 2).

Table A4.   Biggest Mandated Project Arrangers in 2012
(Bold: Non-Equator Bank).

1.	Mitsubishi UFJ Financial Group (Japan)
2.	**State Bank of India (India)**
3.	Sumitomo Mutsui Financial Group (Japan)
4.	Mizuho Financial Group (Japan)
5.	**Korea Development Bank (South Korea)**
6.	HSBC Holdings PLC (U.K.)
7.	Crédit Agricole CIB (France)
8.	Société Générale (France)
9.	BNP Paribas SA (France)
10.	BBVA (Spain)
11.	Lloyds Bank (U.K.)
12.	Commonwealth Bank of Australia (Australia; EPFI since 2014)
13.	ING (The Netherlands)
14.	National Australia Bank (Australia)
15.	Standard Chartered PLC (U.K.)
16.	IDFC Ltd (India)
17.	UniCredit (Italy/Germany)
18.	**ICICI Bank Ltd (India)**
19.	**Axis Bank Ltd (India)**
20.	ANZ Banking Corp (Australia)
21.	Citigroup (USA)
22.	RBC Capital Markets (Canada)
23.	KfW IPEX-Bank GmbH (Germany)
24.	Santander (Spain)
25.	**Oversea-Chinese Banking (China)**

Source: Thomson Reuters (2013, p. 2).

THE INFLUENCE OF PROFESSIONAL ASSOCIATIONS ON ORGANIZATIONAL ETHICS: THE CASE OF VETERINARIANS

Howard Harris

ABSTRACT

The first veterinary school was founded in 1761, as a professional school not as a trade school. This has had a lasting impact on the role of the veterinarian in society, in industry, and in organizations. This paper recounts the circumstances of the founding of that first school in France and discusses the impact that professional institutions can have on ethics in organizations more generally.

Keywords: Professions; veterinarians; ethics; beliefs; values; virtue

INTRODUCTION

This paper first considers the implications of the transformation over 250 years ago of veterinary practice from an economic or social activity to a profession. After a brief consideration of the innovation of Claude

The Ethical Contribution of Organizations to Society
Research in Ethical Issues in Organizations, Volume 14, 161–175
Copyright © 2015 by Emerald Group Publishing Limited
All rights of reproduction in any form reserved
ISSN: 1529-2096/doi:10.1108/S1529-209620150000014007

Bourgelat in the establishment of the Royal Veterinary Schools in France, the paper identifies common elements of the profession as perceived by Bourgelat and by contemporary professional codes. The paper then discusses the way in which the profession as an organization affects the practice of its members and the ethics of the organizations in which they operate, using veterinarians as an example. The final section considers the profession-organization conflict, especially in relation to the ethical challenges which face employed professionals in a profession where the traditional professional commitment to put the client first has to be balanced with the unalienable need to consider the health, welfare, and respectful treatment of the animal.

A PROFESSION WAS FOUNDED

In 1761 Claude Bourgelat, already Inspector-General of horse-breeding establishments in Lyon, was invited by the French King, Louis XV, to establish a veterinary school. This was the world's first and in 2011 veterinarians around the world celebrated the 250th anniversary of that event and many histories and memories were published, including individual articles (Caple, 2011), special issues and series (Baker, 2011; Larkin, 2011), critical reviews (Reed, 2013), radio programs (Williams, 2012), and websites (Vet2011, 2011). The historical background is, therefore, well reported elsewhere. It is not the founding itself that was so much the cause for celebration among veterinarians as the nature of the foundation and its lasting influence. What Bourgelat founded – not perhaps what the King and their mutual friend the Controller General of Finance Henri-Léonard Bertin had expected – was neither a superior school of horsemanship nor an establishment focused on the eradication of cattle disease.

It was the middle of the eighteenth century, the Enlightenment was well established in Europe, and within 30 years the French monarchy would fall. Bourgelat was a much a philosopher as a veterinarian, corresponding with Rousseau and Voltaire, contributing to Diderôt's *L'Encyclopédie*. He conceived the role of the veterinarian not as economic, concerned with "the prevention of cattle disease, the protection of grazing land and the training of farmers" (Vet2011, 2011) but as a doctor (Robin, 2002) with the oaths and commitments of a profession. Two quotations from his "philosophical testament," the "Rules for the Royal Veterinary Schools" (1777) demonstrate this:

The doors of our Schools are open to all those whose duty it is to ensure the conservation of humanity, and who, by the name they have made for themselves, have won the right to come and consult nature, seek out analogies and test ideas which when confirmed may be of service to the human species and we have realised the intimacy of the relation which exists between the human and the animal machines; this relation is such that either medicine will mutually enlighten and perfect the other when we discard a derisory, harmful prejudice. Then we shall no longer fear that we may degrade or debase ourselves if we study the nature of animals, as if this same nature and truth were not always and everywhere worthy of exploration by whoever is able to observe and reflect.

To "be of service to the human species," "to ensure the conservation of humanity," "to observe and reflect" are at the heart of what Bourgelat was founding. A profession was clearly in his mind as he included in the Rules that graduates of the schools would be "securely anchored in honourable principles ... [and] will prove by their behaviour that they are all equally convinced that riches lie less in the goods one possesses than in the good one can do." Should there be any doubt that this was a radical undertaking, Mitsuda (2007) gives a full account of how the failure of medical doctors to concern themselves with the diseases of animals, and the disinterest of equestrian academies beyond the welfare of saddle horses led to the foundation of the profession.

That Bourgelat had chosen correctly can be seen from the rapid spread of veterinary academies across Europe – first in Paris and then to Vienna, Turin, Copenhagen, Skara in Sweden, Hannover, London, Madrid, Budapest and elsewhere in Europe, 15 establishments before the end of the eighteenth century, all with founding links and leaders from the original Bourgelat schools in Lyon and Paris (Vet2011, 2011).

THE HEART OF THE PROFESSION

What is it that defines a profession? Why is it that we can be confident that professionals were being educated at the Bourgelat school? The traditional professions such as law and medicine established rules for their governance many centuries ago. These included not only rules for members of the professions, such as the Hippocratic oath for doctors first enunciated four centuries before the Common Era (Hippocrates) but also regulation of the relationship between the profession and the state (Watson, 1988). More recently, as other groups have sought recognition as a profession – engineers in 1818, accountants in 1870, for instance – numerous attempts have been made to capture the nature of the professional calling.

One of these, the 1996 Review of Engineering Education in Australia (*Changing the Culture: Engineering Education into the Future: Review Report*, 1996), concluded that there were seven features of a profession. These were:

- a distinct identifiable group;
- a social contract between its members and the community;
- special area of knowledge based on scientific principles and a history of engineering practice;
- application of knowledge and balanced decision making in the context of a social contract;
- code of ethics;
- disciplinary procedures – maintenance of standards; and
- competence, including continuing education/development.

The relevance of such a description to professions beyond engineering is apparent if one replaces "engineering practice" (the single mention of the discipline in the description) with "veterinary practice" and then compares this with the twenty-first century description of the veterinary profession found in the core principles of the Australian Veterinary Association:

- collegiality: we respect, listen to, and support our colleagues
- integrity: we tell the truth, behave ethically, and do what we say we will do
- knowledge: we base our decisions on evidence and actively seek out knowledge
- animal welfare: the health and welfare of animals is our key concern
- innovation: we recognize that creativity and new ideas will help lead the way to the future.

This comparison demonstrates the consistency in the attributes of a profession across disciplines, a point made more generally by Bayles in his discussion of professional power (1986, p. 28). It can be augmented by another, the consistency over time, for vets from 1761 to now, or for doctors over the two thousand years since Hippocrates. The profession has been maintained as an organizational form. This organizational form has, as I will show below, had an impact on the nature of the profession, on its practice, and on the ethics of the organizations with which professionals have dealt. To confirm the consistency over time for the vets compare the "be of service," and "to observe and reflect" from the 1777 *Rules of the Royal Veterinary Schools* with the collegiality, integrity, and innovation of the contemporary code; or the "decision making in the context of a social contract" and the continuing education of the Australian engineering review.

There is therefore, as many others have found (Bayles, 1986; Chadwick, 1994; Cowton, 2009; Davis, 1998), a core of agreement about the nature of a profession, even if there are uncertainties and ambiguities and it remains a contested concept (see for instance Cheney & Ashcraft, 2007). In the context of professions as organizations that have an influence on ethics I now turn to consideration of the particular form of organization of a profession.

THE PROFESSION AS AN ORGANIZATIONAL FORM

A profession is not a business enterprise, nor a joint stock company listed on the stock exchange, nor a partnership, nor a cooperative. Neither is it a social club, nor a registered trade union. But it is an organization, for "the existence of an organization" is one of the three identifying characteristics of a profession according to Michael Bayles (1986, p. 27). Whilst there have been many studies of professional identity, and of the role of the profession in helping to form or maintain that identity in various situations (see Barbour & Lammers, 2015 for a recent review), the nature of the profession as an organizational form has been less considered. As an organizational form it has been under-examined, "given very little time," notwithstanding the "extremely important part" that professions play in contemporary Western societies (Hall, 1946, p. 33) and the "profound influence [they have] on organized activities and society broadly" (Barbour & Lammers, 2015, p. 38). Although the organizational structure of the profession is partly determined "by the legal frameworks and economic systems prevailing in the field" in which its members operate (Barbour & Lammers, 2015, p. 40) this does not fully determine the nature or form of the professional organization. Thus while the structure of the medical profession is in part influenced by the nature of hospitals and the laws relating to medical practice, and that of the engineers or veterinarians by the situations in which they work, this discipline-specific element does not wholly determine the nature of the professional organization.

There is a well-established body of empirical evidence showing "that an individual [draws] on his or her profession for values, beliefs, standards of judgment and intellectual stimulation" (Barbour & Lammers, 2015, p. 43). In particular, it was for the important beliefs relating to "evaluations of what is good, legitimate, and appropriate" that the profession provides a resource, according to the seminal 1957 study by Gouldner (cited in Barbour & Lammers, 2015). This is both support for the proposal that the profession as an organization has impact on the ethics of its members, and a hint as to the distinct nature of the organization that the profession is (of which more later).

The concept of institutional logics can be used to tease out some of the distinctive features of the profession as an organizational form and then to show how this has of itself had an effect on organizations more generally, especially those in which professionals work, and thence on ethics. According to the institutional logics approach "institutions exert influence on individuals and organizations in part through identity and identification" and institutional logics "provides resources for the understanding the interplay of institutional and organizational structures" (Barbour & Lammers, 2015, pp. 43, 44). There is an interplay in which collective identities become institutionalized, develop particular institutional logics, and reinforce patterns of identification within the group and the key elements of that interplay are belonging, attachment, and beliefs, where beliefs can be "articulated as statements of what *should* be" (Barbour & Lammers, 2015, p. 44, emphasis in original).

A recent study of over three thousand professionals showed that beliefs are important elements of professional life and cannot be subsumed as aspects of belonging or professional attachment. The study measured a number of aspects of professional and organizational attachment including beliefs in autonomy and self-regulation and found "that belonging, attachment and belief are related but independent" (Barbour & Lammers, 2015, p. 51). Recalling that for Barbour and Lammers beliefs are inherent in the institutional logics, that they are "statements of what *should* be," it can be argued that the distinctive purpose of a profession is to provide statements of what should be. No other organization has such a role. Many organizations have mission statements, but these are expressions of overarching goals, a declaration of core purpose, a state it is desired to achieve and do not carry any moral force or sense of ethical obligation. The requirement to provide statements of what should be places a distinctly ethical responsibility on the profession as an organization and requires that it have a distinctly ethical purpose.

Moore (2012) makes a somewhat similar point to the idea that the role of the profession is to provide what should be when he proposes the concept, within the framework of MacIntyre's virtue ethics, of the need for a "practice" within an institution (taken in the MacIntyrean sense) with the responsibility or purpose of maintaining the institution so that the practices which constitute the institution are sustained, providing a way for the governance and a crowding in rather than the crowding out of virtue. Further consideration of this virtue-focused approach may provide "a better foundation for our own understanding of business and professional behavior" (Zinaich, 2004). Virtues are such because they are required elements of the good life, the *eudaimonia* of Aristotle's (1953) *Nicomachean Ethics*. For a virtue ethics to be effective there must be a measure of agreement about the *telos* or good life (Zinaich, 2004). A professional organization is one in which there is a shared view of the good life. In the study of professionals referred to above, attachment and belief were the most distinctive features of professional identity (Barbour & Lammers, 2015, p. 51). Even those who might be inclined to think that a profession is better described as "a conspiracy of powerful occupational workers" and are skeptical regarding the particular view of the good life the professionals might hold in common, acknowledge the collective power that a common view of the good life can have (May, 2013, p. 52, after Evetts).

The ethical responsibility of the profession is recognized in a different way by Berger, Cunningham, and Drumwright (2007) in their paper about corporate social responsibility. They describe companies where the market for virtue is inside the organization, where it is not determined by external market forces, but where corporate social responsibility (CSR) actions are "incorporated, structured, managed, and diffused within organizations [and] where they are considered part of the 'mainstream' agenda" (Berger et al., 2007, p. 136). The success of this "mainstreaming" of CSR relies on the creation of an "authentic and vibrant internal market for virtue" (Berger et al., 2007, p. 147); Similarly, I would argue to the role of a profession in the creation of an authentic and vibrant culture in which what should be done is internalized and mainstreamed.

For much of their history the professions have been based in the West (and its colonial outposts) and the discussion in this paper has thus far been exclusively Western. Hall, over 50 years ago, argued that the nature of the profession as an organization "should be interesting merely for the fact that in no other type of society have they developed in comparable fashion" (Hall, 1946, p. 33). Some have argued that professions had an important role to play "in the creation of [the] modern capitalist order," (May, 2013, p. 52) suggesting a symbiotic relationship between professions and Western society. The importance of beliefs in the development of professional identity may go some way to explaining why no distinctly non-Western notion of the profession has emerged – Confucian or Islamic, say – and why no professions as we know them in the West emerged autonomously in the East. This is not a topic to be pursued here.

Barbour and Lammers talk of professions "more or less well established" (2015, p. 54). I would suggest that "well established" might properly refer to how well the beliefs were established, to how well they were "incorporated, structured, managed and diffused" (Berger et al., 2007, p. 136) rather than to the length of time that had elapsed since the profession had been formally established. Thus the vets, who emerged with values and beliefs fully founded, might have a double advantage over those professions whose foundation began more recently and with a rather more commercial and less clearly ethical focus.

THE PROFESSION AS AN ORGANIZATION AND ITS INFLUENCE ON ETHICS

In this section, I consider the influence that the professions, that "workable, organizational model, based on self-regulation by individuals with standards and integrity, and value systems that emphasize the good of society" (May, 2013, p. 52) have had on ethics. The discussion will be based on the example of the veterinarians. The influence of a profession arises from the nature of the profession and its identifying characteristics (Bayles, 1986, p. 29), and as there is a commonality in the identifying features of professions the use of one as an example is warranted, even though each profession is to some extent influenced by its context and the societal and disciplinary context of the veterinarian is clearly distinct from that of the medical doctor, engineer, or lawyer. The vets are a useful and valid example, not least because the discipline is distinct in a way that accountancy or management is not, because the anniversary in 2011 occasioned a flurry of conferences and publications about the place of the veterinary profession in society and that material is available to support this discussion (see for instance Beggs, 2011; Wathes, Corr, May, McCulloch, & Whiting, 2013), and because of the variety of ways in which veterinarians relate to society. Three distinct ways in which the veterinary profession has influenced ethics are in the influence the profession, as an organization has had on the practice and ethics of vets over the centuries; in the way in which vets, influenced by their profession, have influenced ethics across the world; and in the example of vets as professionals in a relationship with an organization.

One way in which professions influence ethics is by developing members' identity. We have already seen that identity is a key feature of professional life and although the means by which a professional organization "signals" to its membership the key aspects of "what should be done" remains unclear there is little doubt that there is a "connection between identity and institutional order" (Barbour & Lammers, 2015, p. 39). All professions have an organizational base. It provides the collegiality, defines the group through membership criteria, is necessary for the establishment and continuance of the social contract between profession and state, administers the code of ethics, and provides the machinery for the internal disciplinary process. Without this organizational structure, the seven features of a profession mentioned above could not be maintained. A recent examination of the efforts being made "to strengthen ethical behavior across our organisations and institutions" draws attention to the importance of institutional structures in any effort to strengthen ethical behavior, calling these structures "a necessary component of civil society" (Donnelly & Bowden, 2012, p. 65). Indeed members of the professions, who through their participation in the life of the profession have come to "understand the ethical framework of their value system" might well have both the capacity to take part in the wider debate about the nature of society and a "broader social responsibility" to do so (May, 2013, p. 52). Through the organization, ethics is influenced at personal and societal levels.

Professional organizations also engage in more formal continuing education. For veterinarians the institutions – first the schools and then professional bodies – have played this role for over 250 years. The inclusion of schools or professional academies in this alongside the formal professional bodies is instructive. The early history of the veterinary profession in Australia is one of interplay (some might say competition and dispute) between accreditation bodies and educational institutions as they worked out how the specific needs of the Australian colonies would be allowed to influence the practices and beliefs of the UK-based institutions (Baker, 2011; Caple, 2011). The organization that emerged, the Australian Veterinary Association, has clear lineage to the Bourgelat foundations and its core principles are written in the form of statements about what should be done. Perhaps as a result, veterinarians, in Australia at least, are among the most trusted of professionals (Flynn, 2014).

Two other aspects of continuing education activity by professional organizations relate to capability development. Ethical competence among members can be developed by the promulgation or advancement of the beliefs and values inherent in professions. James Rest's four-step model of

ethical decision making (Rest & Narváez, 1994) reminds us that ethical problems are not confined to dilemmas, where it is hard to discern the correct
course of action. The engineers (in the features of a profession listed above)
talk of "balanced decision making in the context of a social contract."
Sometimes it is the action step that is the most difficult, bringing oneself to
do what is clearly right. Ethical action requires courage, fortitude, strength
of will, as well as analytical discernment (McCoy, 1985). These are attributes or virtues best developed in community, and the professional organization is well placed to provide relevant examples and exemplars.

Another aid to ethical decision comes in the form of decision guides or
heuristics, made available to assist ethical decision making and problem
identification. Some of the best known of these are developed and distribu-
ted by professional associations (see for instance the American Accounting
Association's AAA test in Grace & Cohen, 2010). Although such aids can
be seen as formulaic, their association with the professional body can be a
reminder to users that judgment is the province of the professional, in
Bourgelat's words "to observe and reflect" rather than to follow a formula.

Professional organizations, with a responsibility to state what should be
done, influence ethics at personal and societal levels, provide examples of
organizations which have ethical responsibilities, and contribute to the
development of ethical capabilities among their members.

ETHICS IN THE PROFESSION-ORGANIZATION
CONFLICT

A social contract is often said to be at the heart of the professional relationship. In its typical form, the contract provides that "in exchange for the
statutory restriction of [certain acts] to the profession, [members of the pro-
fession] must act in the interests of society and its members" (May, 2013,
p. 46). Traditionally, the professional was a sole practitioner and thus had
only the relationships with client and society to consider. Today, many professionals are employed by governments, corporations, or local practice
groups. That makes the "balanced decision making in the context of a
social contract" element of professional practice more complex and
demanding. So much so that it has been identified and studied as the profession-organization conflict. An individual who is the member of a profession and an employee, manager, or director in an organization has an
identity as a member of his or her profession and another identity as a
member of the organization.

This immediately complicates ethical decision making by making the choice of a value set against which to form ethical judgments anything but trivial. Both organization and profession may have well established, clearly expressed values and beliefs and they will not always be congruent. The Institute of Chartered Accountants in England and Wales has responded by developing two codes of practice, one for sole practitioners and one for accountants in employment (Chartered Accountants Joint Ethics Committee, 1996).

The profession-organization conflict is difficult enough in itself, as the "professional identity is distinctive among the sorts of identities experienced at work because of its extra-organizational character ... It is by definition multilevel involving the individual, the organization and the institutional" (Barbour & Lammers, 2015, p. 43). The situation for physicians and other professionals with responsibility for individual living clients is even more complex, while for vets the equation includes the animal, client, and society. The majority of the ethical dilemmas for vets arise from this triangular relationship and the resolution depends on "the concept of the profession held by the individual clinician" (May, 2013, p. 50), taking us back to the matter of professional identity and values. Trust can be abused, especially when the veterinarian has a clear knowledge advantage and the client is emotionally distressed, or when a single issue such as animal rights advocacy gains supremacy. The individual practitioner may find it difficult to maintain a balanced view, despite acculturation and professional collegiality, and additional resources may need to be devoted to development of the capabilities necessary for members to make recognize moral issues, to make reasoned judgments, and to act upon them in a way consistent with the clearly articulated beliefs of the profession. It would seem "reasonable" that professionals were able to understand their responsibility and to cope with ambiguity (Pritchard, 2006, p. 6), and this is the goal of many professional degrees and continuing professional development programs. For a wider discussion of professionalism and agency in the veterinary context see May (2013), and of the role which professional societies can play in the practice of the profession see the chapter on "protecting engineering judgment" in Davis (1998).

THE VETERINARY PROFESSIONAL AS ROLE MODEL

Certain aspects of the work of veterinarians have meant that they have been abundant providers of role models for the placing of professional identity and values above those of employers or commercial interest. The vet as quarantine officer, as livestock inspector, or as the veterinary officer at the racetrack or equestrian competition provides a very public example of the professional doing his or her job according not to the immediate commercial interests of the employer, nor to the owner or rider, but by placing the professional commitment to the welfare of the animal above all. And doing so in a belief that welfare to animals is for the good of society. Throughout the centuries, the veterinary profession's professional bodies, whatever called, have supported their members in this professional endeavor. The organizations have influenced the ethical behavior of their members, and by providing role models and exemplars, have influenced the ethical behavior of professionals more generally.

Not all problems have been solved. Contemporary veterinary practice provides many examples of ethical problems, both dilemmas and matters of will. How to respond to the pet owner who refuses to accept well-founded advice that the pet is in distress and the best action is termination of life in the surgery? Should the animal be returned to the owner when it is obvious that this will not promote the welfare of the animal? Regardless of the local regulations, does the vet have any moral obligations, and to whom?

In public health, how are the economic interests of the home country to be balanced in quarantine decisions with fairness or concern for people in less developed countries? To what extent should one allow imperfect science to be used to support decisions which are designed to achieve partisan or economic outcomes? Should racehorses be whipped? That the veterinarian, supported by the profession, is an active participant in the discussion of these ethical questions and yet remains one of the most trusted professionals (Flynn, 2014) shows that vets have, at least in part, been successful in operating within the social contract and consistent with the values of the profession.

CONCLUSION

Two hundred and fifty years ago Bourgelat founded a profession. He recognized that France needed animal doctors and veterinary schools, not solely for their ability to halt the then rampant spread of cattle disease or to train farmers, but also for their valuable contribution to society. Professionals to observe and reflect, to apply knowledge and render balanced judgments.

That requirement remains. The context in which the veterinarian operates is perhaps more complex, more interlinked than it was in the eighteenth century, but the ethical component of professional practice is as essential now as then. The example of the vets has allowed us to consider the form of organization that the profession is, one dedicated to instilling beliefs within its members, to the statement of what should be. Such a profession can influence ethics, through the professional development of its members and as an organization that engages in reasonable debate about contemporary issues both directly and by supporting its members as they engage in ethical debate in the community and in the organizations in which they work.

ACKNOWLEDGMENTS

An earlier, shorter version of this paper was given as an address at the conference of the Australian Veterinary Association in Adelaide in 2011, on the occasion of the two hundred and fiftieth anniversary of the founding of the Bourgelat school. The comments from participants and organizers at that conference, and those from reviewers for this journal, are gratefully acknowledged.

REFERENCES

Aristotle (1953). *Nicomachean ethics*. Harmondsworth: Penguin Books.

Baker, H. J. (2011). 250 years of veterinary service to animal and human health. *Journal of Veterinary Medical Education, 38*(3), 209. doi:10.3138/jvme.38.3.209

Barbour, J. B., & Lammers, J. C. (2015). Measuring professional identity: A review of the literature and a multilevel confirmatory factor analysis of professional identity constructs. *Journal of Professions and Organization, 2*(1), 38–60. doi:10.1093/jpo/jou009

Bayles, M. D. (1986). Professional power and self-regulation. *Business & Professional Ethics Journal, 5*(2), 26–46.

Beggs, D. (Ed.). (2011). *Australian veterinary association 2011 annual conference*. Adelaide: Australian Veterinary Association.

Berger, I. E., Cunningham, P., & Drumwright, M. E. (2007). Mainstreaming corporate social responsibility: Developing markets for virtue. *California Management Review, 49*(4), 132–157.

Caple, I. W. (2011). A short history of veterinary education in Australia: the 120-year transition from education for a trade to education for a profession. *Australian Veterinary Journal, 89*(8), 282–288. doi:0.1111/j.1751-0813.2011.00810.x

Chadwick, R. (Ed.) (1994). *Ethics and the professions*. Aldershot: Avebury.

174   HOWARD HARRIS

Changing the Culture: Engineering Education into the Future: Review Report. (1996). Canberra: The Institution of Engineers Australia.

Chartered Accountants Joint Ethics Committee (1996). *Guidance on ethical matters for members in business.* Milton Keynes: The Institutes of Chartered Accountants In England & Wales, Scotland and Ireland.

Cheney, G., & Ashcraft, K. L. (2007). Considering "The Professional" in communication studies: Implications for theory and research within and beyond the boundaries of organizational communication. *Communication Theory, 17*(2), 146–175. doi:10.1111/j.1468-2885.2007.00290.x

Cowton, C. C. (2009). Accounting and the ethics challenge: Re-membering the professional body. *Accounting and Business Research, 39*(3), 177–189.

Davis, M. (1998). *Thinking like an engineer: Studies in the ethics of a profession.* New York, NY: Oxford University Press.

Donnelly, A., & Bowden, P. (2012). Institutionalising ethical behaviour. In P. Bowden (Ed.), *Applied ethics* (pp. 63–80). Brisbane: Tilde University Press.

Flynn, H. (2014, July). Who do we trust? 2014. *Readers Digest Australia,* 34–37.

Grace, D., & Cohen, S. (2010). *Business ethics* (4th ed.). South Melbourne: Oxford University Press.

Hall, O. (1946). The informal organization of the medical profession. *Canadian Journal of Economics and Political Science, 12*(1), 33–40. doi:10.1017/S0315489000018995

Hippocrates. Hippocratic Oath (F. Adams, Trans.). *Works* (Vol. 1). New York, NY: Loeb.

Larkin, M. (2011, January 1). Pioneering a profession: The birth of veterinary education in the age of enlightenment. *JAVMA News.*

May, S. A. (2013). Veterinary ethics, professionalism and society. In C. M. Wathes, S. A. Corr, S. A. May, S. P. McCulloch, & M. C. Whiting (Eds.), *Veterinary & Animal Ethics: Proceedings of the First International Conference on Veterinary and Animal Ethics, September 2011* (pp. 44–58). Wheathampstead, UK: Universities Federation for Animal Welfare.

McCoy, C. S. (1985). *Management of values.* Marshfield, MA: Pitman.

Mitsuda, T. (2007). The equestrian influence and the foundation of veterinary schools in Europe, c. 1760–1790. *eSharp, 10.*

Moore, G. (2012). Virtue of governance: The governance of virtue. *Business Ethics Quarterly, 22*(2), 293–318.

Pritchard, M. (2006). *Professional integrity: Thinking ethically.* Lawrence, KA: University Press of Kansas.

Reed, W. M. (2013). What it means to be inclusive and why it is imperative for the veterinary profession. In L. M. Greenhill, K. C. Davis, & P. M. Lowrie (Eds.), *Navigating diversity and inclusion in veterinary medicine* (pp. viii–xi). West Lafayette, IN: Purdue University Press.

Rest, J. R., & Narváez, D. (Eds.). (1994). *Moral development in the professions.* Hillsdale, NJ: Erlbaum.

Robin, D. (2002). Bourgelat et les ecoles veterinaries. *Bulletin La Société d'Histoire de la Médecine et des Sciences Vétérinaires, 1*(1). Retrieved from http://sfhmsv.free.fr/SFHMSV_files/Textes/Activites/Bulletin/Txts_Bull/B1/Robin_B1.pdf

Vet2011. (2011). *The birth of veterinary science.* Retrieved from http://www.vet2011.com/en_bourgelat1.php. Accessed on November 21, 2010.

Wathes, C. M., Corr, S. A., May, S. A., McCulloch, S. P., & Whiting, M. C. (Eds.). (2013). *Veterinary & animal ethics: Proceedings of the first international conference on veterinary and animal ethics, September 2011.* Wheathampstead, UK: Universities Federation for Animal Welfare.

Watson, J. G. (1988). *The civils.* London: Thomas Telford.

Williams, R. (2012). 250 years of veterinary education. *Ockhams Razor* [Radio], Australian Broadcasting Corporation.

Zinaich, S., Jr. (2004). Returning to virtue theory: Some problems and challenges. *Global Virtue Ethics Review, 5*(4), 50–89.

FROM LAWYER TO LEADER: AN ANALYSIS OF ABRAHAM LINCOLN'S MORAL SELF

Elizabeth C. Vozzola, Paul A. Cimbala and Karen Palmunen

ABSTRACT

Moral exemplars provide us with important case studies of optimal moral flourishing. Although most historians rate Abraham Lincoln as the most moral American president, their analyses do not utilize the perspective of moral development theory or research. This project asked whether such a perspective could contribute to a better understanding of Lincoln's abundantly well-examined self and actions. This study examined the moral self of U.S. President Abraham Lincoln through close textual analysis of his brief autobiographical writings and his ethical turning point, his 1854 Peoria Speech attacking the morality of slavery. Even the limited sample of one major speech and three brief writings about life events provided evidence for the usefulness of McAdams' method of examining life narratives for central themes and textual elements and for Colby and Damon's (1992) method of interviewing exemplars and identifying common traits. Our methods allowed for no carefully constructed interview or clarification questions but rather relied on historical texts constructed for

The Ethical Contribution of Organizations to Society
Research in Ethical Issues in Organizations, Volume 14, 177–188
Copyright © 2015 by Emerald Group Publishing Limited
ISSN: 1529-2096/doi:10.1108/S1529-209620150000014008

political goals. Major figures in the exploration of moral selves suggest that the centrality of morality to people's sense of self lies at the heart of moral motivation and action. Studies of historical moral exemplars provide individuals and organizations with powerful role models for optimal ethical functioning and highlight the importance of fostering the centrality of morality in organizational leaders.

Keywords: Moral exemplars; Lincoln; leader

Polls in which historians and political scientists are asked to name the greatest United States president invariably put Abraham Lincoln at the top of the list. For example, with a rating scale running from -2 (failure) to 4 (great), the oft-cited 1996 Schlesinger poll gives Lincoln a mean score of 4. Invariably, Lincoln is cited as not only the greatest American president, but also one of, if not *the*, most moral. His life and accomplishments have been examined in literally thousands of books and biographies, some focusing specifically on his ethics and virtues; and yet these analyses did not utilize the perspective of moral development. Thus, the research question for this project asked whether such a perspective could contribute to a better understanding of Lincoln's abundantly well-examined self and actions.

Our method involved four lines of inquiry: (1) an in-depth exploration of the psychological literature on moral exemplars and the moral self (e.g. Walker, 2013); (2) an immersion in well-regarded biographies of Lincoln that focused on his ethics, virtues, or morality; and (3) a close textual analysis of three brief autobiographical writings (Abraham Lincoln Online) and (4) of a primary document that marked a major turning point in his life, his 1854 Peoria Speech in response to the repeal of the Missouri Compromise. In this pivotal speech that resurrected his political career, the successful Illinois lawyer attacked the morality of slavery itself. Although this paper focuses on applying the lens of moral development theory and methods to sample passages from the Peoria Speech and Lincoln's autobiographical fragments, our interpretation of that evidence is also supported by our deep reading of extensive biographical information.

PART I: THE MORAL SELF/PERSONALITY AS KEY TO MORAL MOTIVATION AND ACTION

For many years the field of moral development has grappled with the implications of research demonstrating a gap between people's scores on measures of moral reasoning complexity and their actual moral behavior. Gus Blasi's work moved from his classic review documenting the judgment action gap (1980) to a compelling theoretical argument (e.g., Blasi, 2004, 2009) that the concept of *moral identity* best integrates "moral cognition and moral personality within a framework that better explicates moral behavior" (Walker, 2004, p. 2). Very briefly, Blasi's self theory proposes three major components of moral functions:

- *Moral self*: It is defined as the extent to which moral considerations and values are central to a person's self-identity.
- A sense of *personal responsibility for moral action*: Blasi, like many other theorists, suggests that the sense of a moral obligation to act on our moral judgments may be rooted in early attachment relationships.
- *Psychological self-consistency*: People strive to be seen by themselves and others as good person – a motive that can either result in Freudian rationalizations or actual consistency between beliefs and actions.

Blasi (2004) has noted that the moral self may only become fully constructed and integrated in adulthood and we will argue that analysis of Lincoln's 1854 Peoria Speech, made when he was 45 years old, provides compelling retrospective evidence that (a) the moral value of opposition to slavery moved to the center of his identity; (b) he felt a deep sense of personal responsibility to speak out against its further spread; and (c) his moral beliefs and public actions came seamlessly together in the mature moral self that has been universally recognized and respected.

With the central and overarching goal of exploring the emergence of Lincoln's mature moral self, we used concepts from McAdams' life stories research paradigm to analyze key passages in Lincoln's 1854 Peoria Speech; especially the self-identified *turning point* in Lincoln's life narrative and construction of self. We also applied a literary analysis approach in which we examined evidence of how Lincoln's choice of language and imagery in the speech reflects Lincoln's personality traits and compared them to those identified in moral exemplar research.

PART II: THE HISTORICAL CONTEXT FOR LINCOLN'S SHIFT IN IDENTITY: THE 1854 KANSAS–NEBRASKA ACT

During the first decades of the 19th century, the fledgling American democracy had held together an uneasy union of Northern and Midwestern states increasingly appalled at slavery and its extension, and Southern and Western states increasingly concerned that the right to own slaves was under assault. The famous Missouri Compromise of 1820 had barred slavery north of the 36°30′ parallel of the Louisiana Purchase territory. Both free states and slave states made significant concessions but, in general, especially in Northern states, the act was viewed as a *sacred compact* legislated in good faith. And then in 1854, the Kansas–Nebraska Act, sponsored by the "Little Giant," Illinois Senator Stephan A. Douglas, upended the fragile compromise by repealing the 1820 prohibition of slavery in what was then called the Kansas–Nebraska territory. Douglas argued for "popular sovereignty," or letting the voters of the territory decide for themselves whether to come into the union as a free or slave state. Lincoln and other Whigs and free-soil Democrats worried that the act would not only open the door to the spread of slavery but also possibly lead to its eventual nationalization (Lehrman, 2008). On October 16, 1854, Lincoln and Douglas publicly aired their conflicting views before large audiences in Peoria.

PART III: LINCOLN'S TURNING POINT

"On the extension of slavery I am inflexible. Have none of it. Stand firm. As with a chain of steel."

Dunlap and Walker's (2013) study of psychological factors underlying brave actions suggested that different kinds of exemplars might show unique patterns of traits. Thus, we hypothesized that we might find traits reflecting Lincoln's unique historical time, place, and role. Indeed, even though after 1854 we see a definite shift in Lincoln from the highly successful lawyer willing to take on pretty much any case that comes his way (Miller, 2002) to a morally centered self committed to containing the spread of slavery; he remained nevertheless a shrewd and effective politician throughout his life. In short, the political context for both his speech and his autobiographies matters and has to be acknowledged in any close analysis of public documents and speeches (Horrocks, 2014).

In his insightful book identifying the Peoria Speech as Lincoln's turning point, Lewis Lehrman (2008) concludes: "Master of himself and master of his political and economic philosophy, the forty-five-year old lawyer became a master of men" (p. xviii). The abstract principles that would later inform his great moral actions — the Emancipation Proclamation of 1863 and the abolition of slavery in the Thirteenth Amendment in 1865 — were there first "joined to a bold but prudential wisdom, expressed in unforgettable argument" (p. xviii).

Lincoln's Moral Self Through the Lens of McAdam's Narrative Method

Lincoln was known not only as a great president but also as a great story-teller. That attribute ultimately steered us to select as one lens for our analysis Dan P. McAdams' (1993, 2013) method of viewing identity as a life story or personal myth. Like Colby and Damon (1992), McAdams (1993, 2013) employs an interview method rooted in a respectful mutual relationship between the listener (researcher) and the participant (storyteller). To guide the life story construction, his participants are asked to divide their life into major chapters and briefly describe each. They are then asked to describe in great detail eight key events in their life stories: a peak experience, a nadir experience, a turning point, the earliest memory, an important childhood memory, an important adolescent memory, an important adult memory, and an additional particular event from their past that stands out. The method arises from McAdams' belief that " identity is a life story ... a personal myth that an individual begins working on in late adolescence and young *adulthood in order to provide his or her life with unity or purpose*" (1993, p. 5). His research suggests that people come to know themselves by creating, both consciously and unconsciously, "a heroic story of the self" (1993, p. 11), organizing their stories around the lines of two central themes: *agency* and *communion*.

McAdams (1993) has found that the first two years of life "leave us with a set of unconscious and nonverbal 'attitudes' about self, other, and world, and about how the three relate to each other" (p. 47). These attitudes set the "narrative tone" for the myths we construct in adulthood. McAdams does not, however, argue for a simple correspondence between life history and narrative tone. Rather, he believes that constructed life stories or personal myths "involve an imaginative reconstruction of the past in light of an envisioned future" (p. 53).

McAdams (1993) has noted, "We don't know what personal myth Abraham Lincoln developed for himself. But it is quite clear that Americans since have employed an antithetical strategy (rags to riches, bad past/good present, etc.) in constructing and celebrating their understanding of his life" (p. 104). Although we may not have sufficient autobiographical material to determine Lincoln's life myth, a careful textual analysis of his autobiographies and his Peoria Speech allows us to examine one piece of the construction of his moral self in some depth.

In the second part of their interviews, McAdams' participants are asked to describe a key life *turning point*, defined as "An episode wherein you underwent a significant change in your understanding of yourself ... in retrospect, you see the event as a turning point, or at minimum as symbolizing a significant change in your life" (1993, p. 258). Given our specific interest in the point at which Lincoln publically manifests a mature moral self, we were lucky to find him addressing the issue of his life turning point explicitly in two of his three autobiographies. In 1859, at age 50, as the 1860 presidential election approached, Lincoln wrote a brief autobiography for a Republican friend to be published in a Pennsylvania newspaper (a common campaign tactic of the day). The four-paragraph piece contains this terse description: "*I was losing interest in politics when the repeal of the Missouri Compromise aroused me again.*" A year later, in 1860, a Chicago reporter requested an autobiography that he could use to write a campaign biography. Lincoln wrote a longer piece in the third person with description of his rise from humble beginnings sure to resonate with Western and Northern free labor voters who believed "that one could improve one's station in life through 'hard work and self discipline'" (Horrocks, 2014, p. 3). And, as he did in the second autobiography, he ended this third text by highlighting the major turning point of his life to that time: "*In 1854 his profession had almost superseded the thought of politics in his mind, when the repeal of the Missouri Compromise aroused him as he had never been before.*"

One way then in which the moral development perspective may enhance the many rich and extensive historical studies is to do a close analysis of the developmental processes by which he integrated his political self with an increasingly central and mature moral self. Lawrence Kohlberg, with his conception of cognitive development and role-taking ability providing necessary, but not sufficient, conditions for moral development, would likely have loved the fact that this brilliant but self-educated wise-cracking lawyer emerged from a period of deep research into the laws and history of slavery as a very different man – a morally self-educated man.

And although that morally self-educated man left us no memoir and only snippets of campaign autobiographies about his own life story, we do have the major narrative of Lincoln's Peoria Speech – the story of slavery – that provides us with ecologically valid insights into the moral self telling that story. Despite the fact that Lincoln went into this period of research having been exposed to all the prejudices and biases of a person of his time and place, historians frequently note that something about him from his early years suggested an emerging humanitarian bent to his personality. In his ethical biography of Lincoln, William Lee Miller (2002) paints a picture of a remarkable shaping of self for a man of his time, place and humble upbringing:

> Young Lincoln did not, if he could avoid it, hunt, fish, swear, fight, farm, perform manual tasks, gamble, despise Indians as many around him did, vote as his neighbors did, join the church as his family did, believe what his neighbors did: what he did do, when he could, was to read. (p. 44)

This independent, open-minded thinking set the stage for his increasing concern about moral issues such as slavery.

Dismayed at the implications of the passing of the Kansas–Nebraska Act, Lincoln commenced a period of intense self-study and research and emerged more cognitively complex, more large-spirited, and deeply confident of his moral purpose. The following is the empathy and moral centeredness in one of the most famous passages from his speech:

> But if the negro is a man, is it not to that extent, a total destruction of self-government, to say that he too shall not govern himself? When the white man governs himself, that is self-government; but when he governs himself and also governs another man, that is more than self-government, – that is despotism. If the negro is a man, why then **my ancient faith teaches me** that '**all men are created equal;**' and that **there can be no moral right in connection with one man's making a slave of another.** (Lincoln, 1854)

In a second passage from the Peoria Speech, note the way in which Lincoln's words soar with emotion beyond his initial, rational lawyerly case for over-turning the Kansas–Nebraska Act, to become the moral exhortation of a virtuous leader to his fellow citizens:

> Our republican robe is soiled, and trailed in the dust. Let us repurify it. Let us turn and wash it white, in the spirit, if not the blood, of the revolution. Let us turn slavery from its claims of "moral right" back upon its existing legal rights, and its arguments of "necessity." Let us return it to the position our fathers gave it; and there let it rest in peace. Let us readopt the Declaration of Independence, and with it the practices and policy, which harmonize with it. Let north and south—let all Americans—let all lovers of liberty everywhere—join in the great and good work. If we do this, we shall not only have saved the Union; but we shall have so saved it, as to make, and to keep it, forever worthy of the saving. (Lincoln, 1854)

It is interesting to look at this passage through the lens of a developmental personality theory with a strong focus on the moral self. McAdams (2013) has proposed a three-layer conception of personality comprised of dispositional traits, characteristic adaptations, and integrated life

narratives. He has found that midlife Americans who score highest on measures of generativity tend to see their own lives as narratives of redemption.
In the Peoria Speech, Lincoln proposes a redemption story for the nation
itself, using moral language and imagery: the need to "repurify" the "soiled
republican robe," to "wash it white," to readopt the principles of the
Declaration of Independence, thereby saving the nation and "keep[ing] it,
forever worthy of the saving."

In terms of Blasi's theory (2004), we see a man for whom moral considerations and values are central to his self-identity, who feels a sense of personal responsibility to take moral actions on the basis of those
considerations, and whose confident tone suggests the achievement of psychological self-consistency between his political and moral self. He reveals
this sense of personal moral responsibility by including himself (using the
first-person plural) in his repeated pleas to action: "Let us repurify ... let us
turn ... let us return ... let us readopt." At this point, he is a politician taking his listeners and the larger national audience as far as he believes they
can go.

Lincoln's Moral Self Through the Lens of Moral Exemplar Research Findings

One may also study the "Our republican robe is soiled" text by applying
Colby and Damon's common traits of moral exemplars: being principled,
consistent, brave, inspiring, and humble. This short passage alone gives evidence, for example, of Lincoln's ability to inspire: his evocative imagery,
his use of repetition and amplification: "Let north and south—let all
Americans—let all lovers of liberty everywhere." It also strongly suggests,
through his appeal to morality and to the "practices and policy" of the
Declaration of Independence, that he is a man of principle.

Other sections of the speech also evoke Colby and Damon's moral
exemplar traits. In a radical departure from both the norms of the times
and his own prior tendency to use his clever wit to cutting advantage,
Lincoln began his speech on a principled note by promising Douglas and
his audience that Douglas's points will "receive such respectful attention as
I may be able to give them."

> I wish further to say, that I do not propose to question the patriotism, or to assail the
> motives of any man, or class of men; but rather to strictly confine myself to the naked
> merits of the question.

> I also wish to be no less than National in all the positions I may take; and whenever I take ground which others have thought, or may think, narrow, sectional and dangerous to the Union, I hope to give a reason, which will appear sufficient, at least to some, why I think differently. (Lincoln, 1854)

Today we are so jaded about politicians and their speeches—usually written by someone else—that we need to remind ourselves not only that Lincoln wrote his own speeches but also that the historical record shows that he lived up to the promise of respect in this speech for the rest of his all too short life.

In a later passage, one that we judge to be the moral turning point of the speech, keep in mind that Lincoln is speaking to an audience in which even those who opposed slavery held attitudes about the inferiority of blacks that would be abhorrent to people today. For all the careful, political calculation in this speech, Lincoln is now attempting to move his racially insensitive countrymen towards his own emerging humanist vision through his personal and passionate response to the inhumanity of slavery (Striner, 2012). After finishing his summary of the history of slavery in America, Lincoln tells his audience "we have before us, the chief material enabling us to correctly judge whether the repeal of the Missouri Compromise is **right or wrong**." Like the good lawyer that he is, he makes sure to hammer home his point by repeated use of straightforward moral terms and emotions.

> I think, and shall try to show, that it **is wrong**; **wrong** in its direct effect, letting slavery into Kansas and Nebraska—and **wrong** in its prospective principle, allowing it to spread to every other part of the wide world, where men can be found inclined to take it.
>
> This *declared* indifference, but as I must think, covert *real* zeal for the spread of slavery, I can not but **hate**. I **hate** it because of the **monstrous injustice** of slavery itself. I **hate** it because it deprives our republican example of its just influence in the world—enables the enemies of free institutions, with plausibility to taunt us as hypocrites—causes the real friends of freedom to doubt our sincerity, and **especially because it forces so many really good men** amongst ourselves into an open war with the very fundamental principles of civil liberty—criticizing the Declaration of Independence, and **insisting that there is no right principle of action but self-interest**. (Lincoln, 1854)

This excerpt further emphasizes exemplar traits, through its strong moral language ("monstrous injustice") and appeal to principle ("the very fundamental principles of civil liberty") as well as its inspiring rhetoric centered on Lincoln's own hatred of the injustice of slavery. (Note the repetition of the words "I hate.") This passage and others also reveal *consistency* in Lincoln's attitude toward slavery, *courage* in attacking a controversial social institution, and a *humble*, respectful attitude toward his audience –

all traits of the moral exemplar. Analysis of this and other passages in the speech provides evidence for Lincoln's mature integration of the overarching life narrative themes of agency and communion (Colby & Damon, 1992: Frimer, Walker, Lee, Riches, & Dunlap, 2012; McAdams, 1993).

To be sure, Colby and Damon (1992, pp. 320–325) used a method of intensive semi-structured interviews to identify common traits in the contemporary moral exemplars they studied. Much of the richness of their work and findings arises from their method of assisted autobiography, in which the participants collaborate in both the exploratory and interpretive phases of the project. We were at all times fully cognizant that, in contrast, our methods allowed for no carefully constructed interview or clarification questions but rather relied on historical texts constructed for political goals (Horrocks, 2014) (Note: as did Frimer et al., 2012, in their more extensive analysis of influential historical figures). Furthermore, a political speech is a self-presentation with information selected for the purpose of presenting the self in a certain light. We know that Lincoln was re-engaging with politics and was selecting information he believed would be useful for campaign purposes. Yet even with those caveats, a textual analysis using Lincoln's words from the Peoria Speech, noting specific patterns, arguments, and rhetorical devices, reveals an integrated political and moral voice and supports the utility of using Colby and Damon's exemplar trait categories to examine a historical figure.

PART IV: CONCLUSION

The work of numerous outstanding historians and biographers (e.g., Burt, 2013; Donald, 1995; Horrocks, 2014; Kearns Goodwin, 2005; Lehrman, 2008; Miller, 2002) provided us with a rich trove of resources for understanding the ways in which the various ecosystems described by Bronfenbrenner (1994) had influenced Lincoln's moral development. Yet historians are generally very deliberately a-theoretical and for years even those writing psychobiographies tended to reflect a psychoanalytic bias (Houghton, 2009). However, we believe that the method of conducting an in-depth analysis of textual evidence from a major life turning point supports our argument that the academic field of moral development's work on the moral self and moral exemplars adds an important and rich explanatory dimension to the more descriptive analyses of Lincoln's life and self to date.

Even using the limited sample of one major speech and brief writings about life events Lincoln selected to share for campaign purposes, we found evidence both for the usefulness of McAdams' method of examining life narratives for central themes and textual elements as well as for Colby and Damon's (1992) method of exploring exemplar traits. Historians (e.g., Oakes, 2013) have amply demonstrated not only Lincoln's consistent anti-slavery position after the Peoria Speech, but also his unwavering commitment to the speech's ethical arguments. His later letters, speeches, conversations, and legislative accomplishments provide additional concrete evidence that his words and actions continued to be congruent with the "moral exemplar" political persona we have identified in the texts we examined.

Blasi's theoretical framework and the methods of exemplar and life stories research add explanatory power to Miller's (2002) cogent conception of Lincoln's exemplarity. Unlike moral exemplars who retreat from the world into communes or libraries or preach lofty yet idealistic moral messages, Lincoln represents an exemplar who engaged "in collective undertakings – political parties, legislative bodies, governments—in which his decisions and actions" had to "take account of the decisions, actions, and convictions of others" (p. xv). As a politician, he could only achieve his moral goals "in the fragments and distortions possible in a particular time and place" (p. xv).

By examining Abraham Lincoln from the perspective of moral development theory and in the context of his "particular time and place," we found abundant evidence of the emergence of a central moral self that would guide his moral actions throughout the coming years of great moral challenges and great moral accomplishments. In his transition from lawyer to leader, Lincoln crafted not only a politically compelling personal myth of his own rise from humble beginnings, but also a morally compelling national story: the potential rise of the American nation above the "monstrous injustice" tearing it apart through return to its fundamental principles. This principled, consistent, brave, inspiring, and humble man used all the formidable legal, political, and moral skills at his command to convince a nation: "No man is good enough to govern another man without that other's consent."

REFERENCES

Abraham Lincoln Online. *Lincoln autobiographies of 1858–1860.* Retrieved from http://www.abrahamlincolnonline.org/lincoln/speeches/autobiog.htm

Blasi, A. (1980). Bridging moral cognition and moral action: A critical review of the literature. *Psychological Bulletin, 88,* 1–45.

Blasi, A. (2004). Moral functioning: Moral understanding and personality. In D. K. Lapsley & D. Narvaez (Eds.), *Moral development, self and identity* (pp. 335–348). Mahwah, NJ: Lawrence Erlbaum Associates, Inc.

Blasi, A. (2009). The moral functioning of mature adults. In D. Narvaez & D. K. Lapsley (Eds.), *Personality, identity, and character: Explorations in moral psychology* (pp. 396–440). New York, NY: Cambridge University Press.

Bronfenbrenner, U. (1994). Ecological models of human development. *International Encyclopedia of Education* (2nd ed.), *3*, 1643–1647.

Burt, J. (2013). *Lincoln's tragic pragmatism: Lincoln, Douglas, and moral conflict*. Cambridge, MA: The Belknap Press of Harvard University Press.

Colby, A., & Damon, W. (1992). *Some do care: Contemporary lives of moral commitment*. New York, NY: The Free Press.

Donald, D. H. (1995). *Lincoln*. New York, NY: Simon & Schuster.

Dunlap, W. L., & Walker, L. J. (2013). The personality profile of brave exemplars: A person-centered analysis. *Journal of Research in Personality, 47*, 380–384.

Frimer, J. A., Walker, J., Lee, B. H., Riches, A., & Dunlap, W. L. (2012). Hierarchical integration of agency and communion: A study of influential moral figures. *Journal of Personality, 80*(4), 1117–1145. doi:10:111/j.1467-6494.2012.00764.x

Horrocks, T. A. (2014). *Lincoln's campaign biographies*. Carbondale, IL: Southern Illinois University Press.

Houghton, D. P. (2009). *Political psychology: Situations, individuals and cases*. New York, NY: Routledge.

Kearns Goodwin, D. K. (2005). *Team of rivals: The political genius of Abraham Lincoln*. New York, NY: Simon & Schuster.

Lehrman, L. E. (2008). *Lincoln at Peoria: The turning point*. Mechanicburg, PA: Stackpole Books.

Lincoln, A. (1854, October 16). The speech at Peoria, Illinois. In R. P. Basler (Ed.), *The collected works of Abraham Lincoln (1953)* (Vol. 2, pp. 247–283). Brunswick, NJ: Rutgers University Press.

McAdams, D. P. (1993). *The stories we live by: Personal myths and the making of the self*. New York, NY: Guilford Press.

McAdams, D. P. (2013). Narrative identity. *Current Directions in Psychological Sciences, 22*(3), 233–238.

Miller, W. L. (2002). *Lincoln's virtues: An ethical biography*. New York, NY: Alfred A. Knopf.

Oakes., J. (2013). *Freedom national: The destruction of slavery in the United States, 1861–1865*. New York, NY: W. W. Norton & Company.

Striner, R. (2012). *Lincoln and race*. Carbondale, IL: Southern Illinois University Press.

Walker, L. J. (2004). Gus in the gap: Bridging the judgment-action gap in moral functioning. In D. K. Lapsley & D. Narvaez (Eds.), *Moral development, self and identity* (pp. 1–20). Mahwah, NJ: Lawrence Erlbaum Associates, Inc.

Walker, L. J. (2013). Moral motivation through the perspective of exemplarity. In K. Heinrichs, F. Oser, & T. Lovat (Eds.), *Handbook of moral motivation, theories, models, applications* (pp. 197–214). Rotterdam, The Netherlands: Sense Publishers.

AGENCY AND COMMUNION: THE MORAL MOTIVATION OF MIEP GIES

Rebecca J. Glover

ABSTRACT

While much of the existing research regarding moral exemplarity has focused on living individuals, examination of the lives of historical figures can also prove invaluable in understanding moral motivation. Consequently, this paper sought to apply Frimer and Walker's (2009) reconciliation model and methodology in examining themes of agency and communion in the motivation of Miep Gies. Frimer and Walker's (2009) Self-Understanding Interview and the VEiN coding method (Frimer, Walker, & Dunlop, 2009) served as guides for examining published and audio-recorded interviews, biographical and autobiographical information, as well as video-recorded speeches given by Gies. Aspects of an integrated moral identity appeared evident in the personality of Miep Gies as indicated in statements reflecting an overlap of both agency and communion. The study was limited in its reliance on publically available documents about or by Gies. Further, reliance on these documents, as opposed to a "live" interview, limited the ability of the author to identify responses to all questions included in Frimer and Walker's (2009)

The Ethical Contribution of Organizations to Society
Research in Ethical Issues in Organizations, Volume 14, 189–200
Copyright © 2015 by Emerald Group Publishing Limited
ISSN: 1529-2096/doi:10.1108/S1529-209620150000014009

interview or fully utilize the VEiN coding method (Frimer et al., 2009).
Exploration of life narratives of historical figures can provide insight into
an integrated moral identity as well as examples of developmental cross-
roads Frimer and Walker (2009) cited as essential in their reconciliation
model. Comprehension of this reconciliation process is critical to under-
standing what lies at the heart of moral motivation and action as well as
the ability to promote such growth in the lives of others.

Keywords: Moral exemplarity; moral motivation

On a Monday morning in 1933, a young woman arrived at Travies and Company in Amsterdam and inquired about a job. She was interviewed, quickly hired, and began work as a jam maker (Gies, 1987) with a group of individuals that would ultimately include, among others, Victor Kugler, Johannes Kleiman, Bep Voskuijl, Hermann Van Pels, and the man who had hired her, Otto Frank (Van der Rol & Verhoeven, 1992). Although limited in her skills as cook, she reminded herself she could accomplish anything she set her mind to, followed the recipe she had been given, and made jam. After mastering those skills, she moved a month later into the main office where she assumed clerical responsibilities. Nine years later, in the Spring of 1942, Miep Gies would still be at Travies and Company when Otto Frank approached her to ask if she was willing to share in the responsibility of caring for his family and others in hiding from the Nazis. Her ready response ... "Of course" (Gies, 1987, p. 88).

Although Kohlberg's (1969) cognitive-based theory laid the foundation for research related to moral functioning, many have argued it was inadequate in its ability to address moral motivation (Frimer & Walker, 2008). Rest defined moral motivation as the process by which an individual determines a situation to be moral, is aware of what action should be taken in such a situation, and makes the decision to act in ways consistent with the individual's moral perspective (Thoma & Bebeau, 2013). Vozzola, Cimbala, and Palmunen (2015) noted research by Blasi (1980, 2004, 2009) in understanding the judgment and action gap in moral identity as well as the work of Colby and Damon (1992) who defined characteristics of moral exemplarity in individuals whose lives demonstrated consistency in moral judgment and action. Also relevant has been the research of Walker and colleagues (Frimer & Walker, 2008, 2009; Frimer, Walker, Lee, Riches, & Dunlop, 2012; Walker, 2013) and their focus on understanding the development of moral motivation through the integration of agency and communion.

Walker (2013) contended the alignment of morality with the self was critical to examination of moral motivation. Posing the question, "Why be good?," Walker (2013) noted most theoretical explanations require moral individuals to act out of duty and/or obligation while simultaneously ignoring personal interests. He maintained a key issue with such explanations of moral motivation was that we must act in ways that disregard needs of the self and which provide no "moral credit" in promoting interests of the self (Walker, 2013, p. 198). Walker (2013) has instead proposed the idea of moral centrality, defined as "the extent to which morality is central to one's sense of self" (p. 199), arguing action aligned with our moral concerns would work to enhance the self, while failure to act would be denial of that same self.

Citing dominant themes of agency and communion in the study of moral motivation, Walker and colleagues have explored the integration of the two in several empirical studies using the reconciliation model presented in Frimer and Walker (2009). Historically viewed as competing interests, agency has been noted as being self-enhancing and resulting in action motivated to advance one's own interests (or "getting ahead"). Alternatively, communion (or "getting along") has been noted as being more other-enhancing, resulting in action motivated to contribute to a more collective good (Walker, 2013). Frimer and Walker (2009) argued that as both agency and communion are central to moral motivation, competition between them results in disequilibrium, the resolution of which may occur by ignoring one theme in favor of the other. Consequently, depending on which theme is abandoned, they argued this disequilibrium results in unmitigated agency or unmitigated communion, either of which represented poor moral functioning. Poor moral functioning could then be reconciled by coordinating themes of both agency and communion into one integrated moral identity, a type of transformation Frimer and Walker (2009) described as being similar to an Eriksonian crisis and representative of a critical crossroad in development. This reconciliation model, Walker (2013) concluded, better illustrates moral centrality, providing a more integrated answer to the question, "Why be good?" − "Because promoting the interests of others [i.e., communion] can be fundamentally enhancing to the self [i.e., agency]" (p. 210).

Moral motivation has been investigated in life narratives of both contemporary (Colby & Damon, 1992; Walker & Frimer, 2007) and historical figures (Damon & Colby, 2015; Frimer et al., 2012) through the use of interviews as well as examination of existing documents. While Damon and Colby (2015) noted reliance on subjective, retrospective reporting of events might function as a limitation, they simultaneously contended the use of such methodologies allowed for the examination of lives which reflected moral awareness and intention. This paper sought to apply Frimer and Walker's (2009) reconciliation model and methodology to examine the integration of agency and communion in the moral motivation of Miep Gies, particularly in her actions to save the Frank and Van Pels families as well as Dr. Pfeffer (Gies, 1987), a decision Gies described simply as "self-evident" (Plukker & Van der Sluis, 1998).

METHODS

Miep Gies

Hermine Santrouschitz was born in Vienna, Austria, in 1909, five years before the beginning of World War I. Food shortages at the time resulted in her becoming undernourished and ill, and at the age of 11, Hermine was sent to live temporarily in the Netherlands as part of a program established to revitalize starving Austrian children. There she lived with the Nieuwenhuis family, enrolled in local schools, was quickly accepted by the other children and given the nickname, Miep. Ultimately, she noted, "My sensibilities were Dutch, the quality of my feelings also Dutch" (Gies, 1987, p. 22), and through an agreement between her biological and adoptive families, the decision was made that Miep would live permanently in Holland with the Nieuwenhuises. Across her adolescent years and into adulthood, Miep increasingly identified with the Dutch culture until by 1931 at the age of 22: "The hungry little eleven-year-old Viennese girl with the tag around her neck and a bow in her hair had faded away entirely. I was now a robust young Dutch woman" (Gies, 1987, p. 23).

As noted earlier, in 1933 Miep first met Otto Frank when she found employment at Travies and Company. Later, she met Jan Gies, a Dutch citizen, whom she eventually married in July of 1941; Miep and Jan would become close friends of the Frank family. As is well known, Otto Frank was the only member of the group hiding in the Amsterdam Annex to survive the Nazi concentration camps, and upon his return, he lived with Miep and Jan until immigrating to Switzerland in 1952 (Gies, 1987). Until her death on January 11, 2010, Miep shared the story of Anne Frank and the others in hiding and participated in educational events and other activities of the Anne Frank House in Amsterdam (http://www.annefrank.org).

Procedures

Frimer and Walker's (2009) Self-Understanding Interview (SUI) as well as the Values Embedded in Narrative method (VEiN; Frimer, Walker, & Dunlop, 2009) guided the methodology used in this study. Building on the work of Schwartz (1992), Frimer and Walker's (2009) interview consisted of 14 items ranging from self-description, identification of significant people and activities in the individual's life, and reflection on what defined the self as well as one's uniquenesses and overall personal growth (p. 1672). Responses to these items were coded using the VEiN method (Frimer et al., 2009) to identify responses reflecting 10 values, two of which focused on agency (i.e., power and achievement) and two of which focused on communion (i.e., universalism and benevolence). Power was reflected in statements referring to personal control or dominant status over others or attainment of material wealth, while achievement was demonstrated in statements referring to personal success based on demonstrated competence and perseverance as well as commitments to achieve. Universalism and benevolence, on the other hand, were focused outside the self. Universalism was reflected in statements referring to appreciation, tolerance, and protection for others in general, while benevolence was reflected more in the goal of preserving or enhancing the welfare of individuals with whom one was familiar. Responses in which themes of both agency and communion occurred together in one "chunk" were coded as overlap and represented moral identity integration.

In that Gies represented an historical figure, and hence unable to complete the SUI, Frimer and Walker's (2009) methodology was modified to examine themes of agency and communion evident in published and audio-recorded interviews, biographical and autobiographical information, as well as video-recorded speeches given by Gies during her lifetime. Review of these materials was guided by the SUI questions, and responses to the following questions were identified as being scorable using the VEiN coding method (Frimer et al., 2009):

SUI, Question 3:	Which of your activities are most important to you?
SUI, Question 8:	What are your major roles and responsibilities?
SUI, Question 11:	How did you get to be the kind of person you are now?
SUI, Question 13:	Is there anything else that defines you or is important to who you are?

"Responses" were coded specifically for evidence of agency, using the values of achievement and power, or communion, using the values of

benevolence and universalism. Evidence of overlap of agency and communion was also explored.

RESULTS

SUI, Question 3: Which of Your Activities are Most Important to You?

Responses to this question related to both Gies' actions to help those in
hiding in the Amsterdam Annex as well as her work to save Anne Frank's
diary following their arrest along with two of their rescuers, Kugler and
Kleiman:

> I could not save Anne's life, but I could help her live another two years. In those two
> years she wrote her diary, in which millions of people find hope and inspiration. When
> I found it, lying all over the floor in the hiding place, I decided to stow it away, in order
> to give it back to Anne when she would return. I wanted to see her smile and her say,
> "Oh, Miep, my diary!" But after the terrible time of waiting and hoping, word came
> that Anne had died. At that moment I went to Otto Frank, Anne's father, the only one
> of the family who had survived, and gave him Anne's diary. "This is what Anne has
> left," I said to him. "These are her words." Can you see how this man looked at me?
> He had lost his wife and two children, but he *had* Anne's diary. It was a very, very mov-
> ing moment. Again, I *could not* save Anne's life. However, I *did* save her diary, and by
> that I could help her most important dream come true. In her diary she tells us that she
> wants to live on after her death. Now, her diary makes her *really* live on, in a most
> powerful way! And that helps me in those many hours of deep grief. It also shows us
> that even if helping may fail to achieve everything, it is better to try than to do nothing.
> (*Anne Frank's Legacy: Miep Gies*; http://echoesandreflections.org/wp-content/uploads/
> 2014/04/EchoesAndReflections_Lesson_Seven_Speech-AnneFranksLegacy.pdf)

In this "chunk," evidence of benevolence was seen not only in Gies'
action to preserve Anne's life while hiding from the Nazi's, but also in
Gies' action to help Anne "live on" by saving her diary. Similarly, Gies'
actions in returning the diary to Otto Frank were interpreted as benevolence as she was able to enhance his welfare by symbolically returning to
him his lost child. Additionally, Universalism was noted in Gies' statement
that the diary also served as inspiration and hope to millions of others not
familiar to her. Achievement may also be noted in Gies' expressions of
personal success and demonstrated competence, "I *did* save the diary."
Moreover, despite her ultimate inability to save the lives of all of those in
hiding and "achieve everything," she had persevered and was able to value
her efforts in at least saving Otto Frank and in returning Anne's diary to
her father. Consequently, it was determined both agency and communion
were evident in this response, resulting in the coding of overlap.

SUI, Question 8: What are Your Major Roles and Responsibilities?

Gies' view of her role and sense of responsibility in educating others to the dangers of discrimination was reflected in her Wallenberg Legacy lecture, given at the University of Michigan in 1994:

> Many children grow up in families where they are told to mind their own business only. When those children become adults, they are inclined to look the other way if people ask for help. ...
>
> In my opinion, education is the best way to improve our world. Children should learn from us that people often do not get in life what they deserve. We should tell them that, for instance, most victims of poverty and discrimination are innocent. ... Therefore, we must help. We should also tell our children that they should always share with others and that caring about their own business only did lead to the death of six million innocent Jews, among them Anne Frank. (Gies, 1994).

Similar ideas are expressed by Gies in *Anne Frank's Legacy*:

> We should explain to children that caring about our own business only can be very wrong. ... Therefore, we should *never* be bystanders ....
>
> I feel very strongly that we cannot wait for others to make this world a better place. *No, we ourselves,* should make this happen now in our own homes and school by carefully evaluating the manner in which we speak and by closely examining the ways we form and express our opinions about other people, particularly in the presence of children. (*Anne Frank's Legacy: Miep Gies*; http://echoesandreflections.org/wp-content/uploads/2014/04/EchoesAndReflections_Lesson_Seven_Speech-AnneFranksLegacy.pdf)

In these responses, we again saw evidence of achievement reflected in the first statement advocating for education regarding the treatment of others. In the second statement, Gies' comment that "we, should never be bystanders" and insistence that we should act to "make this world a better place" further demonstrated achievement in her commitment to "improve [the] world." Universalism was also demonstrated in both quotes — not only did she maintain that caring only for the self can be "very wrong" (see quote from *Anne Frank's Legacy*), but a universal concern for victims of poverty and discrimination as well as the need to share with and help others were reflected in her Wallenberg lecture. Consequently, the co-occurrence of agency and communion in these responses was also coded as evidence of overlap.

SUI, Question 11: How did You Get to be the Kind of Person You are Now?

One response to this question was found in Gies' (1994) Wallenberg Legacy lecture where she described the influence of her adoptive Dutch parents, described as socially-minded individuals. Already rearing five children of their own on what Gies described as a modest salary, she credited them for taking her into their home and sharing whatever they had with others. Their actions, she said, left "a deep impression on me. It made me think I should do the same in my life" (Gies, 1994). These comments reflected the value of universalism as Gies expressed concern for the welfare of others.

A different response, however, was found in an interview given by Gies in 1996:

> I'm born an Austrian girl. For a long time, I was deeply ashamed of my home country. My biggest joy was on the day that I became a Dutch citizen. Then, I felt free to hate all Germans and Austrians because of what they did to my friends. I could not see that there was anything wrong with that. ... Otto [Frank] knew about my blind hate towards them and therefore he would never let me near them. But one day, fate caught me. When I suddenly faced Germans, I jumped at them, calling them everything I could think of. "You always say that you did not know what happened to the Jews. You really want me to believe that you were that stupid?"

> The visitors were clearly afraid of me and backed off to the wall. ... I really had my go at them. In a certain way I even enjoyed it. But then, I was told that these German people had been many years in concentration camps themsel[ves] for opposing Hitler. Can you understand how I then felt and can you see me standing there? I really did not know where to look, or what to say, and how to make good for it. At that moment, I started to understand the wisdom of Otto Frank, who always said that we should never lump people together. "Every person makes his or her own decision," Otto said. "Even parents and their children do not act and think the same." Otto felt very strongly that we should not make the same mistake many Germans once made. (Idaho Public Television, 1996).

In this second response, evidence of power could be seen in what appeared to be Gies' sense of status over Germans. She expressed her social power in the freedom to hate all Germans and Austrians, enjoying her ability to create fear in the people to whom she was speaking as she expressed her incredulity at the claims of Germans in general that they were unaware of what was happening to the Jews during the war.

Examined separately, these two responses may be seen as examples of what Frimer and Walker (2009) described as disequilibrium resulting in poor moral functioning in that the first response could be considered representative of unmitigated communion and the second of unmitigated agency. Additionally, each response, most particularly Gies' description of her ability to "understand the wisdom of Otto Frank" and not make prejudicial assumption of others (in this case *all* Germans and Austrians) might also be seen as reflective of a developmental crossroad Frimer and

Walker (2009) noted as leading to the integration of agency and communion.

SUI, Question 13: Is there Anything Else that Defines You or is Important to Who You are?

Here, we returned to Gies' recollection of Otto Frank's request for help to hide his family from the Nazis:

"Miep," he began, "I have a secret to confide to you." I listened silently. "Miep," he said, "Edith, Margot, Anne, and I are planning to go under – to go into hiding."

He let me take this in.

"We will go together with Van [Pels] and his wife and their son." Mr. Frank paused. ...

"As you will be working on, as usual, right next to us, I need to know if you have any objections?"

I told him I did not.

He took a breath and asked, "Miep, are you willing to take on the responsibility of taking care of us while we are in hiding?"

"Of course," I answered.

There is a look between two people once or twice in a lifetime that cannot be described by words. That look passed between us. "Miep, for those who help Jews, the punishment is harsh; imprisonment, perhaps –"

I cut him off. "I said, 'Of course.' I meant it."

"Good. Only [Kleiman] knows. Even Margot and Anne do not know yet. One by one I will ask the others. But only a few will know."

I asked no further questions. The less I knew, the less I could say in an interrogation. I knew when the time was right he would tell me who the others were, and everything else I would need to know. I felt no curiosity. I had given my word. (Gies, 1987, p. 88)

Evidence of both agency and communion was seen in this response. Gies' willingness to act in taking responsibility for the welfare of her friends demonstrated the value of benevolence. In terms of agency, her "cutting off" Otto Frank with the statement, "I said, 'Of course.' I meant it," later adding, "I had given my word," reflected achievement in her sense of commitment, while power was evident in her decision to not ask additional questions in an effort to control her environment to the extent she could in the event she was later interrogated. Consequently, this response was coded as evidence of overlap.

"WHY BE GOOD?"

Walker (2013) posed the question, "Why be good?" as a means of exploring motivation. In the case of Gies, the question was modified to, "Why help the Franks, Van Pels, and Dr. Pfeffer?" One response was found in Gies' (1994) Wallenberg Legacy lecture:

> I'm deeply moved by the warm welcome you extended to me and I am grateful for all courtesies. For me the best thing, however, is to meet people who share my views about our human duty to help those who are in trouble. Ladies and gentlemen, please, do not look up to me. It does embarrass me, very much. Kindly consider yourself to be my equal in providing support to all who live in fear and pain. People often ask why I found the courage to help the Franks. Yes, it certainly requires some courage, some discipline, and also some sacrifice to do your human duty. But that is true for so many things in life.

> Therefore, this question always surprises me because I simply could not think of doing anything else. ... I myself am just an ordinary woman. I simply had no choice. (Gies, 1994).

A somewhat similar response can be found in *Anne Frank's Legacy*:

> I myself am just a very common person. I simply had no choice, because I could foresee many, many sleepless nights and a life filled with regret, if I refused to help the Franks. And this was not the kind of life I was looking forward to. Yes, I have wept countless times when I have thought of my dear friends, but I am happy that these were not tears of remorse for refusing to help. Remorse can be worse than losing your life. *(Anne Frank's Legacy: Miep Gies*; http://echoesandreflections.org/wp-content/uploads/2014/04/EchoesAndReflections_Lesson_Seven_Speech-AnneFranksLegacy.pdf)

In the former statement, evidence of universalism was seen in Gies' expression of "human duty" in working to provide support to those who live in fear and pain as well as achievement in valuing the sacrifice related to that commitment. In the latter statement, this same sense of achievement was reflected in her unwillingness to lead a life of regret had she not worked to help the Franks and others. Benevolence was also apparent, here, in her reference to her "dear friends" and her actions to help. Finally, in both statements, Gies commented, "I simply had no choice [but to act]," again reflecting the value of benevolence. Therefore, these responses were coded as evidence of overlap.

CONCLUSIONS

This study was limited in that instead of analyzing direct responses of the participant (in this case, Miep Gies) to Frimer and Walker's (2009) Self-Understanding Interview, data was obtained by reviewing publically available documents about or by Gies and identifying material deemed responsive to questions contained in the interview. This modified methodology, consequently, also resulted in the inability of the author to fully utilize the VEiN coding method (Frimer et al., 2009). Nevertheless, despite these limitations, aspects of both agency and communion as well as overlap of these two values did appear evident in the moral motivation of Miep Gies. Ultimately, Walker's (2013) integrated response to the question "Why be moral?" (i.e., "Because promoting the interest of others can be fundamentally enhancing to the self" [p. 210]), might be summarized in Gies' (1994) brief comment, "I simply had no choice."

As noted by Damon and Colby (2015) and Vozzola et al. (2015) examining moral motivation in the lives of historical figures could work to provide powerful models of optimal moral functioning. Exploration of completed life narratives such as that of Miep Gies might provide insight into an integrated moral identity as well as examples of the developmental crossroads Frimer and Walker (2009) cited as essential in the reconciliation of themes of agency and communion. Comprehension of this reconciliation process is an essential element to understanding what lies at the heart of moral motivation and action as well as the ability to promote such growth in the lives of others.

REFERENCES

Anne Frank House. (2015, January 15). Retrieved from http://www.annefrank.org. *Anne Frank's Legacy: Miep Gies*. Lesson 7: Rescuers and non-Jewish Resistance. Echos and Reflections Teacher's Resource Guide. http://echoesandreflections.org/wp-content/uploads/2014/04/EchoesAndReflections_Lesson_Seven_Speech-AnneFranksLegacy.pdf. Accessed on October 26, 2014

Blasi, A. (1980). Bridging moral cognition and moral action: A critical review of the literature. *Psychological Bulletin, 88,* 1–45. doi:10.1037/0033-2909.88.1.1

Blasi, A. (2004). Moral functioning: Moral understanding and personality. In D. K. Lapsley & D. Narvaez (Eds.), *Moral development, self and identity* (pp. 335–348). Mahwah, NJ: Lawrence Erlbaum Associates, Inc.

Blasi, A. (2009). The moral functioning of mature adults. In D. Narvaez & D. K. Lapsley (Eds.), *Personality, identity, and character: Explorations in moral psychology* (pp. 396–440). New York, NY: Cambridge University Press.

200   REBECCA J. GLOVER

Colby, A., & Damon, W. (1992). *Some do care: Contemporary lives of moral commitment*. New York, NY: The Free Press.

Damon, W., & Colby, A. (2015). *The power of ideals: The real story of moral choice*. New York, NY: Oxford University Press.

Frimer, J. A., & Walker, L. J. (2008). Towards a new paradigm of moral personhood. *Journal of Moral Education, 37*(3), 333–356.

Frimer, J. A., & Walker, L. J. (2009). Reconciling the self and morality: An empirical model of moral centrality development. *Developmental Psychology, 45*(6), 1669–1681. doi:10.1037/a0017418

Frimer, J. A., Walker, L. J., & Dunlop, W. L. (2009). *VEiN relationship coding manual*. Vancouver: University of British Columbia.

Frimer, J. A., Walker, L. J., Lee, B. H., Riches, A., & Dunlop, W. L. (2012). Hierarchical integration of agency and communion: A study of influential moral figures. *Journal of Personality, 80*(4), 1117–1145. doi:10.1111/j.1467-6494.2012.00764.x

Gies, M. (1994, October). *Wallenberg legacy*. Ann Arbor, MI. Lecture conducted from the University of Michigan. Retrieved from http://wallenberg.umich.edu/medal-recipients/1994-miep-gies/. Accessed on October 26, 2014.

Gies, M. with Gold, A. L. (1987). *Anne Frank remembered: The story of the woman who helped to hide the Frank family*. New York, NY: Simon and Schuster.

Idaho Public Television (Producer). (1996, November 28). Dialogue: Interview with Marcia Franklin – Miep Gies [Television series episode]. Boise, ID. Retrieved from http://idahoptv.org/dialogue/diaShowPage.cfm?KeyNo=309. Accessed on October 26, 2014.

Kohlberg, L. (1969). Stage and sequence: The cognitive-developmental approach to socialization. In D. A. Goslin (Ed.), *Handbook of socialization theory and research* (pp. 347–480). Chicago: Rand McNally.

Plukker, M. (Producer), & Van der Sluis, W. (Director). (1998). *"I write about you too": Miep Gies' memories of Anne Frank* [Film]. Available from the Anne Frank House, Postbus 730, 1000 AS, Amsterdam, NBLC order number 15488.

Schwartz, S. H. (1992). Universals in the content and structure of values: Theoretical advances and empirical tests in 20 countries. *Advances in Experimental Social Psychology, 25*, 1–65.

Thoma, S. J., & Bebeau, M. J. (2013). Moral motivation and the four component model. In K. Heinrichs, F. Oser, & T. Lovat (Eds.), *Handbook of moral motivation: Theories, models applications* (pp. 49–67). Boston, MA: Sense Publishers.

Van der Rol, R., & Verhoeven, R. (1992). *Anne Frank: Beyond the diary*. NY: Puffin Books.

Vozzola, E. C., Cimbala, P. A., & Palmunen, K. (2015). *From lawyer to leader: An analysis of Abraham Lincoln's moral self*. Manuscript submitted for publication.

Walker, L. J. (2013). Moral motivation through the perspective of exemplarity. In K. Heinrichs, F. Oser, & T. Lovat (Eds.), *Handbook of moral motivation: Theories, models applications* (pp. 197–214). Boston, MA: Sense Publishers.

Walker, L. J., & Frimer (2007). Moral personality of brave and caring exemplars. *Journal of Personality and Social Psychology, 93*, 845–860.

ABOUT THE AUTHORS

Peter Bowden was coordinator of the MBA program at Monash University and subsequently Professor of Administrative Studies at the University of Manchester. His background in institutional strengthening includes extensive advisory work with the World Bank, Asian Development Bank and UN agencies. He lectures in ethics in the Faculty of Engineering; and is an Honorary Research Associate in the Department of Philosophy at Sydney University. In 2013 he edited *Applied Ethics* under the auspices of the The Australian Association for Professional and Applied Ethics (AAPAE). In 2014 he published his research on whistleblowing under the title *"In the Public Interest."* He holds a BE in Engineering, an MSc with Distinction from the London School of Economics and a PhD from Monash University.

Hugh Breakey is a Research Fellow at Griffith University's Institute for Ethics, Governance and Law, Australia. His work stretches across the philosophical sub-disciplines of political theory, legal philosophy, normative ethics and applied philosophy. His articles explore ethical issues arising in such diverse fields as peacekeeping, institutional governance, climate change, sustainable tourism, private property, medicine and international law, published in journals including *The Philosophical Quarterly*, *The Modern Law Review* and *Political Studies*. In 2012 he authored *Intellectual Liberty: Natural Rights and Intellectual Property* (Ashgate). Since 2013, Hugh has served as President of the Australian Association for Professional and Applied Ethics.

Tim Cadman is a Research Fellow in the Institute of Ethics, Governance and Law at Griffith University. He is an Earth Systems Governance Fellow, a Member of the Australian Centre for Sustainable Business and Development, and is on the Editorial Board of the *Journal of Sustainable Finance and Investment*. He specialises in global environmental governance, natural resource management, climate change policy and responsible investment. His book *Climate Change and Global Policy Regimes: Towards Institutional Legitimacy* was published by Palgrave Macmillan in 2013.

Paul A. Cimbala (PhD, U.S. History, Emory University) is a Professor in the Department of History at Fordham University, The Bronx, New York, USA. He is author or editor of numerous books on the American Civil War and Reconstruction including *Soldiers North and South*, *The Great Task Remaining Before Us: Reconstruction as America's Continuing Civil War*, *Under the Guardianship of the Nation: The Freedmen's Bureau and the Reconstruction of Georgia, 1865–1870* and *Veterans North and South: The Transition from Soldier to Civilian after the American Civil War*.

Charles J. Coate a Professor of Accounting and Chair of the Department of Accounting in the School of Business at St Bonaventure University, earned his PhD from the University of Maryland at College Park. His research interests include business ethics, theoretical and practical service based learning, and professional and policy based audit and accounting issues. He has received the Francis Medal (for Service) awarded by the Holy Name Province, OFM.

Rebecca J. Glover (PhD in Human Development, Texas Tech University) is a Professor in the Department of Educational Psychology at the University of North Texas, Denton, Texas, USA. Her scholarship regarding moral functioning has focused on perspective-taking and decision-making across late adolescence and young adulthood. Her work assessing moral content in media contributed to the emerging consensus that moral reasoning affects comprehension of the relevance of behaviours observed and how those understandings are incorporated into interactions with and perceptions of others. She is currently working on a study of moral exemplarity across the lifespan.

Howard Harris graduated in Chemical Engineering and worked in industry and commerce before returning to university to complete his PhD in Applied Philosophy. He teaches applied ethics and related social topics to undergraduate business students at the University of South Australia Business School and online through Open Universities Australia. He is a former President of the Australian Association for Professional and Applied Ethics and Convenor of the Group for research in Integrity and Governance.

Mark C. Mitschow, Professor of Accounting at SUNY-Genesco College, earned his PhD from the University of Maryland at College Park, SUNY. His research interests revolve around business ethics, auditing, small business and behavioural accounting. His research has been published in scholarly journals including *Research on Professional Responsibility and Ethics* in *Accounting*, *Journal of Business Ethics* and *Review of Business*. In 2010 he received the SUNY Chancellor's Award for Excellence in Scholarship and Creative Activities. He is on the editorial board of *Research on Professional Responsibility and Ethics in Accounting* and *Journal of Business and Behavioral Sciences*.

Timothy O'Shannassy is a Senior Lecturer in the Graduate School of Business and Law at RMIT University, Australia where he teaches strategic management and entrepreneurship. He has previously taught at University of Melbourne and was Visiting Scholar at University of Maryland in 2007. Tim has extensive teaching experience with Open Universities Australia, in Hong Kong and Malaysia. He consults to business and has taught on numerous executive development programs for companies including Ford Motor Company and Mandarin Oriental Hotels. Tim is Associate Editor of *Journal of Management & Organization*, the journal of the Australian and New Zealand Academy of Management.

Karen Palmunen (PhD in French, Brown University) is Associate Professor of French, Emerita, and former Director of the First Year Seminar Program at the University of Saint Joseph, West Hartford, Connecticut, USA. Her scholarly projects have included work on Madame de Stael, French food and culture, adult-learner foreign language pedagogy, and development and implementation of First-Year seminar programs.

Charles Sampford graduated top of his class in Politics, Philosophy and Law at Melbourne University, combining those disciplines in his Oxford DPhil. He was Foundation Dean of Law, Griffith University (1991). In 1998, he led a bid for the Key Centre for Ethics, Law, Justice and Governance and was its Foundation Director. In September 2004 Charles became Director, Institute for Ethics, Governance and Law. Foreign fellowships include Visiting Senior Research Fellow, St John's College Oxford (1997) and a Senior Fulbright Award, Harvard University (2000). He has written over 106 articles and chapters and has completed 23 books and edited collections.

Michael Schwartz is an Associate Professor of Business Ethics in the School of Economics, Finance & Marketing at the Royal Melbourne Institute of Technology. He is a past president of the Australian Association for Professional and Applied Ethics. He is a member of the editorial boards of the *Journal of Applied Ethics* and the *Journal of International Business & Law*; and a joint editor of *Research in Ethical Issues in Organizations*. His research in the field of business ethics has been published in the *Electronic Journal of Business Ethics & Organization Studies*, the *Australian Journal of Professional & Applied Ethics*, the *Australian Journal of Social Issues, Ethics & Education, Business Ethics Quarterly, Business Ethics: A European Review*, the *Journal of Business Ethics* and *Research in Ethical Issues in Organizations*.

Elizabeth C. Vozzola (PhD in Applied Developmental Psychology, Fordham University) is the Director of the Honors Program and a Professor in the Department of Psychology at the University of Saint Joseph, West Hartford, Connecticut, USA. She is the author of *Moral Development: Theory and Applications*. Past research explored children's moral perceptions of the Harry Potter books and films and university faculty's moral reasoning about affirmative action. She is currently working on a study of the moral exemplars of emerging adults.

Manuel Wörsdörfer is a Postdoctoral Researcher of the Cluster of Excellence 'The Formation of Normative Orders' at Goethe University Frankfurt. In his habilitation/professorial thesis, he analyses the Equator Principles, a voluntary and soft law CSR-initiative in the project finance sector, from a business and human rights perspective. Manuel's current research interests in business ethics include sustainable finance, political CSR and corporate citizenship, and business and human rights. Most of his research has been presented at prestigious international conferences and has been published in peer-reviewed journals. Manuel has also worked as a visiting researcher at Beijing University, Carnegie Mellon University, University of Toronto and York University.